For Robert Pinsky

In Time

THE UNIVERSITY OF CHICAGO PRESS
CHICAGO AND LONDON

IN TIME

Poets, Poems, and the Rest

C. K. Williams

C. K. Williams is professor of creative writing at Princeton University. He is the author of eighteen books of poetry, including *Repair* and *The Singing*, as well as several books of prose, most recently, *On Whitman*.

The University of Chicago Press, Chicago 60637
The University of Chicago Press, Ltd., London

© 2012 by The University of Chicago
All rights reserved. Published 2012.
Printed in the United States of America

21 20 19 18 17 16 15 14 13 12   1 2 3 4 5

ISBN-13: 978-0-226-89951-0 (cloth)
ISBN-13: 978-0-226-89952-7 (e-book)
ISBN-10: 0-226-89951-9 (cloth)
ISBN-10: 0-226-89952-7 (e-book)

Library of Congress Cataloging-in-Publication data

Williams, C. K. (Charles Kenneth), 1936–
 In time : poets, poems, and the rest /
C. K. Williams.
     pages ; cm
  ISBN-13: 978-0-226-89951-0 (cloth : alkaline paper)
  ISBN-10: 0-226-89951-9 (cloth : alkaline paper)
  ISBN-13: 978-0-226-89952-7 (e-book)
  ISBN-10: 0-226-89952-7 (e-book)   1. English poetry—History and criticism.   2. Williams, C. K. (Charles Kenneth), 1936—Interviews.   I. Title.
  PS3573.I4483A6 2012
  811'.54—dc23
                                    2012007986

♾ This paper meets the requirements of ANSI/NISO Z39.48-1992 (Permanence of Paper).

Contents

Preface ix

PART I   Poetry and Poets

    Unlikely Likes: George Herbert and Philip Larkin 3
    Amichai near the End 21
    Autobiography with Translation 33
    Lowell Later 41
    Odd Endings 47
    Some Reflections on Tragedy 71
    Letter to a Workshop 85

PART II   Answerings: Interview Excerpts 98

PART III   The Rest

    Two Encounters Early On 147
    Literary Models of Adolescence 153
    Paris as Symbol, Idea, and Reality 169
    Letter to a German Friend 189
    Nature and Panic 207
    On Being Old 213

Acknowledgments 227

Preface

The first time I gave a lecture was a terrifying, traumatic experience. I'd had no idea it would be—I was asked by a friend who taught architecture to give a talk on poetry to an assembly of undergraduates; it would be one of my first public appearances, and I was quite excited. I scribbled a page of notes and, fortunately, also brought along my first book, *Lies*, which had just been published.

I took my stand behind the lectern, began to improvise from my notes, and was horrified to discover that at the end of five minutes, I had absolutely nothing more to say—I'd exhausted every idea on that sad single page of scrawl. I stood for a moment in paralysis and panic before I realized that the only thing I could possibly do was to read from my book, which I did for the remainder of my allotted fifty minutes. Though my friend tried to cheer me up afterward, I was really quite miserable, feeling I'd failed dreadfully.

For a long time after that awful afternoon I would simply decline invitations to give talks. Then I was asked to deliver the inaugural lecture for a series dedicated to the memory of my friend Paul Zweig. I felt I had to accept, I did, this time I wrote out my talk in advance, and it went well. Thus began my career as an essayist—I'd discovered that writing prose was rather pleasurable and, in truth, much easier than composing poems, if surely less exciting. I realized, too, that when I was invited to give a talk I'd be able to survive speaking prose before an audience if I wrote out what I was going to say in the form of an essay, and before long I found that I'd written enough for a book, and so published *Poetry and Consciousness*.

Since then, I've continued to write essays, sometimes as lectures, sometimes in response to requests from periodicals, sometimes just because I'd be taken by ideas about poetry and poets I felt I might like to explore, and once because I felt I had something I wanted to offer in the realm of morality and history, which resulted in "Letter to a German Friend."

This book is a collection generated by these various propulsions, as well as a section of brief excerpts from interviews, which has its own introduction. The last essay, "On Being Old," was commissioned by the English Poetry Society. When I was asked for a subject for a lecture, the title for some reason immediately popped into my mind: it had come to me that I wanted to do some summing up of the fifty-five years I'd been immersed in the both gratifying and occasionally maddening struggle with my craft. I've had a life that's been long—rather amazingly so—and full, which is another sort of wonder. Through all my adult years, poetry has been with me, and I think "On Being Old" is an expression of gratitude and astonishment that I managed to stumble into a world the richness of which I really had no idea when I began. I certainly do now.

PART I
Poetry and Poets

Unlikely Likes
George Herbert and Philip Larkin

I

A painter I know tells his students a parable about the creative process: "When you go into your studio and stand in front of your canvas," he says, "about sixteen people are there with you: some of your teachers, a lot of painters from the past and some from the present, some friends, maybe even relatives, and you. As you begin to think about your painting a few of the people get up and leave; when you lift your brush, a few more go; as you advance on the canvas you're down to just one or two, and when you start to paint you're all alone with the canvas, and with the work you're trying to make." I like the story because it encapsulates so much of the artist's struggles, but it also slights a bit other elements of aesthetic decision.

Because when the painter picks up the brush or the poet the pen, it isn't only the obvious artistic influences that make claims on the creating consciousness—the entire world does, every detail of every reality the artist has ever known or even heard of; every belief, every myth and every concept, every iota of every perception the artist has ever had or imagined. That's not even counting those other variables that constitute our personal identities, the assemblages of assets and liabilities, ambitions and gifts and quirks, facilities and flaws that drive or impede us as we confront the more than improbable undertaking of reducing all this to a sheet of linen or the puffs of bent air that indicate that a poem is being spoken.

Really, the most radical decisions an artist or writer has to make concern what of reality to omit from the work. Of course we don't have to be conscious of most of these variables all the time: many of the choices about what to deal with and how to deal with them are made in advance. We're situated at a certain point in history from which we encounter reality, and we are the recipients of a conglomerate of cultural assumptions that eliminate other areas of reality and experience. Then there are those elements of the metaphysical that were inculcated in us and that we "believe in," or wish we did, or once believed in, or wish we didn't or hadn't. Our vision of course is further determined by the language we speak, as well as by the aesthetic forms in which we're fluent.

It's clear then, that every artist, and every poet—I'll speak only of poets now—more or less systematically though not necessarily entirely consciously develops modes of inclusion and exclusion with which to elaborate a vision and to accomplish works in accord with that vision. One might even imagine a scale of inclusion and exclusion as a way to categorize poetic intention. Poets like Shakespeare, Dante, Whitman, Wordsworth, and Yeats would be at one extreme, writers who mean to account for as many instances of reality as possible. At the other extreme would be those poets who for various ends purposefully limit their work in either an experiential or formal way. The reason for such limitings might be to go more deeply rather than comprehensively into aspects of self or nonself or to investigate more subtly rather than inclusively perceptual consciousness or belief. It's in this category in which I would situate George Herbert, whose work is an obvious instance of a conscious limiting of spiritual concern and aesthetic scope, and Philip Larkin, whose systems of exclusion are less apparent but just as rigorous.

2

There's no great puzzle in seeing how Herbert strictly defined his aesthetic intentions: all his poems are designed to serve one single purpose, which is prayer, although this also includes preparation for prayer and despair about not being able to pray, or to pray properly, with adequate conviction or purity of conscience and consciousness. To pray is to praise and thank Christ for the benefits, some not immediately evident, that his incarnation and self-sacrifice have brought to humanity; all other movements of mind, unless intimately connected with those facts, are trivial, distracting, spiritually dangerous, and potentially repulsive. Herbert is alone in his poems with his God, and a listener, one who also presumably wishes to pray. If Herbert participates in a community of human affection, that is incidental to his purpose; if he has aesthetic aspirations for his poetic gifts , they are to be mistrusted, although he is perfectly aware of his talents. For example, in "Jordan II," he writes

> When first my lines of heav'nly joys made mention,
> Such was their lustre, they did so excel
> That I sought out quaint words, and trim invention;
> My thoughts began to burnish, sprout, and swell,
> Curling with metaphors a plain intention,
> Decking the sense, as if it were to sell.
> Thousands of notions in my brain did run,
> Off'ring their service, if I were not sped:
> I often blotted what I had begun;
> This was not quick enough, and that was dead.
> Nothing could seem too rich to clothe the sun . . .

Herbert's genius is so ample that he can command himself to spontaneity, and accomplish it, so richly elegantly and with such unselfconscious abundance do his verses seem to flow from him. And we take more pleasure in his work than he claims to allow himself, for in fact he does bring great areas of the world into the poems—both in their associations and figurations—and intricate and precise examples of worldly reality and personal experience (though now presumably renounced) adorn the poems. Passions, though overcome, are still accounted for; earthly longings, though sublimated for spiritual ends, are elaborately recast. In one of my favorite poems, "The Pearl," Herbert acknowledges his attentiveness to the pleasures of human experience and reveals how much he has incorporated of them.

> I know the ways of Learning; both the head
> And pipes that feed the press, and make it run;

> What reason hath from nature borrowed,
> Or of itself, like a good housewife, spun
> In laws and policy; what the stars conspire,
> What willing nature speaks, what forc'd by fire;
> Both th' old discoveries, and the new-found seas,
> The stock and surplus, cause and history:
> All these stand open, or I have the keys;
>   Yet I love thee.
> I know the ways of Honor, what maintains
> The quick returns of courtesy and wit:
> In vies of favours whether party gains,
> When glory swells the heart, and mouldeth it
> To all expressions both of hand and eye,
> Which on the world a true-love-know may tie,
> And bear the bundle, wheresoe'er it goes:
> How many drams of spirit there must be
> To see my life unto my friends or foes:
>   Yet I love thee.

And then, although Herbert is dedicatedly abstinent, he continues, in one of the most sensual stanzas of poetry in the language:

> I know the ways of Pleasure, the sweet strains,
> The lullings and the relishes of it;
> The propositions of hot blood and brains;
> What mirth and music mean; what love and wit
> Have done these twenty hundred years, and more:
> I know the projects of unbridled store;
> My stuff is flesh, not brass; my senses live,
> And grumble oft, that they have more in me
> Than he that curbs them, being but one to five:
>   Yet I love thee.

3

It's more difficult to see how Larkin made an equivalent limiting aesthetic decision for his poetry. There's a great deal of reality directly and concretely considered in his work; he is vigorously contemporary in his imagery; and his poems incorporate a wide variety of his own experiences, sentiments, and perceptions: he writes of everything from mine explosions to race horses to train rides, country fairs, sadly spoiled love affairs, and dismal rooms in horrid boarding houses. And yet his poetry manifests just as severe a system of omission as Herbert's, and its content and modes of reflection are equally determined by that system.

If Herbert committed his poetry to the ultimate and intimate demands of his religion, the resolution manifested in Larkin's work is perhaps even more radical. Larkin's poems evidence a vision of commitment to absolute personal truth: there is present in the poems only the poet as he actually lived, with no compromising illusions about himself or about the reality in which his life took place. Larkin dedicated his work to an unflinching refusal to allow in it any element of his character that aspired to be other than it really was, which generated illusion or lied to itself or others, that fantasized or aggrandized or mythologized itself in any way.

This can seem to be a rather self-evident commitment for a poet, but in fact it's quite rare. The aggrandizement of the lyric personality is a basic assumption in poetry, and in Romantic and post-Romantic poetry the act of writing itself came to be regarded as redemptive: the poet as the protagonist of his poems became something like a secular priest, or a prophet, recasting modalities of beauty and veracity and redefining ethical and aesthetic boundaries. There are obvious examples: Wordsworth, Shelley, Baudelaire, Rimbaud, Whitman, Yeats, Eliot, and Lowell. But even in figures of apparently lesser ambition, it's the rule rather than the exception for poets to assume implications for their writing that imply a larger-than-life scale and significance. Furthermore, even introspective activities such as self-scrutiny, even an analytic vision of consciousness, point in most modern poets towards a presumably valiant enlarging of lexicons of concern.

Larkin will have none of this. Despite the powerful influence of Yeats on his early work (he famously replaced Yeats as his tutelary spirit with Hardy and declared that this had allowed him to mature as an artist), and despite some later experiments with an Audenesque public persona, and even a Dylan Thomas-like orchestration of the ego, in all his mature work there is apparent what can only be called a renunciation, a refusal to allow the self any deceiving overevaluation, and this discipline brings as decisive a limitation in thematic enactment as Herbert's, and one that is as poetically effective.

Larkin, at heart, was surely an incorrigible romantic, haunted by the transcendence he longs for but knows he can't have, whether that transcendence is in the form of sexual or spiritual fulfillment, and yet this passion is always kept in check, ironized, even sometimes quietly mocked, and finally the strictures on these desires end up constraining anything like the solace they might offer. No more than Herbert will he find pleasure in any manifestation of worldly satisfaction; though he certainly knows their attraction, Larkin will not comfort himself with anything that might be characterized as metaphysically illusory.

There is much else similar in the two poets. Both have an ascetic, even mistrustful attitude towards beauty, yet both are brilliantly accomplished in a wide variety of poetic music, and compose with an inimitable polish. There is even a certain unlikely conjunction in their areas of concern: both write of the seductive absurdity of money, of the temptations of the flesh, and of the illusions of worldly success. Of course we read the poets very differently: his poetic gifts aside, Herbert's spiritual agon, though exhilarating and even inspiring, takes place at a certain moral distance from most of us; his poetry enacts a spiritual struggle that concerns us mostly in a theatrical way.

With Larkin, in contrast, the exertions and tensions of the person moving through the poems are intensely familiar; we live Larkin's experience with him in a way that can afflict us with realizations we would just as soon not have to acknowledge about ourselves. By so completely shedding any pretension towards personal mythologizing, towards situating the self in an overt spiritual or philosophical context, Larkin positions himself unadorned, often, it can seem, even unclothed, flayed of his skin, against the potentially oppressive forces of contemporary moral and metaphysical debasement. The truth Larkin confronts and implements in his work is the insidious, barely admissible suspicion that someone else is possibly closer to the center of the reality one values than one is oneself or, perhaps even worse, that no one is at that center at all, that there might not be a hero in our way of existing. Eliot wrote, "I am not Prince Hamlet, nor was meant to be," but just from his tone we know he doesn't for a moment mean what he says: all his poems are cunningly constructed so as to be certain we take him not merely as the hero of his own poetic moment but also as the culminating identity of a poetical-mythological process spanning all the realms of human angst. Larkin wouldn't dream of saying he wasn't Hamlet or any other dramatic protagonist: he has made the decision, in his poems, where it works often to great effect, and apparently in his life as well, where perhaps it brought about a less happy result, never even to entertain such foolishness; he mocks, vehemently and contemptuously, much more harmless pretensions than this.

At his best, at his most withholding and wise, Larkin's daunting commitment allows him a very effective objectivity; there's a forceful union of self-effacement and skepticism in his poems. He's like the figure at the side of some Baroque paintings who holds back a curtain with one hand while coolly gesturing a welcome into a room presumably previously concealed. Except Larkin's drama is more harrowing, because viewed in another way he is the room; language in its most reflective mode will deal with nothing other than the contents of itself, and, as with any reflective poet, it is most often the space of Larkin's own sensitivity that is the subject of his poems. And the mind he presents to us is not so much self-effacing as self-abnegating; he reduces himself in many of own poems and, in his recounting of events in his life, to a very contingent presence, one who observes, comments, scorns, despairs, and occasionally, very occasionally, exalts, but only rarely pretends to satisfying personal experience or emotions.

If the decision towards truth can be morally unnerving, it has aesthetic implications as well. Herbert's poems, for example, have an inherent propulsive pressure in them; they are in a sense underway the moment they begin: the poet knows and we know what their purpose is, what the universe will be they evoke, what emotional and intellectual and symbolic contexts will determine their trajectory and even their volume. Larkin, conversely, begins each poem in a void, both of meaning and of aspiration. If the world he will deal with is familiar to us, it is familiar in a particularly stripped way: what will be selected from the world to be meditated on, the perceptual sensitivity with which that meditation will be equipped, and, most important, what the mood of the poem will be are completely unpredictable; whatever meaning the poem might be moving towards or sometimes away from will only be revealed in the course of events. Whether any poetic meditation ends up being positive or negative, optimistic or pessimistic, will depend entirely on the success or failure of the inspiration of the poet and the skill with which the poem is accomplished. Every poem, then, is a risky undertaking, both to write and to read; one never knows whether the poem will lift us to the inspirational exaltation of, for instance, "Church Going" or "The Whitsun Weddings," or drive us down again into the grinding skepticism of "Reading," or the obsessive spiritual negations of "Self's the Man" or "Home."

Considered in this way, Larkin's poetry is terribly difficult, not because we have trouble parsing what the poems say—he is never anything but excruciatingly lucid—but because each work presents us with the possibility of subjecting ourselves to a first person whom we will experience with a vertiginous frankness really unlike any other—since every other poet's self-revealings, even the so-called confessional poets at their most embarrassingly sincere, have about them a personal aggrandizement that the very writing of the poem assumes and that is generally taken to be morally consoling. The poet says in one way or another: Behold the audacity with which I position myself before you in this poem, a place from which I will speak truths whose purpose, if not whose conditions, is entirely laudable. The poetic undertaking is assumed to be intrinsically noble, but for Larkin this is simply not the case. He presumes no nobility, not even any minimal personal glorification for his effort: if the experience he has chosen to investigate leads him to an abyss of self, a dismal exemplary of characterological flaw, so be it—this is the truth his poetry risks.

4

The only time I ever found myself strongly disagreeing with Czesław Miłosz, a poet and thinker I admire enormously, was about Larkin. Miłosz was speaking at a conference I attended, and he attacked Larkin, saying in so many words that the darkness of Larkin's vision and his apparent pessimism weren't redeemed by his talent or lyric accomplishments. He insisted that poetry that embodied so little hope and so much outright despair simply couldn't be called great because great poetry always has as its ultimate theme just such hope, for the individual, and for humanity.

I felt that Miłosz was wrong, and I'm still certain that he hadn't then read Larkin's great poems with sufficient attention. Because despite the cynicism of many of Larkin's poems, despite an unpretentiousness in some of them that can seem demeaning to him and to humanity, his poetry as a whole is illuminating and inspiring. Even with Larkin's evident personal dejection—the despondency of his hopes for himself—there is in his best work a redemptive gravity: the refinement and variety of his song, the precision and generosity of his perceptions, do outweigh and by more than a little the more superficial grimness of his view of life.

What we take to be a poet's view of life does of course at some point have to come into play in our reflections. It's finally impossible to consider fully any poet's body of work without considering his or her character, with how it determined the work, and then with how the work may in turn have affected the poet. With some poets, this procedure can seem gratifyingly benign. With Keats, for instance, whose poetry seems to be cultivated in the very earth of our language, our judgment of his person is only a grace note to the poetry. Surely we feel so affectionate towards Keats the man just because the details of who he was are so incidental to the grandeur and purity of his song. With Wordsworth—to continue in the Romantic era—there's more in the poems that makes you want to know about the conditions of their writing: even though "The Prelude" is autobiographical, it feels proper to go back to Wordsworth's person to check it against what that person has had to say about itself. It isn't that we don't trust Wordsworth but, rather, that we want to know him more fully in order to understand what brought forth his abundant and generous poetic sentiments. With Coleridge, more, much more of this: it seems as though we can really appreciate the body of Coleridge's work only by understanding the person. The poems point to a person of such variousness and complexity that we can find ourselves reading the poems as much to illuminate our sense of the person who wrote them as for the intrinsic interest of the work. Not that the poems aren't significant in their own right, but the identity that generates them seems often to be obscured by them.

With Larkin, this is surely the case, with Herbert not at all. We don't know very much about Herbert's life, and yet what we do know seems perfectly adequate to the vision and purpose of the poems and the poet. We can believe what we read from those who knew him that he was a sweet and generous soul, utterly devoted to the clerical calling that came to him relatively late in life. But from the poems we can also tell that he was not always entirely a happy man; there is so much dissatisfaction with himself, so much feeling of inadequacy, that we can sense a certain lurking melancholy in him.

With Larkin, though, the dissatisfactions and self-questionings generally glare from much of his writing, and in reading him we constantly seem to have in mind the caverns of his afflicted soul. We know that Larkin was seriously depressed much of his life; he says so himself, most crudely and baldly in a poem, "The Literary World," one of the many that Larkin knew enough not to publish but that the editor of his *Collected Poems* didn't. In it, Larkin replies to a complaint of Kafka's that he hadn't been able to write anything for five months:

> My dear Kafka,
> When you've had five years of it, not five months,
> Five years of an irresistible force meeting an immovable object right in
>   your belly,
> Then you'll know about depression.

Larkin certainly wasn't the only depressed poet the world has ever known, to say the least. Even Herbert, as I've said, evidences surface shadow, but because of the religious disciplines his poems enact, because of how his dissatisfactions and despair are so firmly embedded in the structures of his spiritual quests, we hesitate even in our diagnostic age to apply any categorizing psychological frame to Herbert the person. Yet in their imagery, their connotative auras, the poems can be nearly as somber as anything in Larkin. In "Mortification," for example, Herbert writes:

>   How soon doth man decay!
> When clothes are taken from a chest of sweets
>   To swaddle infants, whose young breath
>   Scarce knows the way;
>   Those clouts are little winding sheets,
> Which do consign and send them unto death.
>   When boys go first to bed,
> They step into their voluntary graves,
>   Sleep binds them fast; only their breath
>   Makes them not dead:
>   Successive nights, like rolling waves,
> Convey them quickly, who are bound for death.

The poem goes on to register six stages of the life of a man, all of which point to death, are limited by death, contained in death. It is a depiction of the inevitability and pervasiveness of our awareness of death as convincing, if not nearly as overtly harrowing, as that of Larkin's in "The Old Fools," where he constructs a sort of compressed atheist's cosmology, raw, clear-eyed, and fearsome—all the more fearsome because of Larkin's use of the first person plural, which few modern poets use as often or as convincingly.

> At death, you break up: the bits that were you
> Start speeding away from each other for ever
> With no one to see. It's only oblivion, true:
> We had it before, but then it was going to end,
> And was all the time merging with a unique endeavor
> To bring to bloom the million-petalled flower
> Of being here. Next time you can't pretend
> There'll be anything else.

In Herbert's poem, the conviction of his spiritual hope keeps his plaint from casting the same pall on our perception of his personality as does Larkin. "Yet Lord, instruct us so to die, / / That all these dyings may be life in death," Herbert says, and, because of the way he posits his plea, we experience the poem not as the expression of a soul in need but of a consciousness in the speculative mode, the mode requisite for religious undertaking.

Larkin's despair, in contrast, can be all too convincing. The bitterness of his tone is sometimes sadly distasteful: "Get out as quickly as you can," he suggests, in "This Be the Poem," his ultimate statement on parenthood, "And don't have any kids yourself." Or, in his grim little poem about the futility of reading, he ends, in a paroxysm of hopelessness and self-scorn: "Get stewed: / / Books are a load of crap."

The examples are sadly many, including "Self's the Man," a scorchingly sarcastic examination of the way ordinary people live, which has an ending that implies that the alternative to such banality is madness, or something close to it.

> . . . I'm a better hand
> At knowing what I can stand
> Without them sending a van—
> Or I suppose I can.

Larkin in his slighter poems can seem so small spirited that you want to take him as an imaginative figure of his work, a fiction, rather than as himself, although he gives no indication that he means to be read that way. Those all purpose critical euphemisms, "persona" or "mask"—how I wish they could be applied with any kind of conviction to the voice in "Toads," for instance, his poem about the insufferability and meaninglessness of work, or of any effort, for any end at all. I'd truly prefer not to believe it's he himself who allows himself to say:

> Lots of folks live up lanes
>   With fires in a bucket,
> Eat windfalls and tinned sardines—
>   They seem to like it.
> Their nippers have got bare feet,
>   Their unspeakable wives
> Are skinny as whippets—and yet
>   No one actually starves.

Surely it was this sort of extrapolation from personal pathology into poetry that offended Miłosz. Larkin's spiritual depression at its worst sounds an edge of contempt, and sometimes expands from contempt for himself to a similar attitude for everyone else. The "we" at the end of "The Old Fools" asks much sympathy from us and includes us perhaps too presumptuously into an attitude like Larkin's own. He writes about old people:

>   This is why they give
> An air of baffled absence, trying to be there
> Yet being here. For the rooms grow farther, leaving
> Incompetent cold, the constant wear and tear
> Of taken breath, and them crouching below
> Extinction's alp, the old fools, never perceiving
> How near it is. This must be what keeps them quiet:
> The peak that stays in view wherever we go
> For them is rising ground. Can they never tell
> What is dragging them back, and how it will end? Not at night?
> Not when strangers come? Never, throughout
> The whole hideous inverted childhood? Well,
>   We shall find out.

How one wishes one might retrospectively endow Larkin with the spiritual resiliency that Herbert manifests in "The Flower," when after all his self-castigation, all his afflictions of the soul, he says,

> How fresh, O Lord, how sweet and clean
> Are thy returns! ev'n as the flowers in spring:
>   To which, besides their own demand
> The late-past frosts tributes of pleasure bring.
>   Grief melts away
>   Like snow in May,
>   As if there were no such cold thing.

And then his famous sigh of triumphant reaffirmation:

> And now in age I bud again
> After so many deaths I live and write:
>   I once more smell the dew and rain,
> And relish versing: O my only light,
>   It cannot be
>   That I am he
>   On whom thy tempests fell all night.

Would that Larkin, at the end, could have come back to "relish versing," to have used his senses—for his senses and his intellect never did desert him—to give him recompense for so much resolve, so much diligence. But he didn't. As we know from his biographer, at the end of his life his mood about himself became sadder and sadder.

5

I don't intend to say here that our ultimate judgment about a poet can be based on character; perhaps that was the ground of my disagreement with Miłosz. At the same time, it can't be denied that an artist's ambitions are defined to a great extent by who he or she is. This doesn't mean that we have to believe "character is fate": there are too many external conditions that determine what we call fate, even when it's defined most personally, though it is hard not to conclude that what defines character is character. Still, although there are in every artist's biography bruises, spots of triviality, a weakening of moral tissue, we learn to take these as marginal to the work.

But in considering Larkin's accomplishment, because his resolution of total personal truth determined so much of the tone of his poetry, we do seem to have to take his emotional identity into account in a way we don't with many poets. With Herbert, for instance, for us, and for he himself, his personality is a detail to which we pay little attention and to which he simply refuses to give credence. His poems struggle for a purity that is beyond self; his identity, his likes and dislikes are incidentals that he is constantly trying to shuck. He seems to want to appear in every moment like a butterfly emerging from a chrysalis. In its resistance to his spiritual ambitions, Herbert's self can appear to be nearly as repugnant to him as Larkin's, but its offensiveness consists essentially in its recalcitrance, its refusal to enact the requisites a belief in redemption entails.

With Larkin, the contrary is true. In his work, and probably in his life, Larkin makes a kind of Pascalian gamble: he wagers that the stripped, unself-exalting person of Philip Larkin can withstand the risks of possible meaningless and the futility that might be involved in his resolute refusal of pretense. Sometimes it's clear he can't hold out against such peril at all, and a forbiddingly global dejection captures him, and us in reading him. But sometimes the gamble pays off marvelously. In his most successful poems, like "Church Going," "An Arundel Tomb," "The Explosion," and, most notably for me, "The Whitsun Weddings," his extravagant objectivity enables a precision of perception and a purity of sentiment unlike any other poet's. "The Whitsun Weddings" is an unrivaled representation of a particular place at a particular moment of cultural history, of a physical environment and a social structure, and of the way individuals experience all of these elements together, consciously and unconsciously, individually and in collectives. The poem ends in an almost jubilant realization that all human reality can be experienced as connection, as a linking together of rituals of allegiance and community, and that an individual consciousness—the poet's—can discover an order for all of this.

> I thought of London spread out in the sun,
> Its postal districts packed like squares of wheat:
> There we were aimed. And as we raced across

> Bright knots of rail
> Past standing Pullmans, walls of blackened moss
> Came close, and it was nearly done, this frail
> Traveling coincidence; and what it held
> Stood ready to be loosed with all the power
> That being changed can give. We slowed again,
> And as the tightened brakes took hold, there swelled
> A sense of falling, like an arrow-shower
> Sent out of sight, somewhere becoming rain.

Larkin said that he took the image of the shower of arrows from Lawrence Olivier's version of *Henry V*, but the possible militarism of the image is marvelously transfigured into that metaphoric rain, which is suspended in some place of mystery beyond sense and intellect.

In this and in Larkin's other great poems, the objectivity of the poet speaking, his refusal to make any claims for the lyric self that might go beyond its capacity to perceive, acknowledge, and transfigure into verse, becomes a way of deflecting personal moral judgment and engendering a lyric state that embodies poetic meanings never diluted with idle fancies of transcendence. Yet there's no question that his inherent longing for a more romantic vision tempered his hard-boiled secular realism so that there is in some of the poems at least a celebration of forms of empathy and compassion that Larkin seemed to deny himself.

What is projected in the poems rather than any systematic social vision or any concrete system of meaning is a vision that is conditioned by mood, but a mood that generates what can at the end be a nearly ecstatic state of consciousness, in which intellect and emotions are wholly devoted to the poetical apparatus and its workings and never to a dramatic enactment of the feelings the poet might have about his stake in whatever is under consideration. Describing Larkin's method might make it seem less pertinent to the spirit than it is, but surely his poetic attack is as purifying in its way as Herbert's, and its self-abnegation has a nearly equivalent rigor, its force of inspiration arising in a similar way from a transparency of self. Larkin's self, like Herbert's, while never being completely committed to the world, still accounts for the poignant realities of existence and exalts them.

6

Sometimes it seems odd to me how popular Larkin's poetry was, how his poems were greeted with so much enthusiasm, first in the United Kingdom and, then, in America; his work, as I've shown, is very demanding. It might be, though, that he is read with such fascination just because of the great risks he took in circumscribing his work in such a potentially bleak way and, perhaps, even more so because the risks he took are so profoundly connected to the ineluctable conditions of our own spiritual reality. For if we are to tell the truth to ourselves, as presumably we have to if we are to do justice to our consciousness, then we, like Larkin, have to realize that we can't predict whether we will emerge from our meditations with a sense that our endeavors have a purpose or whether, in contrast, the reality we experience will afflict us with a nihilistic meaninglessness, with a dire conviction that our world is spiritually hopelessly lacking. This is the universe with which we are presented when we read Larkin and in which it is our task to find redemptive significance.

Larkin had to have understood this; I think his greatest act of courage, and perhaps his doom, was to accept this challenge and to accept, further, the belief that in a contemporary secular consciousness the positive moments of comprehension and illumination are isolated, because without an overriding system, to any sort of which Larkin refuses to give credence, even our episodes of bliss, of aesthetic rapture, can simply evaporate in the ongoingness of time. Larkin accepted no program of commitment, to connect one potentially redeeming moment of his poetry to any other or to anything else. He would have no philosophical or social-political conviction that might have tempered his intellectual penetration or made it subservient to any merely utilitarian end. Larkin undertook his program of truth telling without knowing whether it might end in such despair that the poetic voice would be reduced to absolute silence, to a condition in which neither imagination nor intellect would be able to find inroads through the overwhelming possibilities of metaphysical and personal meaninglessness. This, we know, was a despair, and a concomitant silence, which did indeed take him painfully in his last years.

This was his personal tragedy, and perhaps the worst of it was that Larkin finally hadn't even allowed himself to make an enduring commitment to poetry; he couldn't grant himself the right to believe as most poets do that the composition of poetry is a personally redemptive act. Even Herbert, while chastising himself for it, takes more than mere pleasure in the act of writing. Though surely Larkin had once believed in his poetry in this way, too, because he couldn't have written his great poems without that kind of faith in poetry, but for whatever characterological reason, towards the end of his life that faith deserted him; not even the process of writing interested or solaced him any longer, so that he wrote nothing but the most trivial occasional pieces after the end of 1977, when he composed "Aubade," his last masterpiece, and one of his very greatest. But it's such a mordant poem. "The mind blanks at the glare," he says, punning on his own powers of perception,

> "Not in remorse
> —The good not done, the love not given, time
> Torn off unused—nor wretchedly because
> An only life can take so long to climb
> Clear of its wrong beginnings, and may never;
> But at the total emptiness for ever,
> The sure extinction that we travel to
> And shall be lost in always. Not to be here,
> Not to be anywhere,
> And soon; nothing more terrible, nothing more true."

Nothing, nothing, nothing. The last two lines close down any possibility of redemption a life of art might offer. And the poem resolves in as distressing a passage:

> Slowly light strengthens, and the room takes shape.
> It stands plain as a wardrobe, what we know,
> Have always known, know that we can't escape,
> Yet can't accept. One side will have to go.
> Meanwhile telephones crouch, getting ready to ring
> In locked-up offices, and all the uncaring
> Intricate rented world begins to rouse.
> The sky is white as clay, with no sun.
> Work has to be done.
> Postmen like doctors go from house to house.

"Work has to be done," the poem says, not meaningful work, not work that brings forth meaning, but work at its most absurd; labor, the hands or the mind mechanically performing what has been given them to perform, for no real reason. "Postmen like doctors go from house to house," the poem ends: they do their work, but the task of delivering mail is the same as the task of healing lives: as repetitive, as rote, as purposeless.

But it wouldn't be fair to leave Larkin at the time in his life when his powers were deserting him. Because Herbert died so young, in his prime, he abides as an inspiring poetic identity; when we look back on his work, we realize that the spiritual solitude of his poetry included much basic human affection. The phrase, "Love bade me welcome," in "Love III," might be his motto.

I sense that Larkin, like Herbert, felt much more love towards life than he was, because of the quirks of his personality, prepared to admit. A profound sympathy informs many of both poets' work, and if less evident than in Herbert, Larkin's compassion and ultimate affection are wonderfully articulated in "An Arundel Tomb," the most touching of his masterpieces. Regarding the earl and countess who "lie in stone," hand in hand before him, he ends the poem with a statement that might be the summary of at least the best of his poetic effort and accomplishment.

> The stone fidelity
> They hardly meant has come to be
> Their final blazon, and to prove
> Our almost-instinct almost true:
> What will survive of us is love.

Amichai Near the End

When we were being mistaught poetry in grammar school and high school, the most off-putting misapprehension our teachers inflicted on us was probably the notion that poetry had something to do with wisdom, that not only did it embody wisdom but, more than anything else, it *was* wisdom. We were given to understand that poetry was a dazzling compilation of sage instruction and profound advice. It is boring just to remember how boring were those compilations of jingly-jangly maxims and supposedly inspired adages that had been extracted for us and that we were meant somehow to apply—a possibility that we knew was absurd. No wonder we ducked—and that most of us stayed ducked.

Strangely, I think that when nonreaders of poems explain their disaffection from the art by bemoaning the lack of rhyme and meter in contemporary poetry, this is often an expression of a nostalgia for this kind of quasi-philosophical counsel, although in truth there is precious little of it in real poetry. If there is anything morally useful in poems, it is to be found, I believe, in their spiritual and emotional drama, just as what is most useful in our own lives is inextricably embedded in our experience and tends to disintegrate when we abstract it and attempt to make it relevant.

And yet, there is in poetry, or in great poetry, poetry like Yehuda Amichai's *Open Closed Open*, a certain intensity of attention, an ethical focus so absolute that there is no question that a significant knowledge is crucially entailed, and wisdom, as a category or a value, seems inescapably germane, no matter how our aesthetic understanding might make us veer away from it.[1] And we do veer: even when Amichai, the shrewdest and most solid of poetic intelligences, finds himself formulating what sound like elements of some ultimate comprehension, he seems to doubt what he is doing and he backs away, and undercuts, and undermines, sometimes with irony, sometimes with humor, sometimes, though only for moments, with something like self-scorn.

For one does not have to accede to the illusion that poetry is essentially didactic to recognize that there is a tradition, of which Amichai is quite clearly aware, of poetry as a summing-up, of long or longish poems that intend to recapitulate the realizations at which a rigorous intelligence and a forceful poetic will can arrive. In a tradition that exists apart from but adjacent to epic and tragedy, probably beginning in the West with Lucretius, it comes to us through Dante, Milton, Pope, and Goethe, among not all that many others. In our century, the two most admired examples of it are Rilke's *Duino Elegies* and Eliot's *Four Quartets*. Amichai seems to have had both those poems in mind in writing *Open Closed Open*: he infuses some of Rilke's metaphoric detail into his own and refers directly several times to Eliot, even going so far as to quote from him several times, most obviously in a passage that elaborates on "what was and what might have been."

Certainly Rilke's and Eliot's poems incorporate ranges of experience that make them worthy of being described as "wise," though as a means of articulating the sort of sanctified sagacity that my teachers fancied they certainly disappoint. Rilke's poem, undeniably one of the masterworks of twentieth-century literature, was taken by some of his more rapt enthusiasts as the basis for a spiritual cult; but if the work is supposed to point toward systems of belief and action, they are even more elusive and inconclusive than what we find in our more sanctioned canonical writings. To be sure, there are readers who take any text short of the sports section as though it was meant to bring about "illumination"—Wittgenstein can, alas, be read like Khahil Gibran—but even for Rilke's most devoted countesses it was hard to find much

---

1. This essay first appeared in the *New Republic* as a review of *Open Closed Open* by Yehuda Amichai, trans. Chana Block and Chana Kronfeld (New York: Harcourt, 2000). All quotes are from the translations in the book.

heartening ground for faith in the *Elegies*. The poem concludes in a rapture glorifying "lament," and what that might indicate as a spiritual directive is impossible to say. The *Four Quartets* have evoked a similarly hopeful reverence in some of its readers, not least because Eliot set out quite consciously to echo liturgy; the poem employs various prayer-like devices of repetition, rhythm, and phrasing. Both works are imaginatively inspired, and they treat aspects of experience that are rarely elucidated in any way. And yet even these vatic masterpieces are not of much use, if it is a coherent metaphysical or ethical doctrine for which one is searching.

Amichai's new book of poems comprises a sustained outburst of inspiration, and it has a similarly complicated relation to wisdom and to matters of the spirit. There are differences, of course. Amichai's work is longer, and it incorporates a personality distinctly different from Eliot's and Rilke's. Amichai is a Jew, and an Israeli, and he is exquisitely aware of the conditions entailed by those identities, both historical and spiritual. He is on a much more familiar and easier footing with the traditional term "God," and his unexpected, almost casual intimacy with divinity seems much closer to traditional piety than anything found in either of the other poets. Amichai surely meant his poem—again, in a deep sense *Open Closed Open* is one long poem composed of many parts—to consider the same grand and fundamental issues of life and death, but his yield of meanings, his "wisdom," is unmistakably his own.

Amichai is a poet of powerful feeling, of nearly boundless appetites and affections. He is attached, with a commitment that sometimes drives him to distraction, to the things of the world, to the natural and the human, to the other and the self, to the divisions of his own body; but his poetry is informed by a skepticism, a rage for objectivity, that is just as vigorous. Several times near the beginning of his book he uses the image of two heavy grindstones—"the spirit is ground up as by two heavy grindstones, / upper and lower"—and there is no doubt that the genesis of the image is to be found in the seemingly irreconcilable aspects of his imaginative and moral struggles. He adores the world, in detail and in large, as much as any poet who has ever lived, but a part of his mind is taken with a wild doubt that drives it relentlessly towards lucidity.

Amichai despises all the disfiguring and degrading illusions attached to so much of human life, public and private, present and past, but he also allows no room in his poetry for avoidance, for omission, for a prematurely resolving subjectivity. His own overfull consciousness is his subject and his object; and he vividly demonstrates, and tries to rectify, the way that even our best intentioned drive for understanding is susceptible to sentiment and to wistful self-delusion by our reflex to make the world fit our seemingly admirable preconceptions and longings.

At the same time, there is in the poems the sense of a synthesis and an acceptance—an acceptance that triumphs not in the negation of doubt but in the incorporation of the poet's perplexity into an ardently comprehensive awareness. Amichai has lived, and has distilled in his writing, a life of really singular richness. His own adult life has been almost precisely coeval with the history of his country. He has led as energetic and as rewarded a literary career as any of his contemporaries, anywhere. He has fought the wars of his nation, and the wars of love and marriage and parenthood, and the struggles of self-overcoming that the life of a conscious artist demand. Now, he is saying to himself, now that you have seen and felt everything, and caused yourself to feel everything in poetic reflection again, felt it backward and forward, in elation and despair—now what have you come to? And his answer is: a negation for every assertion, to guard against falsehood; a speculation counter to every supposition, to guard against self-deception; and an unaccomplished act remembered for every seemingly admirable but possibly falsely valued accomplishment.

His methods for working through all of this are various: paradox, irony, reversal, commentary, contradiction. He can bring himself to say, "we cannot be fooled. Yes, we can be fooled," and then, just a few pages later, "We can be fooled. No, we cannot be fooled." He proposes alternative narratives for personal experience, for history, for myth. With biblical myth, the results can be fanciful, and enchanting. One section of the book is a retelling of biblical stories in forms not unlike some of the zanier passages of *The Waste Land*.

> King Saul never learned how to play or to sing
> nor was he taught how to be king.
> Oh he's got the blues.
> he's nothing to lose
> but the moody tune
> on his gramophone
> and David is its name-oh. David is its name,
> its name its name its name . . .

> Our father Jacob, on the beaten track,
> carries a ladder on his back
> like a window washer to the VIPs.

He does God's windows if you please. In "Jewish Travel: Change Is God and Death Is His Prophet," Amichai marvelously recasts biblical history by having Moses write the Torah "as a travel book."

> a memoir, every chapter with something very personal
> that was his alone—like Pharaoh's daughter, like his sister Miriam,
> his brother Aaron, his black wife, the Ten Commandments.

Then, in one of the most endearing passages in the book, he returns to the story of Abraham and Isaac:

> Every year our father Abraham would take his sons to Mount Moriah
> the way I take my children to the Negev hills where I once had a war.
> Abraham hiked around with his sons. "This is where I left
> the servants behind, that's where I tied the donkey to a tree
> at the foot of the mountain, and here, right here, Isaac my son, you asked:
> Behold the fire and the wood, but where is the lamb for a burnt offering?
> Then, up a little farther, you asked for the second time."

And he goes on, so intimately, so lovingly:

> After Abraham died, Isaac started taking his sons to the same place.
> "Here I lifted the wood, this in where I got out of breath."

And ends:

> And when Isaac's eyes were dim with age, his children
> led him to that same spot on Mount Moriah, and recounted for him
> all that had come to pass, all that he might have forgotten.

There are also moments in which the past and the present, the mythic and the personal, fuse even more clearly and intensely. About intimacy and love, Amichai is always more gentle and forbearing than about anything else; and about love he evokes emotions grounded in the pure origins of affection.

> Every woman in love is like our mother Sarah,
> lying in wait behind the door while the men inside
> discuss the beauty of her body and her future.
> She laughs into her palm, her hollow palm, as into a womb,
> ocarina of a future, like the light cough of a clever fox . . .
> And every loving woman is like Rebecca at the well, saying
> "Drink, and thy camels also." But in our day Rebecca says:
> "The towels are on the top shelf in the white closet
> across from the front door."

Yet Amichai's purposes are not always so uncomplicated. He means to confront, to demand, to analyze everything. Nothing may be allowed to escape his exigent, mordant scrutiny: not history, not belief, not his nation, not his self. He questions gender foolishness, as when he challenges the casuistical puritanism of the ultra-Orthodox by expressing what sounds like an innocent desire to be prepared for burial by women, for them a sin. And he juxtaposes the intimate and the horrendous in combinations that can be chilling, for instance, when he evokes the Angel of Death during the exodus from Egypt:

> standing over them, legs wide apart . . .
> crotch gaping male and female
> like a bloody sun in the thick of frizzled black death.

And God, too, especially God: Amichai's is a God composed of absence, of negation, of accusation, a God of excruciating nearness and agonizing inscrutability, of power and of impotence. Sometimes the closeness, the approachability, of God brings forth a tone of fondness, even of conviviality.

> The Jewish people read Torah aloud to God
> all year long, a portion a week,
> like Scheherazade who told stories to save her life
> By the time Simchat Torah rolls around,
> God forgets and they can begin again.

Or:

> The God of the Christians is a Jew, a bit of a whiner,
> and the God of the Muslims is an Arab Jew from the desert, a bit
>   hoarse.
> Only the God of the Jews isn't Jewish.

More often, though, the relationship between Amichai and his God is harsh, painful, a matter for dark and fearsome questioning. "I declare with perfect faith," be writes (in an old liturgical phrase that becomes a refrain in the poem,)

> that prayer preceded God.
> Prayer created God,
> God created human beings,
> human beings created prayers
> that create the God that creates human beings.

And, finally, because he is a Jew, because, as he says, he is "not one of the six-million," he adduces (again with the aid of a phrase from the prayer book) also the God who is both intimate and maddeningly lax.

> "Our Father, Our King." What does a father do
> when his children are orphans and he
> is still alive? What will a father do
> when his children have died and he becomes
> a bereaved father for all eternity?

And history. Has any people ever lived so many vagaries of history, in their very flesh, as the Israelis? And has any Israeli lived them more intensely than Amichai? First as a Jew:

> After Auschwitz no theology:
> From the chimneys of the Vatican, white smoke rises—
> a sign the cardinals have chosen themselves a pope.
> From the crematoria of Auschwitz, black smoke rises—
> a sign the conclave of Gods has not yet chosen
> the Chosen people.

Then as a citizen, a soldier—for surely no nation more than Israel has been so caught between history's many narratives and has so often gone forth in fierce obedience for the great cause of national and religious survival and then been brought up by so many stoppings to think, so many changes of mind:

> When I was young I believed with all my heart
> the Huleh swamp had to be drained.
> Then all the bright-colored birds fled for their lives.
> Now half a century later they are filling it with water again
> because it was all a mistake. Perhaps my entire life
> I've been living a mistake.

This is Amichai's personal experience of what amounted to the national recantation of one of the founding symbols of Israeli statehood, the draining of the swamps near Galilee, which had been nearly as much an article of Zionist pride as the Jewishly blooming deserts. A later generation realized that the reclaiming of the swampland was an ecological disaster, so they were flooded again. And even recent history must be written again, and the relationship to enemies and to friends reconsidered.

Amichai broods on the propensity for communal legends to deceive; but this is not the customary literature of disillusion. He is too much of a realist, he is too experienced in the perversities of history, to be surprised or outraged by the crude discrepancies between political rhetoric and political outcomes. Still, he comes close to disdain when he refers to modes of public remembering, at one point scrutinizing one of the memorials to the War of Independence, a scattered column of burnt-out tanks and armored vehicles along a highway, by adding to them his own mementos about the vagaries of death and destiny:

> The skeleton of some other car, charred in a traffic accident
> on some other road.

And in another context:

> Tova's brother, whom I carried wounded from the battle at Tel Gath,
> recovered and was forgotten because he recovered, and died

in a car crash a few years later, and was forgotten
because he died.

And Amichai knows, too, the resigned and sad stoicism of the Israeli, living as the conditional in the psychoses of other nations, as a parent who, in an armed and hating world, must send his children off to military service. In a wrenching simile, he regards his son's face in the window of the bus taking him away to his army base "like a stamp on an envelope." Later he must behold his daughter's face as her bus takes her away and find nothing but the same terrifyingly impersonal figure to employ. Then, the crying out:

> Oh, those stamps, those letters sent off into the world,
> those letters we send. These names, addresses, numbers,
> those colorful stamps, those faces . . .

There are so many stunning metaphors in these pages. Amichai has always had a dexterous and supple metaphorical imagination, and now the force of his feeling, the necessity that he has imposed on himself to come to conclusions, takes him to astonishing lengths. Every perception, experience, reflection, emotion, and tradition presents itself as the potential half of a simile. Sometimes his metaphorical passion seems nearly to rend itself to pieces in trying to do so much labor of transfiguration. In a passage in which he surely has himself in mind, he writes:

> The singer of the Song of Songs sought his beloved so long and hard
> that he lost his mind and went looking for her with a simile map
> and fell in love with the images he himself had imagined.

Everywhere there are figures of wrenching poignancy. In the section called "Evening Promenade on Valley of the Ghouls Street" (which echoes the "They all go into the dark" passage in the "East Coker" section of Eliot's *Quartets*, and through there to Dante), he writes of

> A few remain standing at the crossroads of empty streets
> like windsocks at the airport. But each one
> is blown a different way, each in the direction of his flight
> by his own wind, his own spirit.

And again, in another passage, about visiting the cemetery of the village in Germany where he was born:

> There's the name of my mother's
> mothers, and a name from the last century. And here's a name,
> and there! And as I was about to brush the moss from a name—
> Look! an open hand engraved on the tombstone, the grave of a *kohen*,
> his fingers splayed in a spasm of holiness and blessing,
> and here's a grave concealed by a thicket of berries
> that has to be brushed aside like a shock of hair
> from the face of a beloved woman.

Sometimes Amichai's figurative work can be as charming and as fanciful as his work with the Bible. In "Jerusalem, Jerusalem, why Jerusalem?" he exalts for his beloved city and frets about the way the world obsesses about it, lamenting, "Why, of all places, Jerusalem?" He proposes other possibilities, Babylon, Petersburg, Rome, and finally (of all places) Vancouver:

> why not Vancouver with her salmon
> that ascend to her from the sea, crawling
> on their bellies up the hard mountain slope
> like atoning pilgrims, kosher pilgrims of fin and scale . . .

There is so much sheer imaginative force in this book. In a single sequence, about a visit to a museum, Amichai generates enough similes for whole volumes of lesser poets.

> A collection of ritual objects . . . : spice boxes
> with little flags on top like festive troops
> and many fragrant generations of sacrifice,
> and the memory of many Sabbath nights that did not end in death.
> And happy menorahs and weepy menorahs and oil lamps
> with the pouting beaks of chicks like children singing,
> their mouths wide open in desire and love . . .
> Seder plates that rotate at the speed of time
> so it seems they are standing still, and kiddush cups
> in a row on the shelf like soccer trophies.
> . . . A collection of ritual objects

like the gaudy toys of a baby god, the gift
of an aged nation, like the strange instruments
of a ghost orchestra, like some odd motionless
bottom fish deep in the waters of time.

Perhaps, at this level of transformative power, when consciousness manifests so astonishingly its ability to elevate the particular to the conceptual grandeur of the general, it is only metaphor itself, and the mind as the master metaphor, that can mediate between the irresolvables of self and other, trust and mistrust, reflection and action. And it may be that finally the most decisive element of poetic worth might have to do with the sheer quantity of this transfiguring metaphorical energy. That, and a certain sensual and intellectual assurance that one is capable of dealing with the manifold complexities of existence, and that imagination is capacious enough to contain and to recast all those complexities, without aversion or exclusion. By these measurements, no poet alive has more claim to stature than Amichai.

If there really is such a thing as wisdom, it might well reside in the character that a master such as Amichai can fashion for himself, and so for us. Our connection to anything ultimate, in other words, is more aesthetic than moral, and to understand this is to understand also that this connection is never, in any way, dogmatic. To sojourn with Amichai in the vast, rugged, sympathetic domain of his imagination is to be given leave to linger in one of those privileged moments when we are in a confidential and confident engagement with our own spirits, when we know with certainty that such a process of imaginative self-investigation is proper and just, regardless of the substance or the occasion of our thoughts.

The wisdom of Amichai's poetry consists of an essential mistrust of any prescriptive thought or act, from any source, from any community or nation, from any constricted notion of self. There is much we cannot know about ourselves, and about the universe, but at the same time this condition must not prevent us from keeping all that disorderly material as a vital part of our consciousness, for it is what enriches and gives resonance to our self-conception. It is a limitation that launches us. Whether the admirable equilibrium that Amichai achieves in *Open Closed Open* is accessible to us is our own affair; but we have to be grateful at how much he has bestowed of his own harrowing experiment of self-realization, and thankful, too, that the outcomes at which he arrives at for himself are, in the end, so benign and so exalting.

> All my life I played chess with myself and with others
> and the days of my life were chess pieces, good and bad—I and me,
> I and he, war and hope, hope and despair,
> black pieces and white. Now they're all jumbled together,
> colorless, and the chessboard has no squares,
> it's a smooth surface blending into night and into day.
> The game is calm and has no end, no winners,
> no losers, the hollow rules
> clang in the wind. I listen. And I am quiet.
> In my life and in my death.

Autobiography with Translation

A few years ago, when I gave a reading at a TED conference, one of a series an old friend of mine initiated for people from various fields—scientists, inventors, architects, designers, show-biz folk, and even this time a poet, me—my friend said to the audience after I was finished something about how moved he was to think of all the years I'd spent, had to spend, working by myself, all alone, and, he implied, lonely. I was startled: I'm quite a gregarious person, and sometimes I do become lonely, but it's something that never happens to me during the hours I'm at work. When I'm at my desk, my room is filled, overflowing with the presence of a vast number of poets I love, and some others I don't know at all, whose books or poems have recently arrived but who are there waiting for me to become acquainted with and possibly love, too.

Here are some of the poets that are with me on my desk or the table next to it as I write this: two different translations of Osip Mandelstam's poems; a book of translations of Giacomo Leopardi; a collection of Thomas Wyatt; another of Gerard Manley Hopkins; an anthology entitled *New European Poets*, which includes poems from every possible nook and cranny of Europe; a book of essays of Eugenio Montale, as well as his last book of poetry, *It Depends*, the astonishing singularity of which I only recently came to appreciate; a collection of Blake; *Alcools* by Guillaume Apollinaire, in French; a book of translations of early

33

Celtic poetry, with those magical strings of modifiers; a translation by Marilyn Hacker of a contemporary French poet, Guy Goffette, whose work I'm not familiar with, but which I plan to read soon; and several anthologies of English and American poetry.

What I find striking about this list of the works of poets I'm studying, or restudying, is how many different languages, cultures, and moments of history are represented in it. When I first began to write poems in college, we were offered in our courses no poetry whatsoever in languages other than English, except very rarely as exercises in language classes. Still, somehow the first two poets to whom I found myself intimately attached were the French poet Charles Baudelaire and the German, Rainer Maria Rilke. Furthermore, when I was released from the university (or perhaps I should say paroled, since I've ended back in them for my livelihood), I found myself, during the first years of my apprenticeship, which seems never to have really ended, spending almost all my time with poets from languages and cultures other than American and English. To mention just a few, there were Pablo Neruda, Cesar Vallejo, García Lorca, and Miguel Hernandez, in Spanish; Baudelaire, again, still, French; and Rilke, German, still as well. Then a little later Rimbaud, Jean Follain, and Francis Ponge; the Polish poets Miłosz, Rosewicz, and Herbert; Montale, Ungaretti, and Pasolini from Italy; the Alexandrian Greek Cavafy; Tomas Tranströmer from Sweden; the Russians Akhmatova, Mayakovsky, and Mandlestam; the classical Chinese, Du Fu and Li Po particularly; as well the centuries of Japanese haiku masters; even quite a lot of poetry from cultures without a written tradition that were being collected and published or republished around then. And this, as I say, is a very partial accounting.

The question that comes to me now is why? English certainly has a great poetic tradition—it might actually be the very greatest—so why was I driven so forcefully to other languages and cultures? And I should add that I certainly wasn't alone in this: there was a terrific amount of translating and reading of translations of poetry going on at that time. Many literary journals in the early sixties were crowded with translations from every place in the world, and for awhile my impression was that there were as many books of translations being published as poetry in English. Again: why?

I've thought sometimes that there were extraliterary reasons for this. Much of this turning outward, this searching for new poetic resources, came during the years of the Cold War when America took on, or had imposed on it by circumstances, an imperial sense of itself, an identity of power from which we have suffered and caused much suffering since. There might be something to this, and something also to the fact that there were such profound social changes underway in race and gender relations in America at that time. But I'm not really sure about how much either of these were the reasons for what was happening in poetry. Perhaps because so much of my attention has been devoted to poetry, learning to write it and learning about it, I'd feel disingenuous if I didn't limit my reflections to the areas in which I can be less speculative.

It's one of the miracles of art that no matter how many times we experience a poem or a painting or a piece of music, no matter how much time we spend reveling in it and analyzing it, each time we return to it, it feels utterly spontaneous, seeming to be improvised anew as we experience it. Furthermore, if a work even on a tenth reading or viewing or listening, or a hundredth, doesn't convey that quality of freshness, of renewal, it will seem moribund, perishing before our eyes like a fish on a beach.

The truth is that the creation of art is laborious, or if that's not quite the word, it certainly is the case that all art is generated out of the necessities of an aesthetic system, its demands and restrictions, as well as its opportunities, its propulsive energy. Such systems are dauntingly intricate, though fortunately many of the variables of an art form will have been absorbed into what might be called the unconscious of the artist before a creative act is undertaken.

Another characteristic of creative systems, what are usually called styles, is that they have a strong conservative tendency. Styles are always striving to perfect themselves, by which I mean that styles have inherent in them the potential for enactments that no longer depend on anything but the demands of the style itself: neither matter or content nor, in other words, world. Stylistically, art is always moving from the transparent to the opaque, from trying to make encompassing and as comprehensive as possible its relations with reality, to a state in which its formal dexterity comes to be its most essential requirement. When this happens, usually during the late moments of an artistic era, the execution of style becomes an end in itself, *the* end in itself: art becomes style displaying itself, preening, showing off.

This is when an artistic style becomes decadent. Decadence in itself isn't intrinsically bad—it's unavoidable. And some of the very greatest art is created at the end of the innovation-decadence cycle. What happens then, though, is that some subtle line is crossed, and the gloriously decadent becomes offensively empty and sterile, and, with no portion of the quest of the artist's blundering soul any longer a part of it, produces work that is lifeless, stillborn.

This isn't any great revelation, surely. We all know that when a contemporary painter paints an impressionist painting, no matter how deftly it may be done, no matter how seductive it might appear, it offends, seems at best kitsch, a trivialization, at worst a painful violation, hardly worth being deplored. And when a contemporary poet generates a Keatsian sonnet that isn't driven by anything in the spiritual cosmos of his or her time, if there is nothing of our difficult contemporary reality infused in the work, and of the poetic history that informs that reality, then experienced readers will find it inert, without essential energy, not worth the effort of bothering with.

Serious artists or writers or composers are acutely aware of all this. At some point in a style's cycle, and not even necessarily during the decline to decadence, there is the realization that the assumptions that have been informing the style have become rote and are being executed in accord with formulas that produce nothing but simulacra of the authentic work they once enabled. And, perhaps not surprisingly, this is something that many of the practitioners of an exhausted style experience at almost the same time.

This is what happened to me and to many other poets during the years of the late 1950s and the early 1960s, when much of the poetry being written in America seemed to have become overly formalized, self-referential, stale, and if I dare use the word, spiritually lifeless. Artists are always ranging over their own traditions, searching for viable models of inspiration, but I believe that our mostly unconscious realization during those years that we were at a dead end drove many of us to ransack literatures other than our own, no matter how grand our own surely was. We needed, desperately, it felt then, other cultures, other histories, other poetries in order to discover aesthetics that would disrupt those we'd inherited. We wanted new models that would make unfamiliar demands and offer new freedom, new inspiration.

And the poems from other languages that came into English then brought with them much that became immediately essential to me. As I've noted, English literature is certainly one of the richest, if not *the* richest, in the world in the sheer number of great poets and great poems; we have somehow managed since the Renaissance to produce astonishing poets in just about every period of our history. I could very well have spent my life reading nothing but English-language poets and been gratifyingly recompensed, but I was searching for something then that without my ever quite understanding it had less to do with the greatness of the poems themselves than with quite other matters.

For many of those poets I read in translations seemed to offer clues to my own poetic identity in a way that very few American or English poets had. Of course I labored to digest my own tradition, but though the poets of that tradition would ultimately have to be the models for much of my own work, in those starting-out days, they were my masters only in matters of technique: I was learning from them essential matters of language and sound. But what the poets from other cultures offered were varieties of what I'll call poetical-spiritual identities, ways of conceiving of myself in poetry that weren't available to me from the poets in English, either because they were too far removed from me historically or because the model they offered was too predetermined, too much a part of a culture I felt only marginally a part of and quite intimidated by. There would come a time later on when I could conceive of myself as being in a poetic cosmos with the English masters, perhaps because my own poetic identity had become firmer, but back then, I needed poets who arrived on my desk without my having any literary or cultural preconceptions about them: they were, in a sense, as naked as I was, as unencumbered—as, in some odd way, vulnerable. They were merely the sum of the matter of their poems, and their presence in the universe of my poetic attention seemed as contingent as my own. This of course is beside the quite astounding variety of aesthetic possibilities they brought with them. I was particularly taken then with the use of nonrational modes of association and figuration, discoveries that had been made in delightful, if rather whimsical embodiments by the French Surrealists but that were given a moral and metaphysical edge, especially by the great Spanish and Latin American poets of the thirties: particularly, García Lorca, Hernandez, Vallejo, and Neruda.

Of course this wasn't the only time in English and American literature when there was this kind of reaching out to other sources. At the turn of the century, when the self-consciously decadent pre-Raphaelite and late Victorian poets were setting the aesthetic standards of their day, the early modernists turned from them, finding in French poetry, poetry from Asia, even early Provençal poetry, new visions and new styles. Similarly, in the early English Renaissance, many of the best poets of the time translated Petrarch and other Italian and Latin poets as a way of broadening the scope of what they experienced as a limited range of stylistic possibility. Some of Thomas Wyatt and Henry Howard's most famous poems are actually translations, though often our anthologies don't even remark the fact. And similar things happened in the visual arts: in the late nineteenth century, Monet, Van Gogh, and Gauguin, among others, turned to the Japanese print; Manet went to Goya; Picasso and the other cubists to African art.

In retrospect, needless to say, there were at the time of which I'm speaking poets who were doing serious, significant work, but each of them seemed to have something about them that kept them, at least for me, from becoming the inspiration and examples they were later to be. Ginsberg wrote "Howl" in the fifties, and though it's now almost universally considered a great poem, when it was published it was received by many poets, including me, I'm embarrassed to say, as a work that had more to do with the propagation of a worldview than a new kind of poetry. Perhaps because there was so much publicity hysteria around the publication and attempted censorship of the poem, it was difficult to see what its real virtues were. Also during that period, William Carlos Williams was still writing, better than he ever had—*Pictures from Brueghel*, his greatest book, appeared in the early sixties. But for a young poet, Williams seemed to be more of an ancestor: he, along with Frost, who was also still alive though not writing at his best, were poets from the definite past, to be revered, certainly, but whose work didn't possess that thrust of the unexpected as did poems coming from other languages. Robert Lowell and Richard Wilbur were writing then as well, but until Lowell published *Life Studies*, he and Wilbur seemed to me only the very best of the poets working in the conservative conventions of the fifties: admirable, but not the powerful innovative influence Lowell would become with *Life Studies*—and, even more explosively, with *Imitations*.

Imitations arrived near the middle of that golden age of translation I've been describing that transformed American and English poetry in the late fifties and early sixties. As I've said, there seemed in those days to be an endless supply of unfamiliar and crucial poems being delivered to us across language barriers.

But *Imitations* brought its own unique revelations and released something in me I hadn't grasped had been keeping me from moving ahead in my own work. It wasn't that the book "influenced" me—what happened was much fiercer than that. I didn't know or care then exactly what about it inspired me so, but I realize now it surely had to do with the audacity with which Lowell approached and poached on and cannibalized so many sacrosanct canonical poets and made their work so thoroughly his own. As a translator myself now, and a teacher of translation, I sometimes disapprove of much of what Lowell perpetrated on the original poems, the distortions, the amputations, the mutations. Other times, when I come to the book I again find myself rapt.

On those first readings, though, when I saw what Lowell had dared to do, the presumptuousness with which he had turned poems by everyone from Victor Hugo to Montale to Rilke to Pasternak into grist for his own poetic identity, I had no reservations at all: *Imitations* was a book I needed, the book that without even knowing it I'd longed for. What Lowell had done seemed to strip away the last of the intimidating barrier of sanctity that proscribed the world of poetry from me. I always felt I'd arrived too late to poetry to be a real poet, and besides, I never seemed to feel anything like the "inspiration" other poets spoke of; my composing always felt more laborious, more dogged, more willed than they made it sound. How could I ever hope to place myself among those geniuses? Lowell was a member of that Parnassus, clearly, but he had done something I'd been taught simply shouldn't be done—he had dared to usurp the inspirations of other poets, modifying them, altering, *hacking* at them, really, making them his own in a way I could never have conceived possible. It was his impertinence, his temerity, more than anything he did with the individual poems that made the book mean so much to me: he had brought poetry down to the earth on which I actually lived.

Needless to say, there were poems in the book that were wonderful in themselves, especially Montale's, whose work hadn't yet come to me and which I still admire. And occasionally, when Lowell would go almost completely "free," as he did in "Heine Dying in Paris," he would come up with poems all but unrelated to the original, but splendid in their own right. His recastings of Rimbaud are always fascinating: a fusion of two not dissimilar sensibilities, whose experience couldn't have been more disparate. There are some, too, which I find quite awful; what he did to Rilke is a disaster, unmitigated by any virtue, tonal, interpretive, or otherwise, and "Orpheus, Eurydice and Hermes" is all but perverse in its distortions of the original's metaphoric grace.

I realize now, though, that more than any particulars in the poems, it was that other thing, the sheer presumptuousness with which Lowell attached those various poetic souls to his own that so enfranchised me and was so crucial to my perception of my own possible place in the world of poetry. All this went beyond the mere study of verse, with which I was already feverishly involved, and beyond my being affected by the poems themselves. The poet I wanted to be, the poems I was trying to write, trying, really, to imagine writing, all at once seemed feasible, if not right away, then someday. Lowell apparently conceived and wrote *Imitations* to get past a dry period in his work, which it certainly did; for me, the book simply gave me the right to begin to be myself.

These days, there has been what has come to be called a globalization of art and a nearly instantaneous awareness, especially in the market-driven visual arts but in literature as well, of what is happening in other aesthetics. Whether this is all for the good I'm not certain. While I was reading the anthology of contemporary European poetry I mentioned before, I was struck by how many of its poems tended to sound alike: in too many cases, I couldn't really tell what country or language a poetry had come from until I checked. I thought at first that perhaps the almost universal commitment to free verse was the reason for this apparent homogenization, which is a rather distressing thought. It may have been, instead, because all the translators of the poems in the book were working in American English and hadn't sufficiently taken into account the subtleties of the original languages.

Or perhaps not. Perhaps we are entering in, or are already immersed in, an age in which the singular glories of the poetic traditions in each language are being subtly undermined by a too easy accessibility to other sources. That would be sad for young poets now who are battering against the untranslatability of reality itself and who won't have the revelatory experience of coming across, the way the poets of my generation did, a Wole Soyinka, a Yehuda Amichai, a Zbigniew Herbert—each utterly unique, each embodying his own culture in a way we'd never suspected could be done.

Lowell Later

I. A. Richards wrote but apparently never sent a letter to Robert Lowell that was quoted by William Pritchard in his *New York Times* review of Lowell's *Collected Poems*. Richards is explaining to Lowell (or complaining about) the fact that he can't "understand justly" the poems in Lowell's first publication of his long sequence of free-verse sonnets in *Notebook*. "The tone," Richards says, "the address, the reiteration, the lacunae in convexity, the privacy of the allusions, the use of references which only the PH. D. duties of the 1990's will explain, the recourse to contemporary crudities, the personal note" (and now the most damning, and probably the reason why he never sent the letter), "the 'it's enough if I say it' air, the assumption that 'you must sympathize with my moans, my boredom, my belches' . . . puzzle me."

    The key terms here are "understand justly" and "sympathize," the first stating the not unreasonable lament of a critic confronting unfamiliar and difficult work, the second posing what is actually an ethical demand on an aesthetic issue. Lowell's poems—finally really anyone's poems—don't ask primarily for "sympathy," anymore than music does. Certainly Mozart wasn't asking sympathy for the very bizarre variations on Masonic mythology that are an integral part of the plot of *The Magic Flute*. There are no moral propositions being offered. What Mozart is presenting to us is music, his music, the music that Mozart heard in his mind and brought into the world; it's a music that no other mind in the history of humanity had produced before or ever would again.

It's the same thing with Lowell's music, or Milton's, or Whitman's, or Donne's, or any other truly major poet's. Lowell's was a great poetical musical voice. To read the hundreds of poems in *History, For Lizzie and Harriet,* and *The Dolphin* (the successors of *Notebook*, which include most of its poems) is to be immersed in that voice, even if the matter of a poem can increase or decrease our enjoyment. Lowell's genius, and the genius of poetry, is that we can listen attentively and with pleasure, for so many pages, no matter how apparently incidental the matter or theme or story of any single poem might be. I'm not sure how many of the poems of the three books I can say I love whole-heartedly, and there are many I might wish—as did Elizabeth Bishop—hadn't been written, or at least published, because of their outrageous intimacy, their embarrassing indiscretions about other people's intimate business. But when I'm in the book, none of that finally matters; the poems are there, I listen to them, they're the productions of an enormous musical talent, and that's sufficient: that there are elements in the poems I don't care for, or even have to forgive, is incidental to the elemental experience of being taken again by Lowell's singularly gratifying music.

Any poem has its music, of course, though with less accomplished poets the music can be less efficient, and the unity of music and matter more questionable. Even poems with a striking musical identity can end up lacking the fusion of voice, character, and substance we find in poets as masterful as Lowell. John Berryman's long sequences of poems in *77 Dream Songs* and *His Toy, His Dream, His Rest* were surely the model (never quite acknowledged) that Lowell used for the *Notebook* sequences. Lowell acquired from Berryman the right, we might say, to compose poems that are, in fact, rather well described in Richards's critique: they do reiterate, they do have "lacunae," and they can be terribly private. But Lowell's music lifts his sonnets to a level that makes them continue to be fascinating, while for myself I can't read Berryman's books with nearly the satisfaction I did when they first appeared, and I think this is because of limitations of the music in Berryman's poems.

Berryman's music at first can seem as compelling as Lowell's, perhaps even more so, but the poems depend very much on idiosyncratic devices, unorthodox word order, odd violations of grammatical conventions, minglings of conversational tone, even of dialects, most commonly of African American speech (though it isn't the speech of actual black America Berryman uses; he devises riffs, instead, from the reconfigured language of nineteenth- and early twentieth-century minstrel shows). It's true that when the poems do work, they're unforgettable: "Life friends is boring . . . ," "There sat down, once, a thing // on Henry's heart . . . ," and a dozen others remain central to my view of American poetry. But already by the end of the first book of seventy-seven, there seems to be more than a breath of repetition and tedium. The poetry's music often seems to be being played for its own sake, which is all well and good, but it also begins to feel that it isn't an ample enough music to bear so much sheer usage. By the end of the several hundred poems of *His Toy, His Dream, His Rest*, it's almost impossible to find anything like a satisfying single poem: the poetry has been overwhelmed; there's the claustrophobic sense of being trapped in one self-indulgent aria after another.

Lowell's music, in contrast, by the time he came to write the poems in *Notebook*, had modulated many of the more flagrant idiosyncrasies of his earliest work, very likely because of the influence of Bishop, whose poems' precise conversationality Lowell recognized could carry a broad range of theme and emotion. If Lowell had tried to compose the tonnage of poems in *History* with the percussive—we might say symphonic—music of "The Quaker Graveyard at Nantucket," the poems would very likely have ended up seeming now as nearly unreadable as Berryman's. As it is, there isn't any single poem whose music wasn't stirring to read the first time and very few that don't continue to be satisfying to listen to again, no matter how slight or merely personal their material.

Still, problems arise when we consider Lowell's work during the period when he was exclusively writing his sonnets. Those years represent quite a large portion of Lowell's entire career, and it's hard not to ask whether during that time Lowell put his talent to its best use. Like all truly great artists, Lowell is finally to be measured only against himself, but it's not unfair to wonder whether the work of that period fulfilled as much as it might have the potentials of his enormous gifts.

No poet, even a genius, can be asked to write only hugely significant poems. Nonetheless, we have expectations of poets that to one degree or another can be disappointed. Frost's last decades didn't bring anything like the number of marvelous poems his earlier career did; one doesn't value him less for that, but it's impossible not to remark it.

With Lowell, although during the period of the sonnets there was never the slackening of output there was with Frost, there are still questions. What I keep wondering is whether during that time Lowell may have become too engrossed in his instrument—as singers like to call their voices—so that exercising it became an end in itself. Anyone who has worked for a period in a single form knows how generative that kind of formal commitment can be, how it can draw forth so many unexpected epiphanies. As Lowell put it, "I don't find fourteen lines a handcuff. I gained more than I gave." Furthermore, all poets well know that writing poetry is seductive, not only in that it's difficult to stop doing once you've begun but also because the act of composing brings with it such a sense of excitement that when it's not happening, when inspiration fails, there can come to pass what might well be described as withdrawal symptoms.

Lowell's commitment to his poetry was undeniable—so was his moral seriousness and his erudition and intellectual range. I think it can be asked, though, whether during those years he became too avid to experience again the pleasures—the ecstasies—of composition and so became impatient with his craft. When I read *Notebook* and its successors, it doesn't bother me that the work presumes a preexisting interest in both the poet and his poems: I remain committed to both Lowell and his music, and I never cease to be astonished by the spectacle of his being able to create such engrossing poems out of the most incidental experiences and the most glancing historical perceptions.

And yet, mightn't Lowell's potential ambitions for his poetry have been slighted by his grasshoppering, as it were, over his keyboard? Though "The Dolphin" is a moving sequence, with many Lowellian delights in it, it still seems slight when compared to the marvelous family poems of *Life Studies*. And there's certainly nothing in *Notebook* that has the conceptual scope and the musical audacity of "The Quaker Graveyard," nor was there anything like the emotional complexity and depth there is in the *Life Studies* poems, nor poems that so powerfully fuse the private and the public, the meditative and polemical as "For the Union Dead" or "Waking Early Sunday Morning." Considered as a whole, many of the poems in the sequences seem to be offshoots, somehow, of a poet living a life of poetry, rather than individual performances that could result in poems equal to Lowell's best work.

When Lowell finally stops writing the sonnets and turns to the poems in *Day by Day*, things pick up again, notably. In his last book,

Lowell devised a new kind of poetic reflection, with an intellectual weight and a fusing of abstraction and concrete detail that's completely unique, and it resulted in a poetry of sheer density unrivaled, I think, by anyone's since Donne. Although there are still a number of poems that share the limitations of the sonnet sequences—a certain, yes, day by dayness, and, in truth, much of what Richards characterized as the "It's enough if I say it" syndrome—there's a startling enrichment of Lowell's diction, which was certainly rich enough to begin with. The book has a number of poems unlike anything else, anywhere. "Ulysses and Circe" is one of his great triumphs, a powerful evocative uniting of the mythical and personal, so compressed that in its few pages the poem enacts a drama of remarkable narrative and lyric scale. It ends with a description of Ulysses's return to Penelope, which has become one of my favorite passages in all poetry. The voice crackles here with an utterly original, unfamiliar music, pared down, terse, abrupt, almost curt, a music that can embody the most unlikely chords of anachronistic figuration.

> Volte-face—
> he circles as a shark circles
> visibly behind the window—
> flesh-proud, sore-eyed, scar-proud,
> a vocational killer
> in the machismo of senility,
> foretasting the apogee of mayhem—
> breaking water to destroy his wake.
> He is oversize. To her suitors,
> he is Tom, Dick, or Harry—
> his gills are pleated and aligned—
> unnatural ventilation-vents
> closed by a single lever
> like cells in a jail—
> ten years fro and ten years to.

(I find that phrase " a vocational killer / in the machismo of senility, foretasting the apogee of mayhem" so efficient, so charged with implication, that each word does the work whole phrases would in most poems.)

Lowell never stopped being a great poet, but one can admit to some small regret that during those long sonnet years he didn't put himself to the more difficult task of writing more ambitious individual poems. With all the admiration I have for his work, I feel something like a bit of longing, a sad nostalgia, for those great poems he didn't permit himself. No one in the last half century, with the exception perhaps of Bishop, has written as many, but along with our gratitude for so much given, we can end up with a twinge of disappointment, similar to what we feel about Mozart's early death or that of Keats, wondering how many more great pieces there still might have been.

Odd Endings

How poems end, and why they end the way they do, "closure," has become a subject of much discussion over recent generations of literary criticism. Some of this speculation has led to fruitful insights about literature and our responses to it, but for the practicing poet, the issues involved in endings often seem to be of another dimension entirely. For poets, the basic, forthright, and unavoidable question about endings is whether or not they work and, if not, why not. A poem can come to its end in a flash of inspiration and excitement, or it can finish in ways that are disappointing, may be confusing, and appear to be simply wrong, although, interestingly, sometimes the essential worthiness of poems afflicted this way can still not be called into question. I'd like to discuss examples of both sorts: first, poems whose endings leave me uncertain, even irritated, then two others whose endings continually, faithfully startle and please me.

Poets sometimes speak of poems they've written as being like their children, meaning that if anything like a flaw should be perceived in a poem, it's incidental to the affection the poet feels towards it. I've never used that analogy about my own work, but I do feel that way about certain poems written by other poets, poems I consider indubitably great, major, essential—whatever my adjective of the day is. Those poems are indeed metaphorically like my own offspring, in that I still find them essential to my poetic life, even if I might notice elements in them I find lacking and decisions they enact with which I might disagree. I feel a similar intimate connection to certain poets themselves, they're so close to me, my being in the world, that if they may have poems I don't cherish as much as I might, I'm not troubled: they, like my own children and grandchildren, are beyond reproach.

Perhaps recognizing this has allowed me to admit to myself that some inestimable poems in fact do have not defects but, say, blemishes, and I've noticed that often these blemishes occur at or near the ends of poems. Still, because of the attachment I otherwise feel to them, I've chosen to speak of their endings as odd, not bad or mistaken and certainly not unforgivable—just "odd."

One of these poems, Wordsworth's "Michael," seems out of balance in the way its narrative climax is structured. Another, Robert Frost's "Out, Out—" ends in, to me, a wildly inappropriate tone that seems plainly, inexplicably wrong. I'll consider two other poems that are absolutely basic to my very definition of poetry but that seem to falter in their spiritual, philosophical conclusions—in a sense they fail to deliver what they've promised, or not in the way they've promised it: Rilke's *Duino Elegies* and Eliot's *Four Quartets*. And finally, I'll look at two poems, one by Rilke, one by James Wright, whose endings are wholly unexpected and mysterious and entirely gratifying and influential beyond what their dimensions would seem to indicate.

I should probably concede in advance that there's a strong possibility I might be simply wrong in some or all of my carpings and quibbles about the poems whose endings disappoint me. It may be that I just haven't fully understood these poems, or not yet, and that wiser students of their strategies might be able to set me straight. So in a sense this is a tentative venture, subject to correction or retraction, even disavowal. But so be it.

Worthsworth's "Michael" is rightly considered to be a key work in the development of both the poetical and social outlooks of the early Romantic movement. In its depiction of the lives of a family near the economic bottom of English life, it is one of the first of what might be called socially analytical works that attempt to bring the actual lives of the lower classes into serious literature. The poem is about a shepherd and his wife and son, but, although Wordsworth does use the term once, nothing about them and the way they live has much to do with the ancient tradition of "pastoral" poetry, those recountings of the leisurely doings of mythical sophisticated rustics entertaining each other with lyrical celebrations of the purity of their elemental but not elementary vocation.

Michael, Worthsworth's shepherd, is depicted as confronting the realities of his very difficult vocation and the scant security it affords him. The poem's catalog of the hardships of rural life is rich in particulars and in atmosphere. There are many passages about the great labor such a life entails, the more or less constant expenditure of energy, and the solitude of the shepherd's calling. Michael's precarious financial situation is treated at length in the poem; we learn that he inherited his small parcel of land with a mortgage on it that took years to redeem, and a key element in the plot concerns a guarantee he gave long ago for a business affair of a prosperous nephew, whose fortunes have declined, so that now Michael may have to sacrifice "half his substance" to make good on his pledge.

Wordsworth's portrait of the shepherd and his family and their life is positive and admiring. Although he doesn't scant the difficulties with which they're confronted, the mood of the poem is mostly positive, almost exultant. The characters are stoic and patient and, essential for Wordsworth, for the most part they glory in being so deeply embedded in a life nourished and ennobled by their closeness to nature. The solitude Michael experiences in tending his flocks is tempered by his time with his devoted wife Isabel, and then by the son who comes to the couple almost biblically late in their lives. Much of the poem is given over to the upbringing and moral education of this much doted on son, Luke. The early life and formation of the boy are almost idealized: it would be difficult to imagine a more thoughtful and considerate upbringing than that to which Michael and his wife devote so much of themselves.

The poem ends in disaster: the boy grows up, and when the family is faced with their financial crisis, he is sent to the city to be brought along there by another relative in order for him to be able to earn enough to help prevent a portion of the family's land from being sold off, their only other recourse. There's a long passage of farewell, in which Michael lays a cornerstone of a sheepfold with his son, which he proclaims will be a "covenant" between them. There he makes a plea—moving in the light of subsequent events—that if, while the son is away, he is tempted by "evil men," he should think of their labor together, and "God will strengthen" him.

> "Amid all fear
> And all temptation, Luke, I pray that thou
> May'st bear in mind the life thy Fathers lived,
> Who, being innocent, did for that cause
> Bestir them in good deeds."

The son leaves, and after a promising beginning in the city, he goes bad, takes to evil habits, vanishes into urban anonymity, and finally flees "to seek a hiding place beyond the seas."

The amount of space I've used here to recount what would seem to be a key element in the plotting of the poem probably seems a conventional compression of complex events. The odd thing though is that this isn't a compression at all; I've used only slightly fewer words to describe the fate of the shepherd's son than Wordsworth does in the poem. The events that in ordinary narrative would seem to be the tragic turning point in the destinies of the poem's characters are encapsulated in the following several of the almost five-hundred lines of the whole:

> Meantime Luke began
> To slacken in his duty; and, at length,
> He in the dissolute city gave himself
> To evil courses: ignominy and shame
> Fell on him, so that he was driven at last
> To seek a hiding-place beyond the seas.

That's all. Luke's entire destiny is brought down to these five and a half pentameter lines. It's worth noting that earlier in the poem thirteen entire lines are dedicated to the description of Michael's household's lamp. In the structuring of the poem, there seems nothing untoward in this: an evocation of a revered household object, it serves to reinforce the mood of reassuring domestic stability. It begins:

> Down from the ceiling, by the chimney's edge,
> that in our ancient uncouth country style
> With huge and black projection overbrowed
> Large space beneath, as duly as the light
> Of day grew dim the Housewife hung a lamp;
> An aged utensil, which had performed
> Service beyond all others of its kind.

In the poem's allotment of human drama, there seems something seriously awry in the space devoted to the lamp and to Luke's fate. And again, before the youth leaves home, when Michael reveals to his wife his intention to send their son to the city, Isabel is naturally upset, but she comforts herself with an extended memory, a fantasy really, about a poor "parish-boy" from their neighborhood, who has gone off to London to become "wondrous rich." Her reflections about this other youth, whose story is at best oblique to the plot, continues for fifteen lines.

Yet the undoing of Luke's life, which is absolutely central to the narrative takes up only those few lines, and we never hear another word about him again. Though the poem goes on to recount albeit sketchily the ultimate fate of the parents, the thrust of the destiny of the characters for all intents and purposes seems to come to a stop right there. The first time I read the poem, I remember I checked to see whether there might not have been a misprint in the edition I was reading, that some, or many, lines might have been omitted by a sleepy type-setter.

As we know, Wordsworth, especially in his early work, was a consummate craftsman, one of the greatest in English poetry, and there's surely a way to read the poem to account for the poem's structure. It may be that Wordsworth felt his deeper purposes were already accomplished by what he'd given of his narrative, which would have had to do with the way his old shepherd's spiritual consciousness is sustained by his closeness to the greater rhythms of the natural world, and his stoic dedication: he goes on for the seven years remaining of his life continuing to work on the sheepfold he'd begun with his son, though it's never finished. Or perhaps Wordsworth conceived of Luke's denouement as something like the off-stage deaths of characters in Greek tragedy. But even in tragedy there's always a messenger who elaborates at length on the awful out-of-sight goings-on. Still, no matter how I try to justify the poet's greater purposes, I find poor Luke's fate abrupt, amputated.

(There's another odd moment in the poem. Near the end, the narrator tells of speaking with people who had known Michael, and "what he was // Years after he had heard this heavy news." The text says then, "His bodily frame had been from youth to age // Of an unusual strength." The strange thing is that Wordsworth had used precisely these same words to describe the shepherd near the beginning of the poem. I can't think any other major poem, or any poem at all, which contains the same exact sentence twice.)

Another poem with a rural setting, Robert Frost's "Out, Out—" is a much more abrupt narrative, with an ending as strange and dismaying, but even more unexpected and shocking. The poem again concerns a young man, presumably another farmer's son, whose destiny is also sad, in fact grim, and though the poem is apparently less fraught with ethical implications than is "Michael," its moral tone is layered at the end with what seems to me an inappropriate resonance.

The frame of the poem is the unremarkable rural life of a family. A young man is performing an ordinary farm chore, the cutting of firewood with some sort of power saw. Frost has an uncanny ability to create atmosphere and character in a very few words, and near the beginning of the poem he uses a telling bit of description, some ominous personification of a machine, and a sudden shift of scale of vision to reinforce both the richness and apparent lack of irrelevant complication of at least the idea of life on a farm:

> The buzz saw snarled and rattled in the yard
> And made dust and dropped stove-length sticks of wood,
> Sweet-scented stuff when the breeze drew across it.
> And from there those that lifted eyes could count
> Five mountain ranges one behind the other
> Under the sunset far into Vermont.

The poem continues in this mood of what might be called kinetic serenity for some lines, but then there's an accident: the youth's hand is caught in the teeth of the saw. Frost intensifies the event with an unusually vivid metaphor that at the same time adds a philosophical, even cosmological edge to the event:

> His sister stood beside them in her apron
> To tell them "Supper." At the word, the saw,
> As if to prove saws knew what supper meant,
> Leaped out at the boy's hand, or seemed to leap—
> He must have given the hand. However it was,
> Neither refused the meeting.

We are in a metaphoric universe here in which objects may have minds, in which the dire arbitrariness of cause and effect imply a dimension that, though not inherently good or evil in a moral sense, still has ferocities, systems by which the youth, and all of us, are subject to a violence that seems to have a larger, terribly malignant meaning.

The poem ends:

> But the hand!
> The boy's first outcry was a rueful laugh,
> As he swung toward them holding up the hand
> Half in appeal, but half as if to keep
> The life from spilling. Then the boy saw all—
> Since he was old enough to know, big boy
> Doing a man's work, though a child at heart—
> He saw all spoiled. "Don't let him cut my hand off—
> The doctor, when he comes. Don't let him, sister!"
> So. But the hand was gone already.
> The doctor put him in the dark of ether.
> He lay and puffed his lips out with his breath.
> And then—the watcher at his pulse took fright.
> No one believed. They listened at his heart.
> Little—less—nothing!—and that ended it.
> No more to build on there. And they, since they
> Were not the one dead, turned to their affairs.

There's such an unusual tone here. That "So," to begin with. What does Frost mean by using such a dry term in the midst of such dramatic, not to say tragic, happenings? I really don't know. Seamus Heaney employs the word, which he says is an ancient sort of "Well," to begin his translation of Beowulf, but there's no evidence that Frost had anything like this in mind. Although the writing of the poem is admirable, incorporating Frost's formidable precision and figurative force—"the watcher at his pulse took fright" is an example of Frost's often understated metaphoric ingenuity—I just don't understand what he's up to in terms of the tone of the poem.

Those last two lines, "No more to build on there." And then that "they": there are no characters specified in the poem beside the brother and sister and doctor until "No one believed. They listened." There's a family implied by those plurals, but it's a family with startlingly detached responses and, then, a horrifyingly cold one.

I really can't speculate as to what Frost meant the dramatic function of those last lines to be. Are we simply to disregard what would have to be the grief of the sister, and the others in any normal family, and even the doctor? Is the implication that mere observers can never appreciate the anguish of the participants in such small tragedies? But the characters who would be present wouldn't be mere observers—family never is. What possibly could be the "affairs" to which "they" turn, in the face of such intimate horror? Are they some madly fanatic descendants of the ancient Stoics, for whom the death of a loved one was at least theoretically of no greater moment than anything else?

And what of the title? The association must be to Macbeth's "out, out, brief candle!" in the famous "tomorrow and tomorrow and tomorrow" passage. Or perhaps the "out" from "out, vile jelly" when Gloucester's eyes are plucked out in Lear. But in both cases, Shakespeare's dark vision is tempered by their being so poetically luminous. Might Frost be experimenting with a similar almost nihilistic reflection? Might he be hinting that the implications of the tragic accident he recounts are simply overwhelming, beyond reflection, and that the only appropriate response is to look away from the whole bleak reality in which such things are fated to occur? This is surely the most tolerable possibility. Otherwise, the ending seems merely callous, cruel, even nasty. If there were an aspect of Frost's character anything like this (which his most treacherous biographer suggests), he managed to conceal it impeccably in the rest of his work.

I really don't know the solution to this conundrum, though perhaps there's some clue in the fact that Frost modeled "Out, Out—" not on personal experience but on an article he had come across in a newspaper. But I don't believe that really explains anything either: much literature concerns matters with which the author has no real first-hand experience. And though there is in the abruptness of the tone at the end something akin to the turning of the page of a newspaper or the moving of the eyes from one column of print to another, if that was Frost's purpose, he probably would have let us know about it in the poem itself. As I say, perhaps there's just something about the poem I haven't understood, but it remains for me a kind of shadow on the sensitive and generous person Frost presents in the rest of his work.

Rilke and Eliot now, the oddness of the endings that I want to examine is of a much different order. Rilke's *Duino Elegies*, which many readers, myself among them, consider the greatest single poem of the twentieth century, has a vast range of theme and an equally broad consideration of humanity's enduring dilemmas and their possible resolutions. From its beginning, that rapturous evocation of spiritual desolation, "Who if I cried out?" the poem moves in wider and wider circles, encompassing everything from religious impulse to love and sexuality, to a child's love for and from a mother, and then a father; to a mythical aggrandizement of the overwhelming confusions of young love, to the profound connections between art and life, to the spiritual links poetry can find in nature, and more.

Thematically the poem is simply gigantic: inexhaustible. At its deepest level, it is concerned with what can be expressed intellectually about human life and what in our existence can be transformed to language and poetry, then transfigured finally to what Rilke calls invisibility, by which he means a realm of existence grounded in ours but utterly different in the way it unites the mundane and the metaphysical. "Superabundant being" is what the poem finally proposes and, in many ways, accomplishes. Its primary method is a kind of transcendent metaphor: the bringing together of the most seemingly disparate phenomena, and even categories of being, in order to illuminate reality, but to create new modes of perception ordinarily unavailable to us.

And along with all of this the poem is emotionally terribly moving. I remember many years ago my huge surprise when tears came to my eyes as I read aloud the beginning of the eighth elegy to a friend—it was the first time that had ever happened to me. I still find the passage embodies a profoundly unique way of experiencing nonhuman reality.

> With all its eyes the natural world looks out
> into the Open. Only our eyes are turned
> backward, and surround plant, animal, child
> like traps, as they emerge into their freedom.
> (Translation by Stephen Mitchell)

There are so many more passages of stunning poetic force: the beginning of the third elegy, about young love and the existential gravities of desire; the fifth, based on Picasso's painting "Les Saltimbanques," which is an extended meditation on art, using the street performers in the painting as the vehicles for a dazzling series of symbolic transfigurations that both exalt the figures in the painting and profoundly elucidate how we are ennobled by art.

In some sense then, when I speak of the ending of the *Duino Elegies* as being odd, as having possible shortcomings, I might appear to be ungrateful, but the sense of disappointment with the poem's ending I felt the first times I read it, which at first I chalked up to my own lack of interpretative skill, has stayed with me and in some ways intensified over the decades I've been studying it.

The last, tenth, elegy looks back to the first; like the first, it gets underway with an evocation of angels and continues in a large, exultant tone of poetic triumph.

> Someday, emerging at last from the violent insight,
> let me sing out jubilation and praise to assenting angels.
> Let not even one of the clearly-struck hammers of my heart
> fail to sound because of a slack, a doubtful,
> or a broken string. Let my joyfully streaming face
> make me more radiant; let my hidden weeping arise
> and blossom. How dear you will be to me then, you nights
> of anguish.

The poem goes on into a sentiment on the praise of human misery that only Rilke could get away with: it regrets "how we squander our hours of pain." Rilke considered that his project of transformation would be incomplete if the constant human phenomena of grief and anguish couldn't be a part of it, and going along with him takes some getting used to.

In the section that follows, the poem recounts the devices human beings have generated to inure ourselves to our inevitable sorrows, a brilliant passage in which Rilke posits an angel who "would stamp out" our illusory comforts and goes on to create a scene that embodies the contempt he felt for the deceptive trivialities by which we distort our lives to distract ourselves from our true obligations. The poem refers to a . . .

> city of grief,
> where, in the false silence formed of continual uproar,
> the figure cast from the mold of emptiness stoutly

swaggers: the gilded noise, the bursting memorial.
Oh how completely an angel would stamp out their market of solace,
bounded by the church with its ready-made consolations:
clean and disenchanted and shut as a post-office on Sunday.

(Familiars of Rilke's biography will catch the poignancy here of a man who lived his most intimate life writing and receiving letters, for whom a closed post office was a serious matter.)

Next a passage that encapsulates with wild inventiveness the way our material productions distract us from our more difficult aspirations:

Farther out, though, the city's edges are curling with carnival.
Swings of freedom! Divers and jugglers of zeal!
And the shooting-gallery's targets of prettified happiness,
which jump and kick back with a tinny sound
when hit by some better marksman. From cheers to chance
he goes staggering on, as booths with all sorts of attractions
are wooing, drumming, and bawling.

Then one of my favorite moments in Rilke's work, perhaps because it's so un-Rilkean in how it brings into conjunction the crassest of our false consolations, money and sexuality:

For adults only
there is something special to see: how money multiplies, naked,
right there on stage, money's genitals, nothing concealed,
the whole action—, educational and guaranteed
to increase your potency.

There follows an excoriation of the illusions of inebriation, and the poem returns to the "real," where children are visible and where lovers and even dogs are screwing.

But now, problems. The entity previously called "the figure cast from the mold of emptiness" becomes "the young man," although there's been no indication that there's a young man here at all. Then a little farther on, again with no warning, we discover that the young man is dead and is all at once being "drawn on, farther; perhaps he is in love with a young Lament."

The whole elegy now swings into an evocation of this "Lament," who perhaps "is of noble descent" but who the young man will abandon, because

> Only those who died young, in their first condition
> of timeless equanimity, while they are being weaned,
> follow her lovingly.

"Being weaned?" This is where my sympathies begin to waver. The Young Lament befriends young girls now, and "Shows them, gently, what she is wearing. Pearls of grief and the fine-spun veils of patience."

I don't really wish to diminish Rilke's astounding accomplishment, but I, for one, just can't account for the sheer mawkishness of what comes next. Briefly, the young man finds an "elder Lament" who recounts the history of the Laments, who were once a "powerful race" and who "used to be rich" (as Rilke's many patronesses still were). Then the young man is guided through the landscape of Lament with its ruined temples and castles and "fields of blossoming grief," which the living think are bushes. There are herds and birds and graves of elders, and even the Sphinx, and the whole thing begins to sound like a nineteenth-century fantasy novel, populated by beings who have the anemic ephemerality of figures in bad pre-Raphaelite paintings.

It's only now that we realize the young man is recently dead and, therefore, is too "dizzy" for his sight "to grasp it," presumably the Sphinx. Now there's an owl that brushes his cheek, "the one with the fuller curve," then "the new stars of the land of grief"—a list of constellations, all, again, the most diluted late Romantic glyphs: the Rider, the Staff, the Garland of Fruit . . . Cradle, Path, etc. And last, and surely least, "the clear sparking M that stands for Mothers." The weird story goes on a bit more, until the dead youth, alone now, "climbs on, up the mountains of primal grief. And not once do his footsteps echo from the soundless path."

The first time I taught Rilke, in an undergraduate comparative literature class, I arrived at an extreme though fortunately passing dislike of both him and his poetry: all these delectations of early death, of dead young girls particularly, even if they do ultimately come to be vibrant symbols in the *Sonnets to Orpheus*. And this hapless dead youth wandering through his utterly unreasonable Lament world didn't help.

The elegy, and the poem, end in a passage for which the word "anticlimax" seems to have been invented. After all the splendors of the poem, its absolutely unforgettable beginning, its rich elaborations of so much profound human experience, both ordinary and exalted, I always feel a shock of disappointment when I come to it:

> But if the endlessly dead awakened a symbol in us,
> perhaps they would point to the catkins hanging from the bare
> branches of the hazel trees, or
> would evoke the raindrops that fall onto the dark earth in springtime—
> And we, who have always thought
> of happiness as rising, would feel
> the emotion that almost overwhelms us
> whenever a happy thing falls.

Is that all? That's all: no elaboration of the conceit that might better explain what in heaven's name the poet means, none of the metaphorical transcendence in which Rilke was unequaled. Just that. Finally, the last elegy, to put it mildly, I find to be a muddle, poetically, philosophically, morally. Not only does the ending not deliver what the rest of the poem promises, if you're not attentive, or perhaps I should say tolerant, it can seem to contaminate and dilute the undeniable greatness of basically everything else in this infinitely compelling work. In the end, though, it doesn't because a poem isn't a philosophical system, it doesn't have to possess a systematic consistency from beginning to end. I've even sometimes wondered if in some ways I might love the poem more because of its frailties and the implication that the mind and imagination at work in it is merely human.

Another work of great ambition that's been crucially important to me, T. S. Eliot's *Four Quartets*, shares Rilke's poem's largeness of purpose and even, in fact, its basic thrust. In another context, I've referred to them both as "inner epics," and that's as good a way as I have to describe how both of them enact a sustained reflection on critical issues of life and the spirit, as experienced by a single adventurous poetic imagination. Eliot's poem also shares with the *Elegies* a rather anticlimactic ending, a resolution that doesn't seem to me to come close to fulfilling the intentions the poem has posited.

The beginnings of the poems, however, couldn't be more different. Rilke's starts with a cry to an angel, a proclamation, in a way, of the poem's spiritual purposes. There's also, of course, an implication of religion in the figure of the angel, although there has never been a religion quite like the one Rilke evokes. The *Quartets*, in contrast, begins famously in a tone of philosophical, metaphysical meditation:

> Time present and time past
> Are both perhaps present in time future,
> And time future contained in time past.
> If all time is eternally present
> All time is unredeemable.
> What might have been is an abstraction
> Remaining a perpetual possibility
> Only in a world of speculation.

The poem will move, even more than Rilke's and in a more definite way, into the realm of the religious, but for now the establishment of the poetic tone of Eliot's writing is more speculative than spiritual, with only that term "unredeemable" to give a clue to how the poem will elaborate its religious concerns later on. One critic characterizes the philosophical-spiritual purpose of the poem as a working out in poetic terms of "the immanence theory of time." Surely this is a very partial description of the poem's ambitions, but it does sound as though something like this is taking place, and the poem does concern itself with the function of time in speculative reflection and with elaborations of sense and memory that partake of and exalt the immanent.

One of the central methods of Eliot's poem, like Rilke's, is to be radically inclusive, to touch on a great number of the themes and strivings of a soul that is poetically conscious of itself, of its potential both for fulfillment and for spiritual distraction. The matter that Eliot selects to embody his processes is quite different from Rilke's, as is his method in doing so. His poem is much more committed to quotidian details as ways of opening access to larger questions. The earthly places the poem refers to are much more definite and singular than Rilke's for the most part generalized settings. If Rilke uses a fig tree almost mythical in its unspecificity to speak of the way the soul can hesitate within itself before the project of illumination, Eliot uses details of contemporary England to concretize his spiritual quest.

> The wind that sweeps the gloomy hills of London,
> Hampstead and Clerkenwell, Campden and Putney,

Highgate, Primrose and Ludgate.
From Ludgate, the poem broods:
Descend lower, descend only
Into the world of perpetual solitude,
World not world, but that which is not world,
Internal darkness, deprivation
And destitution of all property,
Desiccation of the world of sense.

It might be interesting to contrast the long metaphoric passage I quoted from the *Elegies* about the crassness of the material world with lines that have a similar purpose in the *Quartets*, the famous "dark dark dark" passage.

They all go into the dark,
The vacant interstellar spaces, the vacant into the vacant,
The captains, merchant bankers, eminent men of letters,
The generous patrons of art, the statesmen and the rulers,
Distinguished civil servants, chairmen of many committees,
Industrial lords and petty contractors, all go into the dark.

The lyric strategies of the poems couldn't be more different though. In detail and in large, Rilke seeks, in his poems, to distill articulated meanings from his meditations; although the *Elegies* are charged with images that are constantly heightened to the status of symbols, those symbols are always a portion of a poetic that, at least until the last elegy, moves toward a kind of experience both spiritually numinous and intellectually accessible. The symbols the poem generates are not poetic ends in themselves; they are always moving towards a more direct intuition that incorporates them as a part of the act of meditation.

Eliot's lyric passages, conversely, are less specifically determined: their meanings—that doesn't seem the proper word here—are embodied, or embedded, in what Eliot himself defined as "objective correlatives." The images, and the passages of pure lyricism, might be described as exciting meaning, hovering above meaning, participating in a much more oblique though just as essential way in the larger purposes of the poem. We never find in the *Elegies* the many passages of pure, apparently nonsymbolic lyrical evocation like the one that begins the last quartet, "Little Gidding."

> Midwinter spring is its own season
> Sempiternal though sodden towards sundown,
> Suspended in time, between pole and tropic.
> When the short day is brightest, with frost and fire,
> The brief sun flames the ice, on pond and ditches,
> In windless cold that is the heart's beat,
> Reflecting in a watery mirror
> A glare that is blindness in the early afternoon.

Although there are hints here, especially in that "windless cold" of some of the symbolic energies with which Eliot charges the poem, there is still a sense of deflection from its direct purposes. It is an elaboration whose method is primarily a reinforcement of atmosphere, of mood.

The poems differ radically in their relation to religion, as well. As I've noted, Rilke's spiritual nomenclatures in the *Elegies* bear little relation to that of any established religion. He may select various symbols, particularly the angel and the saint, from religious iconography (and from his own early poetry), but beyond that they're more indications of an elemental aspiration for larger meaning. Eliot, however, uses the lexicons of traditional religious speculation, mostly Christian but also Buddhist and also indirectly various Indian religions, to reinforce his larger purposes. The following passage relies as much on reverberations from Eastern religions as on any of conventional Christianity.

> The inner freedom from the practical desire,
> The release from action and suffering, release from the inner
> And the outer compulsion, yet surrounded
> By a grace of sense, a white light still and moving.

The amalgamation of different religion experiences allows Eliot to set up resonances between seemingly contradictory conceptions of spiritual consciousness, to fuse these visions with his imagistic clarity, and, crucially, to unite them with the music, the cadences of meditation of which he was such a master. The obsessive rhythms of prayerful chanting infuse the poem with a sense of metaphysical urgency beyond any meanings it might evoke.

Rilke's and Eliot's poems are also alike in that both deal with the psychic risk inherent in their very serious undertakings; they both insist on the potential desolation of such high spiritual ambitions. Again, though, they differ formidably in their articulation of this despair. Rilke's "nights of anguish" are the shucked out midnights of failed poetic inspiration, while Eliot's unattained ecstasies are the exertions of a hypothetical mystic, even of a saint. Eliot's poem can be seen in some ways almost as a handbook of Christian mysticism, and there is always the implication in it that various kinds of anguishing ascetic renunciations will be required for the visionary progress the poem postulates. Even here, though, the poems differ in both the articulation of this spiritual anguish and its grounding. Rilke's poem is always moving forward with a kind of hopefulness; it continually posits a naïve, almost childlike consciousness that is approaching the possibility of illumination for the first time. The past of the poem exists mostly as a repository of moments that are potential epiphanies, that have been waiting to be brought back in a context that will allow them to blossom into their real richness.

In Eliot, though, there's the sense that what is being attempted is the recuperation of other instances of the same project, of efforts wasted and energy having been uselessly expended, and there are many references to futile past ventures, which must be effected again because there is no other choice. Compared to the *Elegies*, there's a sense of weariness, of near exhaustion through much of the poem.

This pattern of negation and renewed striving is in fact one of the *Four Quartet*'s recurring devices. There are many examples in the poem of paradoxes that are both grounds for despair yet that are needed to illuminate—the notorious "Our only health is the disease," for example. There is an underlying dialectic, a tug of war between the desire for action and the sense of action's ultimate futility, a way of looking at acts that are obviated even as they're undertaken. Always the negation that inspires to greater striving, and always the undercurrent of a conclusion that implies that self, mere self, even the luminous poet-self, is insufficient for the higher ends the poem proposes.

> You say I am repeating
> Something I have said before. I shall say it again.
> Shall I say it again? In order to arrive there,
> To arrive where you are, to get from where you are not,
> > You must go by a way wherein there is no ecstasy.

> In order to arrive at what you do not know
>   You must go by a way which is the way of ignorance.
> In order to possess what you do not possess
>   You must go by the way of dispossession.

All of this is a sketchy description of what Eliot is about in his magnificent work. Although at one point in the poem Eliot says, "The poetry does not matter" (and of course the poem reflects at great length on poetry itself, and its own poetic methods, in particular), the poem's greatness resides just in the fact that it is neither ultimately a religious tract or a series of sermons nor, as I have said, a handbook of mysticism but a poem, rich, complex, both thematically and musically various. And it is just this that leads me to describe the resolution of the poem, its ending, as another oddity.

Perhaps I should repeat again that I believe the *Four Quartets*, like the *Duino Elegies*, is a great poem; my admiration for both of them remains unqualified: they have been inspirations and examples to me since I first came to them at the beginning of my writing life. If I'm offering what seem like criticisms of the way they conclude, this doesn't affect my ultimate esteem for them. But I think that both poems at their very outsets establish spiritual, philosophical, nonpoetical tasks or challenges that they don't, and possibly can't, resolve. Rilke, from early in his poetic career, had a notion of spirituality that was grounded in something like monastic ecstasy: *The Book of Hours*, one of his earliest books, is a dramatizations of the devotions of a humble monk, a monk, though, who lived in an imaginary vision of medieval Russia. But the moment of history the poet actually lived in was painfully mundane: the years the *Duino Elegies* took to write bracketed the cosmic horrors of World War I, and though Rilke's participation in and attention to that war was scant, its larger implications on history and culture would have been impossible to disregard. Perhaps it shouldn't be surprising then that the ending of the *Elegies* abruptly abandons anything like a Christian iconography, even the single angel who sets the poem in motion, and moves instead into something like an Egyptian or Grecian cult of the dead.

The problems with Eliot's poem in some ways are very similar to this, and profoundly different in others. *Four Quartets* was written before and during World War II, and if that war is barely referred to in the poem itself, its historical and social reverberations were clearly vivid in the consciousness of the poet: in his prose Eliot shows himself acutely aware of the implications of both conflicts. At the same time, in terms of the philosophical-religious undertakings of the poem, Eliot's trajectory is almost precisely the opposite of Rilke's. The *Quartets* begins, as I've said, with what sounds like a philosophical meditation, but by the end it has moved into a resolution that in its terminology depends almost completely on religious symbol.

> A condition of complete simplicity
> (Costing not less than everything)
> And all shall be well and
> All manner of thing shall be well
> When the tongues of flame are in-folded
> Into the crowned knot of fire
> And the fire and the rose are one.

Now, scholars of the poem can no doubt describe its structure in a way to justify how it arrives at this strangely thin lyrical murmur, with its unconvincing echo of Dante, but for me, in terms of the poem as poem, I feel a serious letdown with this conclusion. Have all those intricate and weighty investigations of spiritual and secular consciousness arrived here, in this rather truncated bit of Christian symbolism? Even musically, the end of the poem is irresolute. This last passage seems to be sung by the voice of a single muted violin, isolated from the highly magnificently chromatic chordal structure of the rest of the poem. There's certainly nothing wrong with this in principle, but the music is perfunctory, plaintive. Rhythmically, the last two lines are slack: there are fifteen syllables in the two lines, of which six are definite stresses, while in the first two lines of the poem—

> Time present and time past
> Are both perhaps present in time future

—nine of the sixteen syllables are stressed. Stress in verse is energy; energy is not at all what defines good poetry, but there's a kind of hesitation in these lines, almost a diffidence, that make them seem inadequate musically as well as contextually to the largeness of the rest of the poem. I'll repeat: thematically and poetically the poem, like the *Duino Elegies* is vast, and vastly satisfying, thrilling. Perhaps Eliot's ambitions, like Rilke's, were simply too large to be accomplished, or perhaps they were attempted at an inauspicious historical moment for such encompassing aspirations. Perhaps in a century that had become so secularized, and at moments of history so fraught with violence and terror, attempting to fuse so many historical and metaphysical yearnings would necessitate a spiritual consciousness with a coherence that is simply no longer available. Might Rilke's poem, composed, after all, less than twenty years before Eliot's, have suffered from the same finally irresolvable tensions?

I have a friend, a master carpenter, who while we were working together once on a simple renovation project that had gone irritatingly awry, offered me a bit of wisdom I find often comes to mind: "Nothing's easy." It might not be quite true that *nothing* is easy, but a lot of things aren't, among which surely is ending poems. Naturally the majority of successful poems have endings that fit their aesthetic and spiritual promises, and there are some that exceed them, two of which I'd like to look at now, another poem by Rilke, "Archaic Torso of Apollo," and James Wright's "A Blessing."

Both poems, I might remark, were terrifically important to me and to most of the poets I knew when they first came to our attention in the early nineteen-sixties. I'm not the first to remark that "A Blessing" was one of the most influential poems for the generation that begin writing when I did, and the Rilke poem, which arrived in America in J. B. Leishman's translation a little later (though it had been published a good while before in the United Kingdom), was as much so. Here is the Wright poem:

A BLESSING

Just off the highway to Rochester, Minnesota,
Twilight bounds softly forth on the grass.
And the eyes of those two Indian ponies
Darken with kindness.
They have come gladly out of the willows
To welcome my friend and me.
We step over the barbed wire into the pasture
Where they have been grazing all day, alone.
They ripple tensely, they can hardly contain their happiness

That we have come.
They bow shyly as wet swans. They love each other.
There is no loneliness like theirs.
At home once more, they begin munching the young tufts of spring in
    the darkness.
I would like to hold the slenderer one in my arms,
For she has walked over to me
And nuzzled my left hand.
She is black and white,
Her mane falls wild on her forehead,
And the light breeze moves me to caress her long ear
That is delicate as the skin over a girl's wrist.
Suddenly I realize
That if I stepped out of my body I would break
Into blossom.

And here is Rilke's, in Stephen Mitchell's translation (Leishman's seems irredeemably awkward now):

ARCHAIC TORSO OF APOLLO

We cannot know his legendary head
with eyes like opening fruit. And yet his torso
is still suffused with brilliance from inside,
like a lamp, in which his gaze, now turned to low,

gleams in all its power. Otherwise
the curved breast could not dazzle you so, nor could
a smile run through the place hips and thighs
to that dark center where procreation flared.

Otherwise this stone would seem defaced
beneath the translucent cascade of the shoulders
and would not glisten like a wild beast's fur:

would not, from all the borders of itself,
burst like a star: for here there is no place
that does not see you. You must change your life.

I won't go into an analysis of the two poems here, though it's certainly worth noting how similar their means are: though Rilke's is an ephrastic meditation, and Wright's a brief narrative, both are illuminated by a series of ingenious, unlikely metaphors, and through the force of their figures, both become infused with an atmosphere of transformation and potential transfiguration that imply genres of mystery, and modes of attention and focus ordinarily unavailable to us. Rilke effects a powerful metaphoric mutation through which qualities of the sculpture's absent head are infused into the surviving torso, the ostensible subject of the poem, and then the gaze of that absent head is transformed into a lamp dimly "suffusing with brilliance" the torso. And the poem continues in an almost metaphysical rapture through churning figurations.

The Wright poem's metaphoric work is less metaphysically (in the special sense of English Renaissance poetry) overt; its images are strikingly vivid, but its metaphors gentler, informed with emotional rather than purely imaginative force. The ponies' eyes "darken with kindness," they come "gladly out of the willows . . . they can hardly contain their happiness." A series of personifications, then a shift of intensity: "They bow shyly as wet swans." And an emotional elaboration: "There is no loneliness like theirs." There is much more factual description in the poem—its tremulous movement doesn't work through figurative alchemizations as does Rilke's: the poet is much more present, much more a receptor of perceptions than a generator of them.

A thorough analysis of the two poems would be worthy of an essay in itself, but it's their endings that concern me here. Both endings are abrupt, they nearly truncate their poems, both are unpredictable, audacious, in some essential way uncalled for, *unreasonable*: both leap in their separate ways out of the world of ordinary concatenation and logic. Rilke offers a preliminary closing: "for here, there is no place // that does not see you." Unreasonable in its own right, the conceit then becomes a command, a cry of warning, or a plea: *"You must change your life."* It is an imperative that seems to go back and set the whole poem shimmering with overtones of meaning for which even the blazing virtuosity of its figurative work couldn't have prepared us.

Wright's ending is in some ways very similar to Rilke's, but also essentially differs. It, too, seems to come from nowhere: rather than the purely metaphoric permutations through which the Rilke works, it implements its images and metaphors to gradually heighten the rapturous mood of the poem. Everything in it is tender, vulnerable; there is the sense that the world being described is being generated even as we experience it and that world is being contemplated with newborn eyes. One of the two ponies takes on the qualities of a human woman, and the poet is drawn ever more closely to her, finally moved to caress her, not by the force of his own poetic transformations, or his own will, but by the "light breeze." It is reality itself that is conspiring in the poem's transfigurations, a reality that has begun to glow with mysterious potentialities. And, again, that ending:

> Suddenly I realize
> That if I stepped out of my body I would break
> Into blossom.

Those final three lines for we poets who were first reading it were a sort of proclamation of a new *ars poetica*. The Latin American surrealist poets, who were just then arriving into the American tradition and who had begun to inform American poetry with unfamiliar ways of objectifying reality through figuration and through the logic of the unconscious and dream, were all at once there for us. Wright, who along with Robert Bly, was one of their first translators, had shown how they could move audaciously into our own canon.

Rilke had plunged into the stone mass of a statue; Wright in "A Blessing" devised a ladder of image and figure to elate consciousness out of its fleshy necessities. The two poems were like two aspects of a single act of liberation. The poetry that I, and many of my contemporaries, had been writing—fact-ridden, history-ridden, intellectually pretentious, emotionally deflected—was all at once offered a dimension that had previously been forbidden to it, although we hadn't until then suspected our quandary.

And the two poems continue to offer their particular luminosities: their "odd" endings still shock and still exalt.

Some Reflections on Tragedy

In the course of working on my translations, I've had the occasion to read a great number of theories about tragedy.[1] With all I've read, though, I've been left, in my own reflections on the subject, with an essential puzzle to which I've never found a satisfactory answer. The puzzle consists of the simple question of why we inflict tragedy on ourselves, why we allow ourselves to be put into an aesthetic situation in which, at the very least, we will be in proximity to terrible anguish and suffering, and why, when we are in this proximity, when we are so close to these obsessions and slaughters, these insane vengeances and self-devouring families, do we feel that something worthwhile is happening to us?

    Aristotle has given us the concept of catharsis, the idea that by beholding the tragic activity, by submitting ourselves to the pity and the terror it entails, we're mysteriously psychologically and spiritually purified, taken out of ourselves and cleansed. But when I consider what actually happens to me when I read or see tragedy on the stage, this isn't a very accurate description of my responses or my thoughts about those responses. All these unlikely goings on, these obsessions and slaughters, these insane vengeances, these self-devouring families: to

---

1. Sophocles, *Women of Trachis*, trans. C. K. Williams and Gregory Dickerson (New York: Oxford University Press, 1978) and *The Bacchae of Euripides: A New Version*, trans. C. K. Williams (New York: Farrar, Straus and Giroux, 1990).

have pity be such a large factor in describing our response to tragedy seems to me not enough. The Greeks, as we're well aware, knew these myths and stories by heart. Educated people even today are presumed to have at their command at least a cursory knowledge of those tales and myths that play such a large part in our cultural heritage. But even if we didn't, we would still quickly realize that the force of the tragic doesn't lie in the surprise or the suspense it offers us; our most effecting, poignant, readings of tragedy are never the first: as with lyric poetry, our responses are instead intensified by our second or fifth or tenth reading.

The terror we feel, then, is at best moderated, because terror implies in some way or another suspense, the unknown, the unanticipated—and in fact, there is almost no suspense in Greek theater. Anxiety, the unknown we fear enough to make us tremble, has finally to do with outcome, with what will or might come to pass to terrorize us, and that is never the real issue in Greek tragedy. Although we hold our breath when in the *Bacchae* we hear the recounting of Pentheus's death and dismemberment, our interest is not in what has happened to him—we are assumed to already know that—but with the poetry in which these terrible events are expressed and, just as important, with how we will respond to them.

I'll offer a counterexample. In a film I saw recently, two characters play a game of Russian roulette, aiming at their heads a gun that has one cartridge in the otherwise empty cylinder and pulling the trigger. I found myself in a state of terrific anxiety as I watched this absurd game: I was actually covering my eyes the way I did in the movies when I was child. I couldn't bear to behold what might happen. Though I knew the characters were fictional and that the actors playing them weren't about to allow their skulls to be blown apart for the sake of their art, it still felt as though what was going on was too much for me, that I was going to be overwhelmed. Needless to say I wasn't, but when I thought afterward about that frightening, really stupid business, I felt cheated, as though my emotions had been trifled with and, more important, that my sensitivity, my capacity to respond to real or potential suffering, had been violated. We never feel this about the great tragedies. Even if we do characterize our response to their dreadful rendings as fear, it is a fear mediated by a different, more complex, probably more mature portion of our consciousness than that with which we reflexively protect ourselves when we cover our eyes or ears.

The function of what we call pity plays in our response to tragedy is more subtle. There is no question we do often feel a quite surprising and rending sympathy for those ancient beings caught in their webs of sad destiny. I once worked for a few weeks with a group of young actors who were doing a production of my version of the *Bacchae*. I'd worked on the translation of the play on and off for ten years and knew it nearly by heart. Yet at the opening performance, at the moment when Pentheus's mother Agave realizes that the head she is carrying is that of her own son whom she's murdered, the actress screamed in grief, and all my familiarity and objectivity vanished, and tears came to my eyes. I had to struggle to keep from sobbing aloud.

Why should this be? I'm not really certain. Pity is an elusive phenomenon. Sometimes I feel that the pity we often pride ourselves on as a symbol of our humanity can, in fact, become an easily available titillation, a spiritual self-indulgence. If there is an Aristotelean catharsis in that compassion, perhaps we should be skeptical about it. Still, even if we can purify our pity of our own gratification, from whence does it arise? Is there an intrinsic complex of empathy for others in our affective system, or is there something that, no matter how hard we try, actually keeps our feelings of pity ultimately directed towards ourselves, at least until we have striven to put ourselves in a disinterested charitable relation with another?

Modern psychology has given us the useful term "identification," and certainly we can identify with Agave's grief, especially those of us who are parents, just as we can all feel another sort of identification with Pentheus, when he suffers the indignation and unreasonable horror of his fate. Somehow though, identification is at the end a limiting term. It describes our marvelous capacity to participate in someone else's anguish, but I think finally the concept isn't a sufficient representation of our spiritual interests. For one thing, it implies a too easy and too complete connection to the person whose pain we are beholding. When we see Oedipus with his eyes put out, we surely know that nothing like this is very likely to happen to us. Neither is there any course of events we can conceive in which we would kill our father, nor that we'd marry and have children by our mother. It is even less likely that we will ever, like Pentheus, have a god appear in our lives to challenge our characters and cause our mothers to tear off our heads.

As we participate in tragedy, this knowledge of our ultimate non-involvement protects us from trivial theatrical illusion, and yet we still feel strongly that our interests, our most personal interests, are somehow bound up with these all but impossible narratives. Our connection to the characters in tragedy and to their grotesque ordeals isn't abstract or theoretical; we don't merely behold them from afar: we use them, and we know that they are productive for us in a profoundly intimate way, but of what does that productiveness actually consist?

I've come to think that the key to understanding why we find these radically implausible events so important to us has to do with certain discrepancies between the way we actually experience ourselves emotionally and the descriptions and meanings our mind has at its disposal to deal with that experience. I believe, in short, that our emotions are too large for us, too grand, that they just don't fit the reasons for them that the world we actually live in makes available to us. Basically, we might say, our feelings are too acute for our cognition of them: without our even being aware of it, they overwhelm our intellectual circuits.

In the *Bacchae*, for instance, the young Pentheus, realizing that all the women and girls of his city have fled to the mountains with a stranger who claims to be a god, becomes furious and desperate and undertakes a series of self-destructive acts. But it doesn't take as much as all that to make us feel and act in ways we know will very likely be counterproductive, if not simply foolish. Merely having one person, if that person is the object of our intense affections, sever his or her attachment to us can be enough to make us act so. We all know what can happen then. We brood, we sulk, we suffer, we become desperate, our whole character and our whole reality are called into question. We find that we are grieving, as though for ourselves, as though we had died to ourselves as well as having been wounded by the other. Finally, if our drama goes on long enough, we focus obsessively not only on our loss but on our offended feelings; we lose control—there is no other term for it—over our minds, over ourselves. We find we are inflicting even more suffering on ourselves through our imaginings and fantasies than the fact of the loss that afflicts us. All reality can become distorted; we become what we call depressed, so that when we look out of ourselves into the world, the misery and the human imperfection, the unreasonableness we see there, reflects and intensifies our misery: everything becomes tainted with its contrary. All we reflect on becomes contaminated with evidences of the meaninglessness of existence, as well as of death. Death, in fact, becomes so insistent within us that we may even begin to believe that death itself, actual death, might be more bearable than this pain that seems so much like death. Sometimes someone will actually try to affect this release, because the reason can become so capsized by the intensities of feeling that it is forgotten that we know that even the most exacerbated emotion one day, however long in the future, will for no particular reason decay and fade, and that the excruciating vacancies of loss will absorb less and less attention. But while our pain is still with us, while any overpowering emotional struggle is actively underway, our vision of what is happening to us isn't adequately served by the concepts and symbols we have at our disposal to describe it. They seem always trivial in comparison to the vast, excruciating violence of the emotions within us, which are so strangely detached from will and from our intellectual effectiveness. Those who can deal rationally and objectively with their own anguish can seem cold, disconnected from themselves, and so from others—in a word, neurotic. Or worse.

My thought is that great tragedy is the enactment of the way we actually, affectively experience ourselves, how we really "feel" about the way we are situated in relation to both the universe and our inner reality, to that conglomeration of sentiment, intellection, and remembered or projected experience that though so mysterious to us finally *is* us. Our inner life, as we experience, it is vast, almost grotesque, in its enormity. The actual reality any human has to deal with seems incidental, nearly paltry, compared to the cosmic emotions and expectations within us: the movements of these feelings of ours are gigantic, their force overwhelming—we gratefully employ the term "irrational" to describe our perception of them.

When Freud turned to tragedy to illuminate his theory of psychological development, I believe the crucial point he was making had less to do with whether the infant boy really wants to murder his father and marry his mother and had more to do with capturing the intensity of our infantile experience, which remains within us and absurdly conflicts with our adult expectations. Murder and incestuous marriage capture much more effectively the violence of the feeling of the mixture of cosmic exclusiveness the child, or the self remembering the child, experiences. Similarly, although there is nothing we call the "Pentheus complex" for the young adolescent who has the sense that because of his inexperience and shyness all his possible amorous partners are forbidden to him, the image of all the women he knows going mad and fleeing from him is of just the proper absurdity to embody the confusion and seemingly irresolvable helplessness he feels about ever accomplishing a sexual and emotive union with one of these unattainable beings of that other, wildly different and obdurately recalcitrant gender.

The illusory world of tragedy presents us with a reality unlike our own, but the events in it match in their intensity the radical drama that is our inner life. That life is mirrored by tragedy in several ways. With a few exceptions, Greek tragedy occurs in the context of a family, a family that always also has some public identity, some essential function in its community. In the *Bacchae*, even the god Dionysus is a member of the protagonist's family: his first cousin. This focus on family, on the first circle of the individual's allegiances, intensifies the connections we feel to our inner reality. For in our social and political existence, there is the much more real possibility for us to be afflicted with the kind of horrors our inner life constantly deals with. We are surely susceptible to the violence of war, to oppression, to various kinds of public disaster; we carry an awareness of those possibilities within us at all times, too, but that menace is of another order.

Although it is clear that in certain circumstances people will involve themselves in public violence—even to their own jeopardy—as a way of making their outer reality match their inner, no matter how enmeshed in matters of larger public violence we become, our experience of such incidents remains by its very nature the exception: it is the abnormal that certainly can entangle us in its snares but that always remains outside us, beyond us. War, as an example, is the material of epic, and our emotional experience of epic is of an entirely different nature from that of tragedy. We don't use the characters of epic the way we do those of tragedy. We are enthralled by them, we admire or despise them, but we don't possess them in the way we do characters in tragedy. We can also admire, or even love, successful political figures, but what they do for us, in life or art, has to do with our identities as parts of social groupings, not with ourselves as beings alone with our ultimate identities and with those puzzling emotions that drag us through a world that can never really account for them.

These are questions that of course are current in all ages and that art in all ages attempts to express. Many contemporary commentators have expressed dissatisfaction with the tragedies that have been written in our own time, and perhaps there is a clue in all of this as to why. In modern drama, the protagonists are not kings, princesses, warriors, or gods; they are our neighbors, or at least those we pass in the street:

lawyers, doctors, workers, salesmen. The destiny of these people is often painfully sad, as wretched as in traditional tragedy. The problem, I think, is that modern protagonists are too close to us, our primary connection to them is identification—we know them too well. In Arthur Miller's *Death of a Salesman*, when Willy Loman is annihilated by his life and by the weaknesses in his character, we know just what he feels; in his shoes, we would feel just as he does, and we would probably act out our grief in the same way. But this knowledge, at least in terms of the real tragic experience, is a disappointment.

Though we might believe we know ourselves better by contemplating Willy's fate, the knowledge we already have of our own spiritual and emotional reality is merely reinforced, it isn't extended. In the characters of ancient tragedy, the impossible distance between them and us and the uncanny discrepancy in the dimensions between the reasons for their suffering and ours are just what makes them crucial to us. That frightening distance is for me one of the very fundamentals of the philosophical identity of Greek tragedy.

And the choruses in tragedy, the function of which can be so difficult for us to understand, serve to reinforce this discrepancy in scale. The chorus in tragedy, a kind of group consciousness, is an enactment of the phenomenon of many minds working as one, and it helps to make the larger experience of tragedy, the connection of self to what is beyond it, even more coherent and compelling. The chorus says everything, proclaims everything, but, except in the purely lyrical passages, what it is always attempting to do is to fuse the analytic and the didactic that are the primary components of moral meditation. The chorus is continually generating ethical energy and, just as continually, consuming or exhausting it; its individual members are not really quite up to the task that defines them.

The psychology of the chorus is further reflected in the characters themselves. Aristotle suggests that before everything else, the tragic character defines itself in action, and this action is determined by what he calls "moral bent" and "thought." By moral bent, Aristotle doesn't mean what we do when we speak of character, or personality; he means the identity of the protagonist as it is revealed in tragic action. There is much debate over what Aristotle specifically means here, but I think he is distinguishing between what we call personality and something more mysterious that these characters from the world of myth and poetry embody. It's very difficult for us to consider humans' actions without also considering their psychological status; psychology is an essential part of our Romantic vision of ourselves as radical individuals. There is no question that the psychological vision is useful, but we should also recognize its limitations.

When we submit tragic characters to merely psychological explanations, they, and our response to them, are taken out of the realm of mystery, removed from the world of those unfathomable forces that possess our inner existence. They become modern, like us, and merely dramatic, rather than tragic. In the dramas of our own time, in the theater or in fiction, it can be difficult not to hope in the course of it that someone will show up to rush its tormented characters to a psychiatrist's couch, to keep them from destroying themselves.

In genuine tragedy, it isn't appropriate, or useful, to think this. The first thing Euripides's Phaedra would do on the psychiatrist's couch would be to kill herself; her role in *Hippolytus* really takes place between her resolve to do just that and a brief period of hesitation. The "reasons" why Phaedra feels what she does are absolutely incidental to her tragedy; they are in fact, in Aristotle's terminology, the "action." Emotions in the tragic sense are merely acts that take place within people rather than between them. Certainly characters in tragedy think about their plight, and about their characters, but the crucial truth in tragedy, and in our own inner world, is that actions begin at the very limit of reflection, at the point at which there is nothing left to think; what is finally effected or not comes after moral argument has been abandoned. There is nothing more to think about because everything has already been thought—and discarded as inadequate to the struggle.

Euripides's *Bacchae* offers a powerful example of this. The sources of the young king Pentheus's struggles in the play are essentially mysterious to him; they are beyond his capacity for self-examination because he cannot believe that such questioning would have anything to do with what is happening to him. The society of which Pentheus is the ruler is being dismembered; he is struggling against that dismemberment, and he believes, not unreasonably, that there is simply nothing more to think or say about this catastrophe. He must act, he must struggle, with all the means at his disposal against what is happening.

The tragedy of Pentheus is that he is not mature enough for real moral reflection; when it is offered him, when Dionysus gives him the chance to approach the rebellious Bacchae in a peaceful, rather than a belligerent way, he misconceives the necessity for patience, for withholding, which social contemplation must entail, and instead takes what Dionysus offers him as an opportunity for self-forgetting and self-indulgence.

Pentheus allows Dionysus to convince him to think about the implication of his actions, about alternatives to them, but then Pentheus loses sight of his social responsibilities as king of Thebes: he allows himself to be seduced into an amputated vision of himself as the sexually curious young man he is. The psychological term "regression" is painfully apropos here. Pentheus regresses from his adult role as a forceful leader, an implement of social cohesion, to that of a voyeuristic adolescent, and then, with Dionysus's hypnotic encouragement, he regresses further, to the intellectual and emotional condition of a small child, whose only desire is to be held in his mother's arms.

The confusions in Pentheus's mind and character that Dionysus plays on, so that Pentheus regresses from imagining himself being carried as a hero on his return from his confrontation with the Bacchae to his being carried instead as a small child in his mother's arms, are terrifying. The lapse Pentheus allows himself seems so slight, so nearly innocent, such a tiny part of his ego lets its guard down, that the punishment he receives appears terribly extreme. Dionysus can be perceived to have acted, as Pentheus's grandfather Cadmus will put it, "With justice, but with too much severity." But in terms of the greater issues of the play, in the conflict between the social and the personal, between family and the larger society, Pentheus's fate is perfectly coherent.

It's crucial to keep in mind that whatever can be said about Pentheus's character, about how young he is, how stubborn, how lacking in wisdom, his social role is firm: he is a king, the symbolic embodiment of his society, the one in that society, we might say, whose task and responsibility is to direct what I have called its moral energies. From this point of view, Pentheus's error, his flaw, doesn't have anything to do with his youth or his impetuousness. It involves, rather, his refusal to realize that the authority he possesses to direct the energies of the community also entails ethical reflection. Pentheus's responsibility to his community lies exactly in this kind of reflection because otherwise the social conscience of that community will be infected with a disorder like Pentheus's own. Dionysus accuses Pentheus of just this: "You don't know what you're doing," he says, "You don't even know who you are." When Pentheus is confronted with Dionysus, he unreflectively defines him as the other, the enemy, and will accept no evidence to support any other perception. When Pentheus feels the data he has been given aren't adequate to the intensity of the instinctive animus he feels, he fantasizes more evidence and offers these fantasies as reality, as justification for his brashness. There's something sadly familiar in the way Pentheus characterizes Dionysus. He sees him as wildly, almost impossibly, sexually potent. Dionysus, Pentheus says, seduces women out of their normal, protected, nonlibidinal environment and leads them into the dark unknown, where he drugs them with alcohol, inducing them to be negligent—irresponsible to their social duties— just as he is irresponsible, obsessed only by sex and intoxication. Dionysus is even physically suspect; although he claims to be a relative of Pentheus, Pentheus finds him to be the wrong color: he is too light, his cheeks too rosy. I won't be so anachronistic to come out and say that Pentheus is a racist, but, just as racism in our own society has often caused our moral energies to go askew, so Pentheus, by his limited vision of the one who is like but unlike him, the stranger, the other, has driven the moral energies of Thebes out of their healthy trajectory and into a system in which the only alternatives to order are violence and exclusion.

The philosopher Karl Jaspers developed the notion of what he calls transition as the zone in which tragedy occurs. Jaspers points out that "prevailing patterns of action and thought . . . do not replace each other suddenly. The old is still alive while the new unfolds itself. The mighty breakthrough of the new is bound at first to fail against the staying power and coherence of the old way of life not yet exhausted." Jaspers uses historical figures, Socrates and Julius Caesar, to show how the "victorious protagonist" becomes "the victim at the border of the two eras." But in the tragedies, the divisions of the transitional zones are even more acute because they are more primal. For the Greeks, the issues that divided zones were not philosophical or political but involved basic questions of civilization, of the separation of the civilized from the barbaric, of the world of morality and law from that of savagery and violence, and, as in the *Bacchae*, of the mythic and the human. For the Greeks, the world of savage barbarism was not far away in either time or space. They were acutely aware that their world abutted boundaries with peoples who did not adhere to the social concords that made Hellenic civilization possible. The centaurs carved on the metopes of the Parthenon, who try to carry off the women and young boys from of the wedding feast of their neighbors the Lapithae, certainly represent in a vividly graphic form the violent, impulsive tendencies that still beset the world of the Greeks. In the *Women of Trachis*, the great hero, Herakles (another son of Zeus, incidentally), lived in two worlds, the human and the mythic. His task was to cleanse the human world of the lethal relics of that mythic world, all the various monsters that still infested the nearly civilized earth, but, as Sophocles depicts him, he is finally destroyed because he cannot commit himself totally to the human world and instead violates, by his actions, the order and decorum that have been imposed on the world by human aspiration and will.

In the *Bacchae*, the division is more complicated. Dionysus, who incarnates so many of the forces that characterize the epoch previous to civilization, is presented as a "new" god: he has just arrived in the world; his ultimate glory, as the chorus says, will be in the future, when "all Greece" will honor him. There has been much speculation on what Euripides was trying to do in this, his last play. Had he become more conservative as he aged? In his earlier plays, he seems to the very embodiment of Greek rationality—sometimes his characters become irritatingly reasonable, as in the *Hippolytus*, when, after finding out that his stepmother Phaedra has killed herself and left a note accusing him of responsibility for her death, Hippolytus, to his father Theseus's rage, engages in a logical, maddeningly reasonable defense of himself. The *Bacchae*, on the contrary, is charged with what at first glance seems unexamined and uncritical irrationality. Unreason, the unreason of a god, triumphs absolutely; at the end, there seems to be nothing left of any representative of the orderly, progressive culture on which the Greeks so prided themselves.

This must have been doubly shocking, for not only were the Greeks aware of their culture as essentially different from the less civilized peoples of their world, but they were also conscious of their own social organization in a way that was entirely new in the world. They were the first society to consider history as an objective fact, which had its own necessities and its own truth; it was not, as in the other societies of the Near East, a panegyric to be rewritten to glorify whatever king or dynasty happened to control the social resources of any given moment. Theirs also seemed to have been the first community to be aware of itself as being in process, to have the sense that their society was developing, and was therefore capable of improvement. For the Greeks, society was formed not merely by the interests of powerful individuals or factions, but by the self-conscious imposition of ideas and ideals as well.

Plato's *Republic*, of course, codified this tendency into the first utopian vision of society, but I believe that this vision of social organization being capable of evolution was also the source from which much of the Greek tragic experience found its substance. In Aeschylus's *Eumenides*, Orestes, hounded by the punishing Furies for having killed his mother to revenge her murder of his father, flees to Athens in the hope of finding justice and a solution to the intricate moral dilemmas of his act. In one of the most amazing moments in literature, what Orestes does, in effect, is to flee across the border from mythic to historical time. The Athens he comes to is Athens at the beginning of Greek history, not of its mythic history but of the history that human beings have affected for themselves, and when he arrives there, Athena, the tutelary goddess of the city, does indeed offer him justice by inventing and implementing the jury system that was such an essential part of the democratic system of Athens.

Euripides, too, would surely have had, as a part of his moral agenda, the fact that Athens was a society in history—and in process. Euripides takes the action of his drama back to a time when the god Dionysus was still living the span of what would have been his human life but, as we have seen, with an awareness of his eternal definition as well. This mix—of the eternal and the transitory, of the divine and the human, of the new and the old—are put into an equation in which it is difficult to attach any kind of reflexive ethical evaluation. When Plato banished the poets from his ideal polis, because of their propensity towards the ecstatic, towards inadequately rational inspiration, what he was suggesting was a policy of exclusion, an attempt to separate from society and consciousness, any disruptive influences.

Euripides, in contrast, brought to the *Bacchae* a restatement, a reminder, as it were, of the often conflicting elements of which any society is necessarily constituted. We don't have to be reminded that Euripides would not have believed that all of these elements are particularly admirable or productive, but it is also clear he believed that the attempt to deny their existence is fatal to the self-reflection that is necessary to the survival of a self-conscious society. To attempt to "deny our mortal nature," as the chorus puts it, is a disaster for both the individual and the community. On the individual level, in which character is crucial, Pentheus's unreflecting attempt to exclude Dionysus and the forces he represents is catastrophic. On the social level, Agave and her sisters, because of their contempt for the god, are forced to abandon their own city; its walls, whose purpose was to keep evil things out, are inadequate for keeping good things in, and the misery Agave and her sisters bring upon Thebes by their recalcitrance toward the forces Dionysus represents is appalling. There can be no question that Euripides is meditating here on the way a society defines and identifies its virtues and its problems. It can seem strange to us that the doings of a king and of a god should have such force for our own social considerations, but they surely can, mainly because Euripides assumes in his tragedy that all humans participate in our own destiny.

Democracy demands that the individual take an active part in the social mechanism and that the citizen reflect on his society. Even if a society is going through a phase of conservative political reaction, as Euripides's was when he wrote the *Bacchae*, this vision of participation is still in effect because once it comes to consciousness, it defines consciousness, both the individual's and the group's; it cannot be repudiated, except with dreadful consequences, as we have seen too well in our own century. In democracy, the individual possesses the ideas and the means of social cohesion, rather than being subjected to powers that require only acquiescence and repression. This sense of Athens possessing itself, rather than the details of its too brief and imperfect democracy, is surely what we find most inspiring in the moral image we have of ancient Athens.

Tragedy embodies for us complexities of experience and emotion that touch on our most profound needs and fears. If it deals with zones of transition, some of the most compelling of those zones are those within us, between our emotional and intellectual existence, and our spiritual and our social aspirations. The use to which the art is dedicated in a democratic universe is the individual's spiritual reality and the reality of the compound individual which is the society. Martin Buber defines a miracle not as the mythic event—the parting of a sea or a moral revelation—that may or may not have happened in a people's past but as the fact that the incident remains a source of inspiration and revelation through eons of history. The miracle of Greek tragedy is the compelling connection it still makes for us between death and life, violence and order, the individual and the community, and, finally, between the tragic urgencies of the world of our emotions and our meditations on our common destiny.

Letter to a Workshop

Over the last few decades, a really daunting amount of commentary has been produced by poets for poets and for poet-teachers on the question of how to generate competent or more than just competent poems. Much of this material has come out of writing programs or summer workshops—craft lectures, essays, interviews with "professional" poets—and there seem to be countless manuals, with exercises for gathering material for poems and for developing systematic procedures of revision that, dutifully pursued, will presumably allow the neophyte or frustrated poet to raise his or her level of skill, even to discover as yet unfulfilled genius.

During the many years I've taught workshops—first mostly in graduate programs, lately undergraduate—I myself have probably expended many thousands of words of counsel to my students. But still, when I remember my own first apprenticeship (I seem to have gone through many, each time I attached to a great poet, but I mean here the very first) I suspect that just the hint of such an intimidating set of suggestions would surely have stopped me cold.

Such well-meant advice might be useful in helping both aspiring poets and those who happen to compose some satisfying verse and would like to figure out how they did it so as to do it again. However, it seems to me that one important issue is never quite articulated, which is not so much how one goes about thinking about the creation of poems but, rather, when you're trying to write a poem, what do you think with and how?

Robert Frost said the poet picks up bits of knowledge here and there, like burrs, and this is probably the case. But it might be useful to have some sense of the mind to which such stickers would attach. This in turn might bring up a number of interesting but probably irresolvable problems, such as how to determine the particular cultural and social issues that should involve poets as much as they do anyone else in the making of a satisfactory self. That's another, surely even more complicated, question, so I'll just pass on here what Isaac Babel's mother said to him: "You must know everything"— the most apt advice I know for an aspiring writer.

Ideally the poet should strive for the curiosity of the ethnographer, the precision of the philosopher, the moral flexibility of the social theorist, the scrupulousness of the scientist, plus . . . Plus what? is the question. What are the qualities of the mind of the poet that might ultimately enable all those virtuous identities yet help to prepare the poet for the very particular and very peculiar act of poetic composition?

I suppose I'm thinking back to that time when I was struggling to get started in poetry, when I'd have liked to know not only how to write poems but also how to think about myself as a poet and, more specifically, how to conceive my mind as a poet's mind. I might in fact be talking to the uncertain self I was in those days, who thrashed about in so many unknowables, not the least of which was how to think about that self and what to ask of it because so much was asked that seemed off the point and had nothing to do with anything except the host of dull imperatives with which it had been conditioned by its very disorganized education. We're inflicted with many lessons about ourselves in the course of growing up, but most such teachings turn out to be not only generally useless but possibly detrimental to any sort of artistic creation. Much of our education teaches us to *do* things and to think about things in order to do them, but poets soon enough come to realize that we can't compel ourselves to be who we're not and do what we can't. Otherwise, we could just read Shakespeare or Milton and say to ourselves: Do that.

I'd like to try to clear a way through at least some of these thickets to consider what we might call the poetic consciousness and some of the ways it functions, as well as some of the methods such a mind might use to enact whatever it is that brings forth poems. Much of what I'm saying here has surely been articulated by other poets in other contexts, and all of it is of course terrifically subjective. Still, I don't think I have to apologize: all of what I'll discuss here is what I've noticed the times I've tried to understand what I've been doing when I write poems, and how I've done it, mostly so I can then go on to try to write others. Finally, much of what I'm able to analyze about composing poems seems to have to do with all the constraints my character has imposed on the activity and with how I've wiggled or tunneled ways around or through the impediments that can make writing a poem not only an unlikely but also an apparently outright impossible task. In some odd way, it feels as though the most abiding element of all this has something to do with having from time to time given myself and the very problematic mind that is my mind *permission* to make a poem.

I've never tried before to begin to make a systematic list of how I've gone about this, and I won't now. What I'll offer instead are some observations I've made about my own procedures, and I thought I'd offer these observations as rights, or opportunities, younger poets might incorporate in their dealings with themselves and their writing. I present them as rights because I know that one of the most persistent, almost appalling problems of being a young poet is confidence, or the lack of it. I once heard Galway Kinnell tell some students after a reading that confidence is 95 percent of composing poetry, and though his number might have been a bit elevated, I've come to agree with his sentiment, so this compendium of rights might be a way of convincing young poets that their work doesn't consist entirely of discipline and duty. While I'm about it, though, I'll also intrude along with these rights some obligations and imperatives it might be useful to consider as well. I certainly wouldn't want any of these observations to be taken as a set of rules or prescriptions—they're thoughts I've had about the poet's task, or plight. I've heard several poets use the expression "having to get out of your own way" when you're writing a poem: if nothing else, maybe what I'm exploring here is what to get out of the way *of*.

So, the first right I'd like to propose sounds odd: it's the right not to know what you're doing, even to not know what you've done. This seems absurd on the face of it: isn't our education, and not only, as I say, our formal education but the self-making, poet-making, that is our life's project, devoted precisely to teaching us that we should know how to do what we set out to? Yet the fact is that much of the best work produced by artists (and maybe everyone else) is accomplished by small or larger leaps into the obscurity out past our intentions; much of what we come to value most in our own work are evidences of that unfathomable phenomenon we call inspiration.

Inspiration is essential to the production of significant art, but considered practically, as a method, a procedure, it's all but impossible to characterize. Inspiration in practice is something either that's happened at some time in the past, even the past of a few moments ago, or that hasn't yet happened. While it is happening, it's not there, or you can't be aware of it being there, because the whole consciousness is taken by its activity—in a certain way you aren't there yourself: there's just the poem being enacted by you and, even more mysteriously, seemingly for you. The hardest thing is that inspiration is neither something that can be willed nor something you can wait around for. If on the one hand you try too hard to bring it about, to force it, but don't succeed—which is what usually happens—the outcome can be impatience and frustration, states of mind not conducive to creation. If on the other hand you sit back and wait too long, it may well never come to pass at all. This is what's troubling, really painful, about the whole business: you need inspiration, it's absolutely essential, but you can't schedule it or count on it or be sure that it's ever going to happen again or that it will happen at all. In the end, we can only prepare a space, a field, for inspiration to occur. This, of course, is contrary to the way we're taught to believe we should accomplish anything: by deciding to do it, then figuring out how, then making it happen. Implied in this view is the notion that learning happens systematically, in increments; that we grope towards something, find it untenable, try something else that works and, along the way, draw conclusions, so that the next time we can skip the inessential rest. We learn, in other words, that the proper way to accomplish anything, especially art, is by developing principles of procedure, which we call "craft," and working from them rather than from trial and error.

In my experience, though, this isn't an accurate description of the whole unlikely process. Anything like a principle I might learn about composition immediately becomes something I no longer have to think about, so I always feel as though I'm working from trial and error, always doing what I don't know how to do, with a sense of blundering towards where I'm trying to go, and I'm always a little surprised if or when I do get there. For a long time I suffered, and still can occasionally, from the feeling that I must be doing this all wrong because if I have to explain, even to myself, what I've done when I've written something I find satisfactory, I often can't.

Lately I've realized that one of the rewards of the labor of poetry is reading something I've written that pleases me and thinking, "How did that happen?" Young poets, or the young poet I was, tend not to know this and can become discouraged waiting for it to happen again. Older poets, by whom again I mean me, can tend, when facing the page, to forget it, too, though if we're lucky we learn that however inspiration happens, all prosaic signs of the self to the contrary, it may indeed take us once more, so we slog on. That "may" is the necessary faith of art, and our most essential right.

The next right I'll consider might not be among the most crucial, but is one that occurs to me now, perhaps because it's connected to my first experience with mind, poet's or anyone's, being discussed as something in itself, to be thought about at all. When I was growing up, my father was much influenced by some inspirational book, the central message of which was that in order to do anything well, one had to *concentrate*, a bit of wisdom he repeated often, very forcefully when my schoolwork didn't meet his expectations. Now, so far as I can tell, I never, through my childhood and youth and possibly until now, have managed to effect what seems to be indicated by the word "concentration." So, I'll propose here the right to *not* concentrate, by which I mean the right to allow one's mind to skip and skid away from any prescribed subject without worrying that some aesthetic or moral commandment is being violated. Going along with this are several correlative rights. The first would be the right to understand that the mind, no matter how far and for how long it strays from the theme or idea to which one wishes it would apply itself, will sooner or later return when it is ready and able to do so and may well be the richer, or wiser, for the diversion and delay. (Bertrand Russell says somewhere that, early in his career as a mathematician and philosopher, he realized that if a problem he was interested in was going to take six months or a year to be solved, it would be solved in that length of time, whether he thought about it or not. This allowed him, he reports, to occupy himself with other questions that interested him. Though Russell's insight isn't quite what I'm talking about here, and I don't think I've ever been able to enact anything like it myself, I like the idea, so thought I'd pass it on.)

Along with the right not to concentrate goes a corollary: the right to vacillate, to wobble, to shilly-shally, to be indecisive in one's labors, and still not suffer from qualms about being irresponsible, indolent, weak. Poems can take a long time to arrive, and to find their final form, so surely patience is the word here, but it's worth emphasizing that what actually happens doesn't seem to have the maturity and dignity the term "patience" implies. There's much more flailing about, and hesitating, and clearing the throat, and taking out the trash—and we need the right to all of it. At the same time, though, there's an obligation that comes with this circling towards patience, which is to know that at some point you have to make your move, even if you don't feel completely ready, and you have to make it with energy and tenacity and—this might be hardest—spontaneity. It might be asked how spontaneity can be willed? But isn't that one of the very basic issues of art, of being an artist? Isn't it really what revision is all about? Trying a thing again and again until the solution finally arrives that surprises and embodies that quality of surprise in itself?

Another, related, right: to be wrong, about anything and everything, and to know that even when your line of reflection or imagining might be viewed as absurdly illogical, you should be able to go on to its however provisional conclusion. This obviously has to do with revision, too: knowing that no matter how wrong, or how awful, a first, or second, or fiftieth draft can be, or an idea can be, or a groping towards metaphor or image, there will always be another chance, another hour for another attempt, and nothing in the meantime is lost except a little time, of which we sometimes have more than we know what to do with anyway. The corollary to this would be to realize that the judgment that something is wrong, or imperfect, or unrealized has a dialectic concealed in it of which one might be unaware and that working through this dialectic in itself can be fruitful. We should be able to regard our inner existence, the part anyway that's raw material for poetry, as a laboratory, in which mental and emotional phenomena are valued according to their potential usefulness for poems and considered harmless unless they demand to be concretized in malignant actions. (It should probably be kept in mind that the ultimate purpose of this sort of reflection isn't action but self-knowledge. Action—creation—comes later.)

From this follows the right of the mind to be able to remark in itself and not repress, or at least not too quickly, anything that comes to it, even such ostensibly inadmissible emotions as, to mention just a few, lust, greed, envy, anger—even rancor, even genres of otherwise unutterable prejudice. We should be able to entertain anything the mind casts up as potentially useful for a poem, while at the same time forgiving ourselves for such, after all, private matters, and this should be a forgiveness that arrives in a short enough time so that any shame or guilt arising from such scary glimpses within will be productive rather than debilitating for the germination of poems. We have to have, for poetry, as accurate an awareness as we can of the quality of our ethical consciousness, but we also need a firm sense of the difference between sins of the heart and sins of the hand: the mind has a life of its own that cares little for the parameters culture and society propose for it, and it is often this inner awareness that is most potentially interesting as an aspect of a poem. At the same time, though, we should probably refuse ourselves, in our poems, too ready an access to a transformative vision of such matters: evil must be perceived as evil even in one's self, and emotions that might threaten to be acted on—such as arrogance, cruelty, contempt, and ungrounded anger—should leave one nauseous, revolted, aghast. We have the obligation to discipline ourselves and our poems morally, to the point of apparent cruelty, but this should be done only for very convincing reasons. We have to recognize that all these rigors are finally for the purpose of making headway against ignorance and inexperience and never as punishment for imaginary offenses, to others or the self. Neither, though, should we privilege the marketability of the moral, in which abides the illusion that someday we'll be judged and rewarded for our ethical efforts, in our poems or out.

More gently: the right to find manifestations in oneself of love (and so of poetry, which is love) in what are apparently evidences of its opposite: coolness, neglect, indifference, stubbornness, even (well-examined) rage (though never violence). Perhaps I'm trying to say something here about the basic trust in the efficacy of poetry, of being a poet or artist, that our efforts have to be grounded even if in the most tenuous way in the conviction that at the core of human existence is, after all else, love, or something enough like it to give us the confidence to send our language packets out to the world.

More practically: the right to move in our work into the realm of abstraction, with neither too much credence in seductive promises of philosophical purity and certainty nor too limiting a skepticism about abstraction's capacity to enlarge on the ordinary and incidental. Abstractions are a useful implement for clarifying the usually muddled impressions that inform our vision of experience, and they're just as useful in poems. In other words, sometimes the old workshop maxim has to be revised from "Don't tell, show" to "Tell: everything you can."

Close to here is the right to recognize and entertain and put to use, at least temporarily, those concrete, platitudinous symbols and implicit metaphors in which many complex considerations are embedded, even those such as "soul," or "spirit," which appear absurdly schematic and timeworn. There seem to be certain configurations of our inner world that can't be fully considered without the use of these ancient constructs, and we have the right to resort to them in poetry, to put them to use if nothing else as starting points, or propulsive stimuli, even though our cultural moment might reject all such terms as merely sentimental.

The right to remember: there's much to be reflected upon about the use or misuse of memory in poetry. One thing seems clear, however: we have the right to cultivate memory. But we shouldn't be too good at it, or reflexive about it, because remembrance can then become an end in itself, which is nostalgia. A corollary to this might be the obligation not to release ourselves too readily from past to present necessities because we can end up then with too compelling a commitment to the present, and the present's future, without adequately taking into account the causes from the past that determined it. We also have to be aware of memory's inherent ambiguities, but we still have the right to inhabit those ambiguities without too daunting a compulsion to strive for accuracy. Remembering is necessarily inventing, and inventing is often remembering, but this doesn't mean there are no standards for judging how things are remembered in poems; on the contrary, the poetic memory is art under oath, but real accuracy has more to do with the aesthetic efficacy of the poem than its fealty to any "real" past.

If the right to remember is taken further, there comes the right to believe with conviction that one is participating in the common history of humanity, to feel, even if only glancingly, even if only for moments at a time, the concrete connection we have to what went on thousands of years ago to certain exceptional, actual or mythical, personages in Greece, or Canaan, or Iceland, or even further back in caves in France or China, and to be able to embody this awareness in our poems. One's own thoughts and acts, however humdrum and banal they may seem, should be able to be regarded as a portion of that same history, or destiny, or tragedy, if tragedy is what one comes to believe it is. (I suppose comedy is another possibility, though sadly these days there don't seem many felicitous or humorous endings gleaming out ahead of us.)

From this comes the right, then the need, to meditate if not directly in our poems then in our reflections on the questions that come before poems, on the nature of our own specific historical identity and to move without qualm from this to general human experience. This has to be done rigorously enough, though, to prevent rash deductions that might jeopardize a scrupulous attention to the single self in terms of the general and vice versa. There should also be the recognition that the ultimate purpose of these reflections may be, in our poems, a kind of forgiveness—of ourselves but also of the groups of which we are, or have been, voluntarily or involuntarily, members. (Sometimes it seems our species itself requires forgiveness.) But in our poems or out of them, we shouldn't be too quick to resort to this sort of absolution: pardoning oneself or one's group should always be difficult; if self-forgiveness becomes programmatic, it degrades the potential seriousness of the debates such issues entail.

History, of course, implies death, so, next, death: to be able to imagine and reexperience the deaths of other people, and one's own future death, as an essential part of general and personal history and of our poetic toolkit—others' deaths perhaps as much as one is capable, less often one's own. We should be able to believe in our own death only in ways that will allow the self to better prepare for an apprehension of the mystery of nonexistence, without inciting a despair that might render meaningless anything but the raw terror of that mystery.

On beauty now, some more general reflections. It seems essential for any artist to realize, and to keep in mind, the ultimate subjectivity of any criteria of beauty, without denying the legitimacy of these criteria. We have to be able to have confidence in our commitment to those elements of our aesthetic that can be categorized, and perhaps denigrated, as "taste." At the same time it seems essential to recognize that taste can only be accurate within the terms of the system it is a part of and that such systems should continually be evolving, as we're exposed to new poets and new poems. We also have to have the right (and again, perhaps the obligation) to liberate ourselves from the strictures of the system of beauty we develop for ourselves and to question how that system and our taste have evolved, because otherwise we can tend to become conservative and hidebound. At the same time, we have to be careful not to undermine our faith in our own taste to the degree that the assurance necessary for creating poems might be imperiled.

Corollary: to be able to keep confidence in one's work flexible enough so that useful criticism of it won't be rejected out of hand. Criticism is always grounded in taste, but it still should occasionally be considered seriously enough to determine whether it might contain helpful suggestions for our own aesthetic processes. It's crucial, though, to recognize when criticism is merely an enactment of its perpetrator's obliviousness to or disregard of the subjectivity of his or her own taste-system.

Corollary to a corollary about criticism: to know with some degree of accuracy the shape of your notions of honor, so as not to believe your honor has been offended when it hasn't, even if something in you wishes to act as though it had.

Corollary to all of that: the right to acknowledge your efforts to yourself and to appreciate them according to criteria of judgment in which you really believe; to reward yourself within a range that neither inflates your feeling of self-worth, thereby reducing your objectivity, nor skimps it so much that the essential and probably inevitable discrepancy between effort and reward becomes disheartening. There should always be an inherent unwillingness to believe that anything in existence really has need of the limited and conditional gestures of which one is capable. But we still should be able to believe in and enjoy now and then our own and other people's appreciation and acknowledgment of what we do.

This implies a certain level of success, so the next step to this would be to not let the seductiveness of possible success contaminate our sense of purpose. The illusion of success is stability, dependability, durability; that illusion is always in negative relation to the uncertainties of artistic labor, and to existence itself. Too great an attachment to success makes one vulnerable to its other properties: capriciousness, flux, and maddening unpredictability. What we call ambition is too much credulity in the illusion of success and an inadequate appreciation of its other properties, of the fact that in ongoing artistic striving, rewards must always be considered fleeting and, finally, symbolic.

I'll end with what is in some ways the primary obligation in writing or trying to write poetry, and that's the reading of poems. It wouldn't seem there'd be a great deal to remark about reading for poets, it's so obvious, but sometimes things can get complicated. I always tell my beginning students that the writing and the reading of poetry aren't really separate acts. The devising of a mind capable of writing poems depends absolutely on knowing how other poets have done it, and, moreover, it's essential that the poems of other poets, their *great* poems, be a part of one's working consciousness. This is probably all self-evident; there's always something to be learned from reading poems, poems you don't know and poems you already know and love. I find, though, that often young poets somehow situate themselves when they're trying to compose at too great a distance from what might be called the poetic cosmos: in their quest to "express themselves" and, a little later, to be "original" in their work, they end up all by themselves in a kind of poetic vacuum, with only their own language rhythms and their own imaginative powers to inform what they're doing. At the same time, I believe paradoxically that we also should have the right *not* to read poems, or even more to the point, sometimes the *obligation* not to read poems, at least some poems, particularly poems by one's contemporaries. Younger poets tend to pore too much over the work of their peers; this is probably an unavoidable component of ambition, and it wouldn't be feasible to specify exactly how much of a poet's reading should be of poems by one's contemporaries and how much from the enormous resource of the many centuries of poetry in English and translation. But it might be worth remarking that too much reading of those whose language and history and vision is by definition close to one's own can seem to overload the world with poems, dilute it, pollute it with poems: poems, poems, poems. It's happened to us all. Sometimes we just have to get up, go out, take a walk.

PART II
Answerings

Interview Excerpts

For the last decades, I've participated in a good number of interviews. Several years ago I was approached about publishing a book of them, which seemed like a good idea, but when I began to read through them again, I realized they were a bit repetitive. This probably shouldn't be surprising: there are only so many questions that can be asked of anyone, and given that the respondent will necessarily have only so much experience, and so many ideas up his or her sleeve, interviews generally suffer from this problem.

Considering this, it came to me to cull the interviews and to excerpt responses that seemed to have had some meaning on their own, either in themselves or as records of my progress through a life in poetry, and to omit the rest of the hill of words from the originals as they were published in journals or, in the case of several that were never published, in manuscripts. This entailed a great deal of editing and frank rewriting, so much so that by now the excerpts often bear little similarity to the original responses. For one thing, they almost all take place in 2009 and 2010, when I polished them. I hope I haven't offended any of my interlocutors by this, and I remain grateful to them all for their interest in what I might have had to say in the first place.

The final revisions for the excerpts were done over a period of time in 2010 and 2011. The opinions and attitudes in them have been pretty much brought up to those dates, that is to say, to the moment I'm closing this book down. Because of the variety of subjects, and the period of time over which the interviews occurred, I've decided to list them alphabetically by titles that seemed to suit the sections.

I would like to thank the following for their part in the original conversations: Greg Conley and Toriell Finch, Tishani Doshi, Alan Fox, David Gewanter, Jeffrey Greene, Edward Hirsch, Lynn Keller, Collin Kelley, Brandon Massey, Efe Murat, Sanford Pinsker, Alan Riding, Alan Shapiro, Peter Sirr, Alan Soldovsky, Christian Teresi, and Ahren Warner.

AN AMERICAN SCENE

I don't really think it's possible to talk about an "American scene" in poetry. Of course, if you get far enough away from anything, you can characterize it anyway you'd like—you might speak of European or Asian poetry, but only if you don't really know anything about them.

I feel that way about American poetry now: it's just too complex to generalize about in any meaningful way. We're in a time of terrific stylistic variety, everything from poems that root themselves firmly in different traditions of English-American poetic history, to performance or slam poetry, to the several self-consciously "avant-garde" movements; and there are different casts to the poems from different regions of the country. America's a huge place, with a terrifically heterogeneous society; it's perhaps surprising that there aren't an even greater number of different poetic styles being written.

Even the language in which our poetry is written is a complicated issue. Certainly one thing American poets would seem to share is language, but that isn't always the case. There are a number of African American and Hispanic American poets who write in what are in some ways separate and unique languages, with their own poetic needs, and if sometimes their work isn't appreciated sufficiently by the larger poetic community, this has nothing to do with its validity. The work isn't written for the "mainstream" culture at all—it has its own poetic conventions and its own audience.

Historically, I suppose there might have been a time, in the nineteenth century, when American poetry could have been characterized as a more or less cohesive phenomenon, but once Whitman's work begins to take effect and the imagists arrive, and the modernists, then the whole thing rather wonderfully explodes.

BISHOP

I have to confess that for a long time I didn't understand what the fuss was about Bishop; her work just didn't get to me. Then one day I was in a library waiting for my son to find a book, and there was a paperback of *Geography III* on a table. I picked it up and almost fell over with the force of it. It's so strange how that happens.

The other night I was talking about Bishop with a friend who's a great poet, and he said he doesn't care at all for her work. I was very surprised, read aloud some what I think are undeniable passages to him—among them that wonderful epistemological section from "In the Waiting Room," which always knocks me down—but he didn't hear her voice at all, still found it all rather blah. And of course I could understand, since for a long time I'd felt the same way: here's somebody using ordinary language in rather ordinary ways to talk about ordinary things, so what's the big deal?

When I did realize how unique and powerful her work is and attached to her—if that's the term—I read her every day for years. It was during the time I was writing *Tar* in which I can see quite clearly her influence, and I still keep going back to her from time to time now. Her purity of vision, the absolute rightness of her figures and the precision of her details never ceases to amaze me and, of course, many other poets along with me. Her subtle use of language rhythms is remarkable, and I'm also often struck by the analytic rigor in her work, the way she dissects perceptions and emotions and ideas so deftly you hardly notice that she's doing it.

CHANGE

In retrospect, I think the change between my second and third books, *I Am the Bitter Name* and *With Ignorance*, was driven by a combination of despair in my personal life, dissatisfaction with the identity I'd made for myself as a poet, and, naturally, by the poems I'd been writing. The assumptions I'd made in the first books about the ways to express my emotions and thoughts I realize now were, if not naïve, then certainly unreasonable. I wrote *I Am the Bitter Name* during the war in Vietnam, a time of great social upheaval in general, and I'd come to believe—I guess it was a part of the common mind then—that poetry could be a direct agent of social progress. But after awhile I finally had to admit to myself, perhaps not quite consciously, that poetry might be a "direct" factor in anything at all was presumptuous—more than presumptuous. I wouldn't say I felt I'd been wrong about trying to be an active agent of the changes in society I hoped for—dreamed of—but I certainly did feel much more uncertain about the possibility of my poetry, or of any poetry, actually having that kind of effect.

At the same time, the social and political conflicts that I had perceived and the attempt I'd made in my poems to link them to my own inner turbulence—and to investigate what in myself had a connection to the deeper causes of social injustice—still seemed to me to be valid. My assumption had been that everyone had an inner life that was much like mine and that there were also only a limited number of ways to look at public reality. And I'd come to feel that I had to investigate what was between one's own psychological, particularly psychosexual, needs and the public manifestation of those needs that drive everyone in a society. I felt the poet's task was to try live consciously in that realm, to work to clarify it in oneself, because if you could help other people see what was in them, it might allow them to understand how the external world really worked in relation to themselves, which would presumably persuade them to change that world.

When I began to write in a more discursive, expansive style, I still believed all that, still felt that those were the areas of my responsibility. But I think I came to see that to be too overt about it was counterproductive, that you couldn't demand that kind of change, because the attempt could be perceived as a kind of attack on the reader: you were demanding that the reader *change.* The implication that if a poem is read properly the reader will change isn't only rather absurd but wildly presumptuous.

In the poems I wrote after that, the impulse towards social change was, and probably still is, a part of my intentions, but I, or the poems, came to work under the assumption that the best way to try to change people was not to let them know you were. My feelings about that, too, have undergone a great deal of evolution over the years, but my initial and probably abiding impulse was to try to make the evidence for change I was presenting more complete, more comprehensive, and to make the injunction (if that's the word) to change less obvious, gentler, more subliminal.

That would describe how I conceived the tasks of my work over a number of years, but since then I've again changed what I ask of my poems. I've become more directly concerned with form in poetry, and with beauty, although I certainly still feel that it's one of the central responsibilities of poetry to engage in the conflict between the public and the private, between obliviousness and injustice.

CHANGE, AGAIN

Change and development are rather elusive concepts and can seem particularly seductive when you are applying them to yourself. We're always supposed to be evolving, developing, and our great fear is that the only progress we're actually making is through time, from one end of our time on earth to the other.

Still, the pure accumulation of experience counts for something—all the mistakes you make that at least you might not make again. And it can seem you've accumulated some craft, although one of the paradoxes of being an artist is that you have to beware of becoming too deft in one's art, too fluent, because then you can be speaking with a portion of the soul that doesn't reach far enough into the true quandaries and mysteries with which we're confronted.

At a certain time in my life I found Machado's statement that "in order to write a poem you have to invent a poet to write it" desperately useful, because I knew well, and was uneasy about knowing, that in fact I was making someone up, a poet, with my name, whom I had only the vaguest hope would someday find congruence with the person I knew I actually was. But that all calms down after awhile, thank goodness. You seem to have to check in at the identity bank a little less often. Maybe it's just one of the benefits of middle age: that whatever you've made of yourself, it's too late to change it.

CHILDREN

The discrepancy between what everybody on earth feels for their own children, and those close to them, and the way our social organizations actually deal with children can be depressing, even tormenting. When

I had my first child, it was such an overwhelming experience, that I naturally tried to write about it. This was during the Vietnam War, when children were being killed almost before your eyes, and I came to feel that the welfare of children should be the primary determinant in any political organization. I still do. These vulnerable creatures are in the most profound sense our most precious possessions; they're greater than us because they have the potential by knowing what we know to be more than we've been. It was inconceivable to me then, and still is, that such an obvious fact shouldn't have a much larger effect than it does.

At the same time, I don't regard children as evidence of our lost innocence. Although I think children are pure, I don't believe they're particularly innocent. I'm a Freudian in this: I think children have the same motivational apparatus we do, the same psychic organization. I certainly don't have any particular longing to be a child again, nor do I think anything is lost by becoming an adult. Unless, of course, you become a neurotic adult, which many of us do, at least for a time.

In some essential way we split in two when we become adults, we're the actor and audience of our lives in a way we almost never are as children, and much of the suffering of adolescence and early adulthood surely has to do with this division that becoming an adult entails. All at once we possess a self who experiences and a self who experiences the experiencing. The child isn't afflicted with this, or only in a rudimentary way. It's not very useful to long towards the undivided self of the childhood, though I relished beholding it in my own children and, now, in my grandchildren.

CIVILIZING

When I was doing the translation of Sophocles's *Women of Trachis*, I became convinced that it's really about civilization, about the moment at which humans become civilized—what Norbert Elias called "the civilizing process." Sophocles's play is the enactment of just that process. Herakles is the pivotal figure; he's from the world of precivilization, but he's the agent of civilization. He's the civilizer, yet he never really quite civilizes himself. I've always been fascinated with that phenomenon as it occurs in the individual. Freud calls it the relation between the id and the ego or the id and the superego. One of the abiding themes of my adult consciousness has been the struggle between instinct and reason, if you would call it reason and if you'd call it instinct—I'm not sure either term in fact is adequate.

The other thing that intrigued me about doing the translations was that when I was a kid my father used to tell me bedtime stories, and my favorites were the labors of Hercules, and so the play had an intimate meaning for me as well.

COMING TO TERMS

I don't myself find any hint in my work that I'm readier to accept the horrors of the world than I ever was, and I certainly don't see how anyone these days could be less "idealistic," if that means clear-eyed, about justice and injustice, given that we've had a crash course over the last years in every variety of it. Still, maybe there is, if not resignation, then something like exhaustion about it all; perhaps I've resorted more to irony than I used to, and perhaps I've sometimes expressed a kind of resigned futility about so many aspects of the great struggles we're involved in against power and its abuses, but my indignation and despair certainly haven't flagged.

Sometimes, to tell the truth, all the terrible crises that seem about to overwhelm civilization feel just too much for me, and it can seem not only futile but self-destructive to maintain that level of passion. I find often lately I just can't bear to hear any more of the details about global warming, environmental disaster, the apparent trajectory America's been on towards an executive branch bent on totalitarianism, even if it still wears the guise of legislative democracy, which it hardly has been lately. We never consider what might have come to pass if Iraq hadn't been such a disaster: what if the Bush administration had been able to claim, and demonstrate, that it had "won" the war? How much more power would Cheney and Bush have demanded and, certainly with the lapdog Congress they had for most of their reign, achieved?

Of course America isn't the only bad example. It becomes clearer and clearer to me over the years that the basic issue about justice and injustice is power, pure and simple. It's about those who desire, and attain, and possess power against the rest of us, demanding we die for them, make them wealthy, put them beyond our influence. I'm in much more of a state of something like despair about all of this than I was when I started writing—a state of hopelessness about human beings being able to achieve any but the most fleeting states of justice or, rather, non-injustice. Perhaps my recent poems demonstrate that. Perhaps in those earlier poems of rage and despair there were elements of hope that now have transmogrified to at best states of . . . if not resignation, then something approaching blindness, forgetfulness, at best disattention.

The old question of what poetry has to do with any of this remains ever alive. I may have actually believed, in my earliest political passions, that poetry could change things, that anything could change things. God, that seems so naïve now, so innocent, so . . . Well, I have to say admirable, jejune but finally admirable.

At the same time, wherever I picked it up, however little it might mean, I still believe that if my poetry is going to have any value, to me if to no one else, it has to strive for and hopefully embody truth—truths. It's odd to realize, as one has to at some point, that poetry can seem to have no particular interest in truth, but when I look closely at the poems I admire, now or from any period, they all, to one degree or another, are fervently involved in finding out the truth. Perhaps that's what makes a certain portion of the poetry that's being written by young poets now difficult for me to respond to: because their poems are given over so completely to the irony I was speaking about before, there's nothing else left. What remains is a world colored deeply by a surrealistic irrationality, a rejection of connection and of consequences. It can seem to be a kind of playground game song, sometimes very beautiful, as children singing is always sort of beautiful, but without the resonance that the philosophical, moral belief in possible truth rings in great poems.

CONFESSIONAL POETRY

I have mixed feelings about the term, and at least in some ways about the poets who enact it, although there aren't really all that many poets for whom the word is just. When the term began to be used, it seems to me there were really only three confessional poets of any note: Sexton, Plath, and Lowell. Berryman is sometimes included in the group, but I don't think he really fits—I'd say he wasn't so much a confessional poet as a poet of narcissism. The great "Dream Songs," the first seventy-seven, seem hardly at all confessional—the personal matter in them is so outweighed by the artifice of the poetry—but when he kept on with the poems, writing those few hundred more, he allowed his great artifice to flag, the poems became self-indulgent, and the confessional element in the poems, I suppose, more prominent.

Lowell's confessionalism, if we can call it that, can trouble me in a different way. He's been very important for me over the years; I've gone through periods when his work has been a model for me, at least in its technique, but his injudicious use of his own and his unscrupulous use of other people's lives has bothered me. When he was incorporating Elizabeth Hardwick's letters to him in poems, in some cases really making poems more or less directly from them, Bishop objected, and I agree with her. There are aesthetic and moral issues in all of this. Besides the question of a poet making significant poems (and Lowell certainly achieved that), there's also the fact that because of your poetry, other people can value your life itself, beyond the poems, because they've been so effected by your work.

Being a poet can be very mysterious; you can write for a long time without it even occurring to you that you are one. But at the same time perhaps you have to be aware that when someone reads and falls in love with a poem, that attachment can spill over onto the poet as a person as well, and there might be some responsibility that comes with that. Everyone's had the experience of reading the biography of a poet and having the person of the poet seem diminished; it can feel like a real betrayal. I remember early on when I was still very attached to Rilke—he was my master, I thought in more than merely matters of poetry—reading a biography that recounted some of his quite reprehensible idiosyncrasies, then finding the same attitudes expressed in his poems, and feeling just that: betrayed. I thought for awhile that his poetry wasn't important enough to offset all the rest. Though I came back to him—I suppose we always do to the great ones—it was a disturbing experience. With Lowell, at least in his "confessional" mode, I suppose I'd ask whether he was attending adequately to that aspect of the poet's function, extrapoetical as it might be, or might he have been misusing his identity in order to keep producing poems? At the end, of course, he's such a great poet that the question becomes a bit moot.

CONSCIOUSNESS AND STYLE

Ordinarily we think that a poet has his or her consciousness and that he or she develops a style to enact it. But I might turn that around and wonder whether, rather than consciousness having gone out to search for its stylistic embodiment, the styles we evolve actually allow our consciousness to find new forms, to change. Certainly when we're actually writing, especially when it's going well, you can feel that things are happening to you, that you're not the cause of what you're writing, that you're being drawn along, sometimes with exuberance, sometimes with real surprise, and, of course, with gratitude.

Beyond that, just achieving a poem adds something to the mind that wasn't there; it becomes an event and an enlarging presence in the field of your thought. These days, for example, I find myself spending a lot of time when I'm at my desk brooding, just sitting there following the flow of my mind, without any particular direction or purpose, in a way I never used to. I suppose the literary word for this is "reverie," but whatever it is, I've been curious about it. My first thought would be that I'm just older now, more "mature," or that at least my life is less tempestuous than it used to be. But there was a period, at the time I was writing the poems of *A Dream of Mind*, when my work became more meditative, and maybe those poems taught me a different way of inhabiting myself. Odd thought.

CONVENTIONS AND DEFINITIONS

I think that there can be a fundamental misunderstanding of what we mean when we speak of "conventions." Poetry has always had several dimensions, several purposes, several potentials. First of all, there's what has always been meant as "art," what might be called the song, the singing, of poetry. The first poetic conventions developed with this as an aim: what the audience desired, and expected, was to hear the poet sing, hear how the language was being transfigured and exhilarated and made sublime by the poet's skill. Any information that the poem might impart along with this singing was—is—relatively incidental. Those conventions of poetry are closest to pure music in this sense: we don't listen to Mozart or Beethoven, or any composer we love, to "learn" anything; there's nothing to learn from a piano sonata, though we can become almost ecstatic in listening to it. Neither do we expect that an ode by Pindar or a pastoral by Virgil is going to tell us anything about our lives, other than the most basic emotions of temporality and mortality. Pindar is so untranslatable because all he was really doing was singing, and to imagine that we might experience his work anything like a Greek audience did is quite far-fetched.

The other function of poetry has to do with the meanings it brings to us, the insights and revelations we need in order to live our lives to the fullest. And although the musical element of this tradition of poetry is essential to it, because it's poetry, not philosophy or polemic, and comes to our consciousness in a different way and to a different place, still, the matter, the information it embodies, becomes as important to us as its singing. This is poetry in the tradition of the epic and the tragic. I think this is where confusion can arise: because so much of modern poetry, really much of poetry since the Renaissance, has its roots in the tragic and responds to the tragic elements of human existence, the enactment of conventions like the pastoral have tended to become secondary, or, perhaps more accurately, they've become resources for poetry rather than ends in themselves. Campion and Wyatt and Jonson were well aware of the conventionality of their lyric poems, of the fact that they were essentially creating variations on themes, just as the composer of a sonata or a symphony is quite conscious of contriving a new embodiment of an existing form. I think modernism, and the advent of free verse, reinforced and accelerated the shifting of the greater part of poetry towards the tragic and away from the lyric. It was surely in reaction to all this that the so-called New Formalists gained their fleeting traction a few years ago, though they seemed, at least to me, to be unaware of how crude their characterizations of modern poetry were. They pined for a return to form, meaning conventional metrics, but seemed to pay little heed, or speak little, anyway, of the dichotomies of these more elemental paradoxes of poetry.

Even the poets who have been great formalists, like Yeats, like Frost, like Larkin and Heaney, have for the most part put their lyric powers at the service of the larger vision of existence they were or are concerned with. Of course you can see the shift in American poetry most vividly in Whitman and Dickinson. Whitman's case is fairly obvious: he developed a vision of human life and at the same time a music to embody that vision. *Leaves of Grass* had to be written in the verse he developed for it—it's inconceivable to imagine Whitman's amplitude and inclusiveness and fluidity of identity in formal verse. The one formal poem he did write, "O Captain, My Captain," is embarrassing in its poetic crudity, although, not surprisingly, considering how revolutionary the rest of his work was, it became the most popular of his poems in his own time. You can call Dickinson a formal poet if you like, but her metrics were obviously quite incidental to her: it's been pointed out often enough how easy it is to reduce the music of her poems to a few set patterns. But she, too, had a powerful vision of the world and of poetry and an absolute genius for figuration and for poetic thinking: the fact that it came embodied in rhyme and meter doesn't at all situate her in the lyrical tradition, that tradition in which the way the matter of the poem is sung determines how we value it. You could call some of her poems pastoral, but they're in the pastoral convention in only the most glancing way. She uses the observation of nature, the events of the cycles of nature, as the traditional pastoralists did but for utterly different purposes: her project was to find and configure the shape of consciousness in the world, in the complexities of existence. It's her intellect that astonishes us as much as her enormous poetic skills: she had a mind like no one else's in history, and the poetry she uses to configure and investigate this mind is only incidentally related to the ancient conventions.

THE DIFFERENCE BETWEEN POETRY AND PROSE

Basically, poetry is language that responds to artificial rhythmic necessities. This has been written about a million times or so, but it can still feel elusive when you try to express it. Poetry happens in a part of the mind that shares our capacity for musical response with our intellect and emotions. It's a very specialized, and I think not very extensive, portion of mind, which might be why poetry isn't more generally appreciated: in a sense, you have to go looking inside yourself to begin to respond to it.

Robert Pinsky has spoken of poetry as taking place in our bodies, as well as our mind—we might say in our voice—and that's a way of characterizing of it, too. Technically, it's even harder to talk about, especially, again, in an age of free verse. There's no question the line between verse and prose has been blurred: some find this offensive, others, like me, find it liberating: the range of poetry, the function it can play in consciousness has surely been extended by broadening the musical resources available to it. And sometimes poetry resorts to prose in a way that makes them superficially quite indistinguishable. I was speaking with an English poet recently about Anne Carson, about whose work I'm very enthusiastic, and he said, "She doesn't know anything about the line," and I replied that she doesn't care about the line. When you try to analyze her best work, there's no way you can account systematically for what she's doing with her music: there are none of the traditional patterns, even free-verse patterns, of poetry to be found in it. And yet it's terrifically effective as poetry: the naked power of her metaphors, which are what make her work so nearly shocking in its emotional and intellectual profundity, doesn't need any of the traditional sounds of verse. She organizes her language very cunningly, her sense of the phrase is devastating, and to want her to write differently would be absurd. I've never been crazy about the prose poem, at least in English; there just don't seem to be that many successful instances of it, yet there, again, you certainly don't want to prohibit it. Some people seem to get riled up about the disorder in modern poetry, the way it keeps redefining itself, violating its own apparent precepts, but you can also think of this as one of its unlikely splendors.

DISCIPLINE

The best advice ever given to me was by a painter I knew in Mexico, Tomás Coffeen, an American who lived for a long time in Tlaquepaque, where I stayed for some months. He never became very well known outside of Mexico, but he was accomplished and terrifically dedicated. Coffeen was a great reader, and one day he mentioned something T. S. Eliot had said: that if you're a poet you have to write poetry every day. Although I don't think now Eliot actually did that himself, it seemed like a good idea, and I took it to heart, perhaps, sometimes, in down times, to my chagrin.

Then Coffeen added his own refinement: that no matter what's going on in your life, you have to keep a certain part of each day to yourself to practice your art, and everyone close to you has to know you're not available for anything else during that time. I took Coffeen's advice seriously—I was twenty-six at the time—and I think it's helped me over the years. I hadn't felt particularly talented when I started out, and I had no early success to hearten me, so I suppose I decided that the only thing I could do was to work hard, as hard as I could, and if I was talented sooner or later it would show, and if it didn't then at least I'd be able to tell myself I'd given my all.

THE DISCURSIVE

I've been struggling over the last years to decide what level of discursive meaning a poem can hold. Of course there are many different ways a poem can mean something; it can move from being almost wholly connotative, in which "meaning" is embodied in the mechanisms of the poem and evoked by them, to being closer to what I'm calling the discursive. It seems our moment of poetry has been almost entirely committed to connotative kinds of meaning, and I've been working with trying to push myself towards the other end of the scale.

I've been exploring, at least for myself, how much you can say of what you'd mean in other modes of language, in what we might crudely call the abstract or philosophical mode, while not sacrificing anything of the musical interest I believe poems should have. Poems that are musically very complex, very attentive, don't on the surface seem to need as high a degree of denotative meaning to be satisfying, but it seems to me that we should be able to put our intellects to use, and our more overtly analytic mental operations, and still have our poems be musically satisfying. Miłosz was the great master of discursive thinking in his poems: the force of his analytic mind combined with his powerful spiritual strivings developed what was an entirely original and, I think, probably inimitable body of poetry.

EARLY WORK

Yeats once made a statement that I used to find very meaningful: he said that at eighteen you are who you are, and the rest of your life is basically spent working out the details. In some paradoxical way, I still believe agree with him, but at the same time I find it completely inaccurate in terms of what I've actually experienced. I suppose I'm genetically the same person I was at eighteen, I suppose I still have the intellectual capacity I did then—though I'm not even sure of that—but in every other way I'm different. Even at nineteen or twenty, when I first started writing—the rather simple, if very needy kid I was then has almost nothing to do with who I am now. I'm not ashamed of that person, of having been him—it's like one of those riddles in which you change all the parts of a mechanism and try to tell whether it's still the article you started out with. I certainly don't renounce the poems I wrote during those first years of striving, I'm just not who I was then. This isn't to flatter myself; you naturally lose something as you move out of that period of earnestness, of unabashed and ignorant effort—sometimes I can even long for the innocence that conditioned so much of what I actually lived day by day—but I much prefer the identity my life has evolved for me over the years.

When I was working at poems back then, I had no idea if I had any gift. Notions like talent or gift at the end just dribble away, though early on they can seem terribly important—the proof is in what you do. All I had when I was young was a kind of blind determination to do the best I could. There wasn't much reflection, in either sense of the word, because I didn't really know how to "think" about poetry, because I didn't know enough of the possibilities of poetry and there wasn't any but the most tentative feeling of accomplishment. I'd learned already that what you did one day very likely could lose much of its value when you went back to work it again. This can drive you a little crazy. For me it still does.

FLESH AND BLOOD

I stumbled accidentally onto the eight-line form of the poems in my collection *Flesh and Blood*. After *Tar* was published, I had a number of unfinished poems on my desk, some of which I'd been lugging around for ten years, even longer. One morning, reading one of them, I realized that it wasn't ever going to be the poem I'd wanted, but that there was one stanza that seemed viable; it was eight lines long, and I worked it into an independent poem. Then I turned to another of the old poems and found another eight-line poem in it, then another. Soon I found myself committed to the eight-line form, and before long I was generating new poems all over the place. I ended up writing a hundred and seventy or so, of which a good proportion ended up in *Flesh and Blood*.

I've wondered why it happened; I may have needed a break from the longer poems I'd been writing, which demanded what seemed sometimes an inordinate amount of time and patience. Maybe I just wanted to write more quickly for a while. The shorter form seemed to allow me to respond with more immediacy to what was happening around me; I liked the feeling of sitting down and writing a poem from start to finish, rather than always gathering fragments and assembling inspirations.

After awhile, having a strict form like that seemed to liberate me in a way I'd never experienced before. I was writing poems all over the place, in the street, in cafés: I once found myself writing in my notebook while leaning on the roof of a car. During one of the summers when I was writing the book, the apartment we'd rented in Paris was too small for me to have space of my own, so I borrowed one in a friend's wholesale fur business. It was an odd place to work, to say the least: the room he loaned me was half filled by fur coats, I had a small table facing a window that looked out into a courtyard, but I was writing in a splendid fury. I'd have lunch with my friend sometimes and say, "I wrote three poems this morning."

Occasionally I miss that time; the writing process seemed somehow so seamless. I even think occasionally of going back to eight lines again, but I feel it would be a regression, a synthetic inspiration, which is a contradiction and a danger.

GOD

I realize there are a lot of references and addresses to god in my first two books, particularly in *I Am the Bitter Name*. I felt in those days that a lot of poetry had a sort of conceptual politeness about it that omitted a great deal of our actual psychic activity. That's one of those egomaniacal things young poets can say to themselves—"Poetry is such and such"—without even being familiar with most of the poetry in the world. At any rate, though, I did feel that the way we actually experience, or try to experience, phenomena like god, or the soul, is much rawer in tone and edge than we generally acknowledge in our poems. So in those first books I very consciously tried to formulate a god, and ways of thinking about and addressing him, that would have the simplicity and directness with which children experience such matters, with a kind of primitive emotional frankness and openness. I think when we're adults we never again experience god in quite that way, as simply him, it, she; as a vivid sensual-mental apprehension, and that's what I was trying to reenact.

Most of the conversations or addresses I made to god in those years had to do with various aspects of theodicy: about god's indifference to injustice, violence, murder—that whole thing. I don't quite know why, but over the years I've become reluctant to talk about the arguments I've had with god. Maybe I've taken too much of that struggle, if that's what it is, into the public realm of poetry, maybe I'm just going through a phase about the whole question that is either very private or, possibly, inconsequential, but it feels anyway as though the moral struggles I used to have that included a divinity were crude, even if heartfelt. Maybe a god who's so much a function of a theodicy argument isn't a god at all, but a convenient invention.

I don't know how I'd make my struggles more refined now. It feels as though I've somehow burnt off everything but the argument; I don't feel much promise anymore about what any god I can conceive of might offer me. Maybe it's because I've been reading a lot of Dickinson lately, and her struggles with her god are so much more complex and rigorous and attentive than mine have ever been. Maybe my labor has always simply been of belief, trying to believe, and I've given the struggle up for now.

I love human beings in their relationships with divinity; I've always been drawn to Martin Buber's definition of a miracle as a people believing over generations that there's been a miracle. I like mantras and mourner's kaddish, but I don't believe they have anything to do with the universe. The only way I can seem to conceive of a god who inheres in any real way in my cosmos is to make him so subtle and difficult that he's beyond my ability to define him. But if I were really able to find a god, I think I'd like him to be unsubtle, concrete, definite, personal. A god who would make the ladder from cosmology to epistemology to ethics as readily apparent as Dante's does.

In my early books, I think I postulated a god with those attributes, though I never really experienced him except insofar as he failed to be what I'd asked of him. I felt then that all the spiritual issues I'd been exposed to, about the soul and life and the world, had been overrefined, that the discussions began after the real force had been intellectualized out of them. The god I wanted to talk to then I thought had made an implicit covenant with creation: that it would be if not always perfect, then at least perfectly understandable. And the god I'd developed for myself, one defined by his imperfections, could appear actively malevolent, or indifferent, which was as bad. God as a sort of laissez-faire conservative, who was letting everything go to pot for the sake of some dubious equations, some absurd moral idealizations. He wanted to have it both ways: to be loved as a loving god and to deal with us as an indifferent one. Now, as I say, I don't really know anymore where he and I are. "It" and I. I don't feel I'm capable of anything like the relation Buber implied by his "Thou," even a disappointed one.

HISTORY

For a long time I had a sort of block against history per se, the history we learn in history classes and books. In school, I never seemed to be able to absorb the history that goes chronologically, from king to king and war to war: it just went through me. It's odd that there are many different histories available to us, but that particular genre, which deals with so-called great men and great events, is the only one that's certified in our culture. I admire Lowell for the way he can take that kind of history and work it into his poems, but I still don't know how to deal with it except in the broadest, almost algebraic way. What I learned about history was by reading in other fields, literature, of course, or art, or religion, or philosophy. Lately I've been reading a lot of economics because it seems impossible to understand our world without understanding at least a minimum about economics, and there's a great deal of history that I'm picking up from that.

At the same time, you have to be aware of just how much innocence can be permitted in reflecting on history, and how much ignorance of it we can forgive in ourselves. I once had an experience in Guatemala, during the early sixties, before I began to be seriously politically conscious. I was traveling with two friends of mine who were doctors through a very poor Indian area, and we struck up an acquaintance with a Bahia missionary nurse, who was the only health care available to about a hundred thousand Indians. She did everything from setting bones, to pulling wisdom teeth, to prescribing antibiotics. It still troubles me how unaware I was of what was going on around me on that trip, of the political situation of Guatemala, which was horrible—a bloody civil war was underway—and even of the absurdity of the lack of medical care those poor people had, which I'd seen with my own eyes. I did finally wrote a poem about this, by the way, "Guatemala: 1964," which was published in *Flesh and Blood*.

The long poem "Combat" is also about our naïveté in dealing with history. I seem continually to be looking back into my past and having to revise what I experienced at the time. That's probably a good part of what our education consists, that revision of faulty perception, but it can so often be dismaying when it happens. We tend to speak about experience as though it primarily has to do with the matters we live in our "real" life, our "outward" as opposed to our "inward" experience, but our lives are obviously an active dialectic between the two things. A lot of my poems that seem to be about "life experience" are actually often created to enact conceptual matters. So many of my poems aren't about things that "happen" but about ideas that demand embodiment in more concrete experience.

HOLOCAUST

There's no doubt that the Holocaust, and my coming to know about it, played a role in my moral education. I grew up with an edge of city, then suburban, childhood and adolescent obliviousness: you didn't have to be aware of anything about anything, social, historical, cultural . . . nothing. Plus, my parents' generation seemed to want their children not to have to know about what happened in the Shoah. They were themselves still stunned by it, I think, and perhaps even ashamed, but whatever the reasons, it was far from being dinner table conversation.

My awareness of the Holocaust came when I was in college, and just after. I was of course shocked by it, but when I look back now the most interesting thing to me about that time is that my knowledge of the Holocaust came at almost exactly the same time as my recognition of the plight of black people in America. In fact, I'd been struggling for months, longer, trying to write the poem "A Day for Anne Frank," and one day I read an article by Thomas Williams about the plight of blacks in America, which I found . . . I don't remember exactly, probably somehow exaggerated. I started to write him a letter and as I wrote I realized that what he'd written wasn't exaggerated at all, that I was just naïve about what was going on around me, and the strangest thing was that trying to write that letter, then stopping, somehow released me into writing the poem . . . Odd, I've probably repeated that anecdote a dozen times; something important must have happened to me that day, that broke down what was left of my ethical complacency . . . If one ever can really say that. We seem to have so many layers of moral obtuseness, it can feel as though one's whole life is learning to dig your way through them.

These days I've tended to become a little mistrustful about Holocaust literature. Although it's certainly essential that those horrors be remembered, and honored, if that's the word, the whole thing has become almost an industry, and I'm hardly the only one who's come to believe that the Holocaust memory evokes a terribly conservative reaction in regard to Israel's struggles and its own all-too-often self-defeating policies. I think that reaction is probably more fraught for some Americans, who find Israel's existence more problematic than Israelis themselves do. I tried to write an essay once—it never worked out—about Jews who are obsessed with the Holocaust; I called them "Miraculists": people to whom the Holocaust has the same kind of spiritual meaning that the resurrection of Christ was for Christians. The Holocaust becomes the most unique and important event in human history: history ends with it and begins again after it, and nothing will ever be the same ever again from then on. I know I went through a phase something like that myself, when my most profound philosophical emotions revolved around the Holocaust and when everything else in history was measured against it. In the poem "Combat," I refer to that period as "the adolescence of [my] ethics," and I still feel that.

And I don't believe I've been alone in this perception. The Holocaust poem many readers feel is the greatest and most enduring is Paul Celan's "Death Fugue," but by the end of his life Celan was so exasperated at being celebrated almost entirely because of that one poem that he'd no longer allow it to be published in anthologies. About the vast volume of Holocaust poems we have now, particularly of the second and third generation, I don't think we finally can know which might endure.

INFLUENCES

The poets who have stayed with me longest are Baudelaire, Rilke, and Yeats. Those are the three who were there almost at the beginning and are always still there. Over the last years, George Herbert has been very important to me, a few years ago I read him nearly obsessively. Before that, Elizabeth Bishop was most important. If I were to say who I think are the poets who've meant the most to me over time besides them, I'd say, Whitman, Dickinson, Frost, Eliot, Lowell, Donne, Milton, Keats, Coleridge—it's really a long list, more than I can keep track of and that's not even counting many of my near contemporaries. And then, of course, Shakespeare; we tend not to even mention Shakespeare because he's so obvious, but you can't write a sentence in English without Shakespeare being there somewhere.

Influence itself is such a fascinating subject that I certainly don't think Harold Bloom exhausted it. I tried for a number of years to get an anthology of influence published in which poets would choose the poems that had influenced them over the years, along with one of their own poems. I could never find a taker until I mentioned it to my English publisher, Neil Astley, and I think he's going to do it himself.

LANGUAGE

I know people refer to the language of my poems as colloquial, but I don't think on the page it really is. The rhythms may come from speech as it's spoken, but the syntax and vocabulary are quite formal, quite "unnatural." I've used that tension quite a bit in my poems—between the apparently naturalness of the speech sounds and the complexity of the actual language.

It's often remarked that the language of much of our poetry these days can be traced to the work of William Carlos Williams because of how devotedly he used ordinary speech. But to take it one step further, I don't think there really have been more than a few American poets this century who haven't written in those rhythms. One of the odd misperceptions of American poetry is that there's a "higher" and a "lower" way of speaking. There were a few years in the fifties when the prevailing mode was a formal verse that seemed quite distinctly removed from ordinary speech, but even then I don't believe that the language of more than a few good poets were very far from what was spoken in the street. The notion that the American speech rhythms had to wait for Williams to find them I think has to do more with the ways he could use apparently (though not really) ordinary ways of thinking and perceiving to create his poems than with his language per se. Certainly Bishop and Moore and even Stevens worked, each in their own way, with "American" language. But Williams's experience and thought was so firmly rooted in the life around him that the discoveries of his poetry were as much epistemological as poetic; he exalted the way we think, as much as the way we speak.

LANGUAGE POETS

I find most of the Language Poets trivial rather than irresponsible. In their polemic and rhetoric, they speak a great deal of responsibility, of the commitment of art to social ideals, and so forth, but you don't see much of it in their work. From a technical point of view, if they're willing to sacrifice the meaning of language to its potential as music, they could be doing a lot more interesting things with the music of poetry than they are. If they're trying to develop a new system of meaning, they're not doing anything much different from what the Dadaists did, and they're much less interesting and zany and inspiring than either the Dadaists or Surrealists. I feel they're mostly driven by a passion for novelty, by the desire to be out ahead of everybody else, to be more "avant-garde," but they're squandering an awful lot in that way.

They demanded a freedom for themselves that was greater than what they knew how to put to good use, and I think that well may be because their perception of the tradition was prematurely determined by their passion for recognition and novelty. Poetry is always an expression or an embodiment of meaning because if you put two words together, language will distill something of meaning out of them, no matter how badly you might want it not to. But it seems perverse to want not to. Life's hard enough to keep meaningful, without cultivating incoherence or nonsense. And this in a time in which there have been, as I said, such a great variety of poems, and so many varied notions of what poems can be.

Of course, I might be speaking here of some poets I don't mean to, like Leslie Scallopino, whose work I often find fascinating, and whom

I've heard mentioned along with the language poets, although I don't find much similarity between her work and the poets who are the core of the movement.

LINES

When I first developed the long line I guess I'm known for, it was because I'd felt too constrained not so much by the length of the lines in the poetry I'd been writing as by the conventions of expression that I'd inherited and learned to use. I've spoken about this a number of times, but basically I just felt I was leaving too much of myself out in the poems I'd been writing; my inner life, my response to the world, was so much more complex than what I'd been honing myself down to fit in poems. I heard my work once characterized as "the act of the mind in meditation," and that for me is a good description of what the poems in longer lines evolved to, what I'd unconsciously felt was feasible for them. Perhaps just as important was the fact that the longer lines revealed cadences of thought and observation that weren't available to me before I began to use them.

I'm often asked lately, as I suspected I would be, why I stopped using the long line exclusively. I think the reason was that I began to feel I needed more constraint, or a different kind of constraint; I guess I became more interested in particles of language, rather than its sweep, though I still use the long line when the music I'm hearing for a poem has that kind of propulsion. I was reading a Seamus Heaney essay recently in which he refers to the "malleable quatrains" he'd been using at one point in his writing, and I found something very apt in that for me. At some point I began to want something more rigorous, like stanzas of shorter lines, that would still be flexible enough not to lose any of the opportunities for exactness the longer line offered. I have the feeling that the reader sometimes won't hear much difference finally in the outcome, but it's been important for me in the process of composition.

MIND

In *Lies* and *I Am the Bitter Name*, I was especially interested in what I called then disjunctive consciousness: ways of charting movements of mind that were similar to some of the methods of what we call (unfortunately, I think) modernism. I was particularly struck, in those days, by the work of Vallejo and Artaud. But I was equally influenced by Freudian psychology, particularly by what is called "primary process" thinking, and, in the crudest sense, by my not being able to make any real sense of how my own mind went from one place to another. We use the rather feeble term "association" to explain that, but the term barely begins to describe how our minds swoop and hover and move in three directions at once. But I still wasn't, and still am not now, satisfied by any of the descriptions we have of how or why the mind works as it does. Vallejo was the first poet I found who seemed to accurately incorporate the way the mind actually does move, through its various planes, if we use a geometric analogy, or through its different levels, if we use Freud's geological paradigm.

At the same time I was trying out these different approaches to charting the mind, I also felt very strongly that our social and political realms took little account of the real workings of both our individual consciousness and the mind we have in common at any given moment. I still feel this, though I have a much stronger sense of how complicated it all is. We live in social systems whose fundamental assumption is that its participants have intrinsically coherent minds, minds that work neatly and logically along rational paths that are laid out for them by various social prohibitions and conventions. Our consciousness is presumed to consist of various strands of intention and evaluation, and our personal morality is supposed to arise from our judicious selection of those we commit to, and obey. But this has so little to do with how we actually live in ourselves as ourselves, with what our instinctual needs are, and with all the amazing deviations from the norm we experience right from the beginning of our adult awareness.

In those first books I think I was trying to take many of those issues head-on, as crudely and truthfully as I could. I wanted the poems to enact all the discrepancies I felt between myself and the social-political world I was trying to live in. I suppose there was some hubris in all of that, but I don't believe I had an overblown idea of what I was doing; I was ignorant, but I had youth and passion to keep me going.

In *With Ignorance* and *Tar*, I began quite intentionally to bury anything that looked like a systematic purpose or "message," if you will, in what I call the unconscious of the poem, the area of response that works more subtly, subliminally, on the reader. Such intentions naturally are worked out in a more disorderly, unpremeditated way than that, but I do think I was trying to describe a world that's closer to the one we experience when we're not being so analytical—a more undramatic, less ruptured reality, with not so many gashes in it. I tried to enact our intrinsic irrationality—and the gap between it and our social structures that pretend to be so "sane"— in less fraught, more unremarkable attitudes of mind. In a way, I thought of the poems as more "lyric," that is, more songs of the self I lived in the everyday, and less "scientific," that is, fewer investigations of reality based on various hypotheses I'd rounded up in my thinking. My verse autobiography, to use Lowell's term, calmed down, and a lot of the issues I had been confronting directly now became part of a less complicated texture. At the same time, many of these ideas, particularly the embodiment of disparate elements of consciousness, are still in crucial to me. They just function in a different system of composition.

MYTH

I've always been fascinated by myth. My father used to tell me the Greek myths as bedtime stories, and they're still very much with me. I feel much more attached to the unteleological worldview embodied in the Greek myths than in those of the Hebrew-Christian tradition. The ones the Greeks developed are less grounded in religious ambitions and more in normal human facts. When I was translating Greek tragedies, I found that mythic world was more deeply enmeshed in my consciousness than I'd realized; portions of them kept coming back to me, and when they did they had the texture of personal as well as cultural memories. How splendid that we have all that within us, the emblematic and the tragic, the brutes and heroes.

At the time I was in college, and in the years after, there was a great deal of interest in myth and religion—Jung, Neumann, Campbell, Zimmer: all the archetypers. And I did my share of reading in them. Most important to me, though, was Yeats; I was fascinated by his way of deepening current historical perceptions by grounding them in older knowledge systems. I've often used myths in my poems, usually under the surface, although sometimes I've let them come close to the surface. I meant "The Shade" in some ways to be a recasting of a morning in the *Iliad*, but set in a decaying modern city. I'm also fascinated by the stern, sad, sexy old men of the Bible. I've been particularly taken lately by Noah, who is the most innocent and impetuous of men and who creates great pain among those near to him.

NARRATIVE

We're really always living at least two kinds of narrative. First there's the one that we call our personal life, which are the stories we tell ourselves about ourselves, past, present, and future, and the other, which consists of our social narratives, the stories that make up our vision of our larger social environment and our situation in it. Our culture is really nothing but a series, or I suppose you could say a system, of narratives to which we give credence or from which we dissent. Furthermore, our relation to narrative is much more elemental than we're given to think. Whatever there is in the structure of our consciousness that makes it so, we have an absolute hunger for narrative: we're like monkeys at a switch who'll zap themselves to starvation to titillate their pleasure centers. I think it was because I sensed all this that I began to move towards narrative in my poems, to deal with chunks of life as experienced by a narrative consciousness; it gave me access to areas of my actual life that had become essentially off limits to poetry.

Now, although I don't know whether I'm ready to clarify this to myself yet, I'm beginning to distrust narrative, for various reasons. For one thing, it may well be that those who govern us may very well ground their power, even their oppressive power, in the way they control our public narratives and are able to colonize our individual consciences, and consciousness, more directly than we like to think. Orwell stated all this rather baldly, but in fact the control of our minds may have begun at whatever point those who had already garnered their power managed also to have themselves inserted into the narratives of the cultural group.

Also, we're so awash in narratives these days, between the novel, whose age we're living out, and its enormous retarded child, television. I sometimes wonder whether we're being blunted, clubbed, and are losing some of our sensitivity to reality, or to imagination, through this endless novelizing. I've written about narrative at length in "Admiration of Form," in *Poetry and Consciousness*, so I'll leave it at that.

NOSTALGIA

I find nostalgia a terrifically sweet but potentially debilitating emotion, sometimes a dangerous one, for the individual and for society. We all have moments, as individuals and cultures—radiant, nearly mythical moments, little ages of gold, you might say—and we have to be thankful for them, cherish them. But nostalgia can be terribly risky, especially nostalgia for innocence.

Innocence is a dangerous idea. We're always trying to find situations and milieus in which we can be innocent, or innocent again. We try to make our personal relationships, especially marriage, in a way that will allow us live in innocence, by which we mean insouciantly and uncomplicatedly yet with great intensity, and we're often disappointed to find that what we've created is a Gordian knot of compromises and painfully lost ideals.

When this kind of passion for simplicity is cast onto a social vision, it can become vicious, as in Hitler's myth-tormented notion of a glorious Aryan past that led to such tragic extremes. Hitler's was a dream of the past, and the Soviet Union promised a future paradise, that in the present generated insane paranoid rapacities, all promised to be redeemed in the name of some future state in which the elect would be able to live more simply and more "innocently." The mean-spiritedness of conservative Republicanism in the United States is informed by a similar nostalgia for a past that never existed, and for a future that will reenact that past and in which we'll all be self-reliant and never need social structures more complex than the family.

Much of this seems to me to come down to the fact that we're always more complicated than our ideas about ourselves; our analyses, our formulas, our equations are always somehow partial, inept, wounded. There's something in our whole way of speculating about ourselves that more and more strikes me as trying to shovel water with a fork. Generation after generation postulating notions of justice, of fulfillment, even of basic matters such as relationship and kinship, and so few of them have anything to do with what we actually are, or are even capable of being: all those guiding ideas can seem off the mark, and partial. We remain fugitives to ourselves, both personally and socially—at this level there really isn't any difference—and the only solutions we keep coming up with have to do with inflicting more rigor on ourselves so that we better fit the broken-down templates and molds we've received in our cultural packages, which all leave out the conflicts we experience between the ideas we're able to have about ourselves and the way we actually are able to convince ourselves to live.

THE NOVEL

When I was starting out, I read a great many novels. Tolstoy and Dostoyevsky were my first loves, then in the twentieth century, Mann, Wasserman, Joyce, but then most passionately the great Americans, especially Faulkner and Melville. Of the contemporaries, I used to love Henry Miller, although he seems to have faded a lot for me—it's strange how that happens—then Bellow and Gaddis, whose *Recognitions* was crucially important to me very early on.

But if I've been influenced by the novel, it's probably been by Dostoyevsky more than anyone else. I've always been in awe of his inexhaustible moral energy. No matter how much you disagree with his vision, his thoroughness is always inspiring, as is the way he's always in touch with the larger questions and, as important, the way his characters exist with so much curiosity and conviction and willingness to risk. He's also for me the most crucial philosophical novelist: his works enact the paradoxes and quandaries of the epoch we've been living through since the French Revolution.

ON LIVING PART OF THE TIME IN FRANCE

There's no question there are benefits to being at a distance from your home place—you can see certain things more clearly if you're not involved in them every day. In France, for example, people have a strong sense of their social rights; they're quick to protest, to call strikes against what they perceive as social or political offenses, much more than do Americans. Americans hardly seem aware of the fact that the last years have seen a huge proportion of the national wealth taken away from the lower and middle classes and given over to the rich and that the working class has been made essentially powerless. Something that momentous would be the subject of heated debate in France, but in America it barely seems to catch people's attention. The right wing has managed to keep many Americans passionately absorbed in cultural issues such as abortion and homosexuality, which they allow to obscure much more significant social and political questions. I don't think it was until I began to live in France, and understand its social mechanisms, that I really appreciated this, although things certainly have gotten worse in the States since I first began coming to France regularly in the early seventies.

At the same time, I've always resisted the idea of defining myself as an expatriate—I don't like the implications of that, of having given up on one's home country. I just want to think of myself an American who sometimes happens to live part of the time in France. My audience is American, and so am I, and I've been careful not to make the setting for too many poems be abroad. Although I've written a good proportion of my poems in France, I've almost always changed those poems that were inspired by things that happened to me there to more generic settings. There are a few poems I've left set in France because I thought it could be an effective strategy to allow the reader to believe they're involved in some rather exotic social question, then have them have realize that what's going on is actually part of their own social universe and their own identity. There's a poem in *Flesh and Blood* called "Racists" that does that quite clearly.

"ONE OF THE MUSES"

I was trying to deal in that poem with a fugitive emotional and mental state that required a kind of analytic approach I hadn't ever tried in poetry. The whole poem is really the analysis of one emotion, loss, or more specifically how we recover from loss. I felt that trying to redeem or account for or come to terms with an experience of that sort required a different kind of approach than any I'd used before. The poem is longer than most of my others, and it's because the experience took more time to come to terms with, and the analysis of it of necessity had to be more capacious. I think the conclusion the poem arrives at, if there is one, is that we need some kind of break, or rupture, to recover from loss. In this poem it's the experience of almost going insane, of going through a radical disassociation, I think the shrinks call it. It did happen to me; I had the feeling things could never get worse for me, that I was probably going crazy, but somehow that feeling brought with it a release, or the beginning of one at least, and the poem grew out of that.

PAINTING

There used to be times when things weren't going well with my poems or my career, when I had the fantasy that I should have been a painter. I used to draw all the time when I was younger, and in those bleak moments I'd managed to convince myself that when I'd started out I'd had more talent in painting than in writing (which I didn't—I was never really much more than a doodler) and that if I had become a painter, I'd be rich, the way a few of my painter friends were.

But there was more to it than that; I've always been jealous of the way painting and sculpting are so involved with the body. Poetry is such a purely mental activity that sometimes you can feel—again, especially when things aren't going well—like one of H. G. Wells's creatures from the future—a stunted white slug with a brain. Painters work with their hands, their eyes, their whole physical being. It's always so gratifying to watch an artist at work. I'm very jealous of them.

PERFORMANCE POETRY

The few times I've actually heard "performance poetry," I've felt it was a different medium from what I think of as poetry, a medium more like songwriting, which has little to do with either the necessities or exaltations of poetry as I conceive them. I should say that my experience is rather limited, but performance or slam poetry always seems to me to have a desperate passion to seduce a larger, more "popular" audience, by decomplexifying it. One of the splendors of poetry is that it offers rhythms and cadences to language that wouldn't exist in it otherwise.

I've heard some performance poets define any poetry that's not oriented like theirs as "academic," and I disagree vehemently with that. The poetry to which I've attached my life has more connection to the work of Archilochos and Issa and Rimbaud than to anything to do with an "academy." I'd also point out that for me all poetry is performance poetry. Poetry is meant to be spoken aloud; even if you're reading it to yourself, if you're not saying it aloud in your own voice as you read, you're not reading it properly. Reciting your poetry to an audience is just saying it a little louder than you say it to yourself. Poetry is the most intimate of the arts; it's the voice of one person's mind and musicalized language speaking directly to the listening mind of someone else. Novels and the dramatic arts usually enact an assumption that the writer is speaking to an audience composed of an indefinite number of other people. That's why we often find in the novel the device of establishing a narrator who's also a character, so that precious intimacy will be simulated. But the connection won't ever be as intense as it is in a poem, because the narrating character is of necessity a fiction, while a poem, at least a lyric poem, is by definition generated by a real person, with a real person's mystery and capacity for pain. Poetry is finally about a fusion between two active, living minds that, at least for serious readers of poetry, doesn't occur in any other medium.

POETRY AND POLITICS

Poets these days sometimes bemoan the fact that poets in other countries seem to have a lot of direct political impact. I don't think that's really the case, although it's true that in places like Latin America and Eastern Europe, where there are obvious social conflicts, poetry seems to be a social resource in a way it doesn't here. In America, since the Civil War anyway, one of the most effective political tactics has been for those in power to pretend that there's no social emergency, even when there clearly is. What we're going through in America these days, with a realignment of class, of economic expectations, of continuing poverty and unemployment, should clearly be considered a sociopolitical emergency, but we have been convinced to regard it simply as a wave in the economic cycle.

I certainly don't think, though, that poetry has much to offer in a direct programmatic way. Whether poetry has a particular political agenda isn't nearly as important as the fact that in its very essence it promulgates a basic human decency, basic values, and a vision of social community. When there is an emergency that people can feel, or are allowed to feel, then they tend to go looking for poetry, for the solace it offers and for the heightened moral consciousness it presupposes. That's what happened during the Vietnam War, when first the college kids and then many other people realized that poetry could speak for them.

I think I'm more radically political than I ever was before, in terms of how intensely I feel about social issues. At the same time, I have less sense of what a political program would be that might avoid the various shoals on which all the existing systems tend to run aground. In the sixties and seventies, when there seemed to be the possibility for activism, for a way to really effect change . . . was all that illusion?

I suffered a great deal back then from the feeling that I wasn't doing enough politically. The really committed people would say, "Put your body on the line," but I had no desire to do that. I went to the demonstrations, but I didn't ever feel truly comfortable with that sort of activism, and I still don't. I feel less acutely guilty about it now, partly because going to the streets these days would be like running around in circles and also because I'm a little more certain that poetry does finally play a part in change and that there's a task for the poet that doesn't involve putting down your pen and grabbing a gun or a bullhorn.

But my discomfort with the ease and prosperity of my life is still something I feel just because I'm in the middle class. I've especially felt that the times I've lived in New York. Part of the reason I think I left New York was because of the tensions I felt, the discrepancy between my life and the life that I had to see around me. And that "I had to see" is the part that I often find myself writing about: having to behold so many people who are condemned to poverty and need, and feeling there's nothing you can do about it, especially at such a reactionary time as the one we're in now.

POLITICS AND POETRY

I do think of myself as a political poet, but that definition is rather complicated. In one sense, every poet is political: we're of necessity in community with an audience beyond ourselves, and we also share ideas that can't exist outside of a cultural-political world. The question, then, really isn't one of definition but of intention. How much of a political poet am I? And how often? How effective? What are the indications of what this possible effectiveness might consist? And what is the business of a political poet: to clarify, cajole, convince, castigate? Perhaps none of them.

It's hard even to characterize other poets. Surely some of the best political poems of the century were written by Yeats—"Nineteen Hundred and Nineteen," "Meditations in Time of Civil War," for example—but I don't think I'd consider Yeats a "political" poet, even though those poems are the very center of his poetry for me. At any rate, the requirements I'd ask of myself for being a political poet would deviate widely from the way I'd define his. Clearly, each person's historical moment has bearing here. The function of poetry as we conceive it is quite different from the way Yeats did, and the place of poetry in politics, of the individual poet's place and possible effectiveness, in the political realm has changed as well. It's even changed over the course of the last decades. What is sometimes referred to as the "rage" in my early poems I think was more a kind of hope. If there was rage, it had to do with the frustration I felt because so much of what seemed self-evident to me about the relation of self to society, of individual psyche to collective, was so adamantly incidental to the world of those with power over us.

I wasn't alone in all of this of course. Where the political world has moved since that time in the sixties and early seventies is terribly saddening. Not simply because of the so-called conservative drift in American politics, not simply because of the outrages and crimes of conscience of so much that's gone on since Reagan, but perhaps more so because the kinds of hope we've been entertaining for two centuries seem to have been usurped, particularly from the young. There's been an enormous sleight of hand perpetrated on the generations who are coming into their political consciousness now. Some of this is due to the chances of history, but much seems to have been quite intentionally, almost diabolically foisted on them. All the so-called necessities of economic activity, the inflations and recession, the deficits, the constant recourse to inculcating insecurity as a way of manipulating people: what a sad consciousness our children have to live with, and how hard it will be for them to generate the hope they need to redeem themselves and their societies spiritually. This is all before we even consider our insane wars.

Since those early books, I've tended to bury my political messages, if that's what they are, deeper into the substance of my poems. I used to think that I began to do it out of a combination of desperation and cunning, and the sense that I couldn't just attack head on the problems I perceived in people's political perceptions and actions, that I had to insinuate my own vision more subtly into the reader. But now I'm not so sure about whether I might not have capitulated to the same kind of hopelessness and barely conscious despair that I see around me. So much of what we feel we will for ourselves, we ultimately find was willed for us.

So, again, am I a political poet? I'd say yes, but not enough of one. Never enough. If the poems don't nearly break with rage as much as they used to, it might be because I'm trying to put more of everything else in them, but my rage and frustration is at least as intense now as it was then.

PROSE POETRY

I've tried several times to write series of prose poems, but I always end up deciding that the form doesn't have enough necessities to generate anything I can believe in. Not having a line to adhere to seems to prevent the language of my poems from being as highly organized as it should be in order for it to have unexpected things happening. I suppose prose is too conducive to "and then, and then, and then . . ."

In French, the prose poem has a lively tradition, although I can't, in truth, appreciate much of it, except Rimbaud's "Saison en Enfer" and "Illuminations" and Francis Ponge's work, some of which I've translated. But even Baudelaire's prose poems strike me as slack and uninspired compared to his poetry. In English, with very, very few exceptions, prose poetry just doesn't come across.

The poem "The Dog" began as a prose poem, but it had almost nothing to do with what the poem finally became: it dealt with a different experience entirely, and the only thing that linked the two poems was that in both versions there was a dying dog. The poem as prose was a story, an anecdote, which was interesting enough, but when I turned to the poem as verse and applied the formal tension that verse of necessity entails, I discovered other possibilities. In particular, I realized that the experience the poem was recounting had to do principally with racism—the racism that educated, well-intentioned liberal people like me have to discover in themselves—and though it hadn't been that when I was working at it as prose, it became the poem's central theme.

Perhaps working in prose doesn't demand as much linguistic energy as verse does, so the investigations it might be making tend to be shut down before their full implications can be realized.

PUBLIC AND PRIVATE

I don't feel there's an obligation for poets to try to move from a more private audience to a more public. It's been suggested that my use of longer cadences is a way of trying for more readers, but framing it that way puts an edge on my formal decisions that I don't feel. "Private" poetry, if that's we'd call it, is after all a very precious tradition. Some of my poems have public themes, but I mean them at the same time to be lyrics because that's what I believe the tradition offers and demands. So the question of public-private doesn't have that much meaning for me.

There is a problem when you're writing poems that have political themes, which is that they risk becoming polemical, agitprop, propaganda—and propaganda is a different, rather scary and depressing tradition. As far as writing poetry about public events: everybody has two identities, one public, one private. You have an identity as a citizen, and you can have strong feelings about things, but that doesn't necessarily mean you have to write poetry about them: you can try to do something in other ways. Do you have to write poems about public issues if you're a poet? Of course you don't. When I do write poems protesting war, I don't ever really believe at heart that they're going to change anything. Maybe the vague hope is they might sensitize one person who isn't really aware of what's happening, or, probably more likely, you might find ways for people who already feel the way you do to articulate what they feel a little better.

REDEMPTION

Do I think poetry is redemptive? Is anything redemptive? Is there redemption? Are we redeemable? If the answer to any of these questions is yes, then my answer is yes.

REVIEWS

Like all writers, I suppose, I try to read only the good reviews. A compliment can be helpful if it gives you more confidence because confidence is a good part of being able to go on with all the roadblocks in writing poetry. Unfortunately, you're generally halfway through a review when you realize it's bad. I read a novelist saying recently that she doesn't read reviews because you forget the positive ones in seven minutes and you remember the negative ones for seven years. It sounds very stupid, but I find unfortunately it's true. So I try to read things about my work aslant. I'm afraid if I look too closely, I might take them too seriously. If someone says I'm lousy then I'll suffer, and if they say I'm good but say it for the wrong reasons, it's almost worse. Recently my English publisher told me I'd received a very hostile review somewhere, and I asked him not to send it to me; I didn't care to read it. I hope from now on I'll always have the chance to do that.

I remember once a well-known critic who had adopted a young poet and was pushing him and helping him make his career—she just really loved his work. At one point in a review she said, "Now he should write more in such and such a way," and I thought, "Boy am I glad nobody ever said anything like that to me." She was the driving force in his career at that point, and for her to say that was really potentially destructive. I mean, what right does anyone have to tell a poet how to shape his soul? Because when a poet changes his or her style, you are really are changing your soul. Another reason not to read criticism head-on.

SCHOOLS

I think it's always an error to classify the significant poets of any moment as a "school"—it rarely occurs to poets themselves and is usually nothing but the crudest sort of identification. Poets crave company, like everyone else, and we like to be in touch, if we can be, with the poets we esteem, but that doesn't put us in definable groups. Even the so-called confessional poets were very different from one another; what they shared in their commitment to intimate disclosure was minimal compared to the variety of the poems they actually wrote. Look at Sexton and Plath, who are sometimes considered the Bobbsey Twins of confessional poetry: their poetry is radically different in its vision, its music, its imagery and figuration. If you were to come across their poems without having any preconceptions about them, there's no way you'd conclude they're connected in any but the most peripheral way.

The self-defined coteries there have been in our time, like the language poets, I think actually debilitated themselves by their commitment to themselves as a movement. Even if you accept the viability of the idea of a number of poets coming together to encourage each other, self-proclaimed schools always seem to me to be doing things backward, cultivating a media identity before they have a body of real work and proclaiming themselves as revolutionaries before they have a clear sense of what they are rebelling against.

STARTING OUT

I was leaving for my first trip to Europe, and on a whim bought a paperback copy of Eliot's *The Waste Land* and threw it into my suitcase along with some novels. I was in no sense an intellectual, and though I'd written one poem, I hadn't really any notion yet that I wanted to be a poet.

I was traveling with a friend, and one night in Florence he went off somewhere. There I was alone and a bit lonely on the fourth floor of a rather rundown *pensione* that looked over a square, and I started to read the Eliot book. Then, as I wrote much later in the poem "My Mother's Lips," I leaned out the window and started speaking aloud poems—imitation Eliot poems, I suppose they must have been. I went on and on and it was terrifically exciting. I have no idea what I might have been chanting—the phrase "innocent dithyrambs" in "My Mother's Lips" speaks to that: dithyramb as ecstatic utterance, being out of yourself, beyond yourself. And something like that happened to me. I presume every poet has an experience like that, a moment when you realize that you can speak with a voice that isn't your own, but in some primitive sense is the voice of poetry itself. Your own voice seems to be doubled, and you feel you're participating in a larger existence than your own—poetry, that would be, however little you might actually know about it.

Of course things change. When you begin writing seriously the joy you feel has more to do with your speaking in your own voice: hearing yourself speaking in verse or some simulacrum of it is so entrancing that no matter what you might actually be saying it feels significant. In teaching composition, especially to graduate students, who one might say are already addicted to hearing their own voice, a good part of the pedagogical task is to convince them that their voice can be enlarged by learning the tradition and the techniques embedded in it. It's delicate, because you don't want a young poet to think his or her own voice is invalid—it can't be, simply because it's there—but you do want to convince students that inserting themselves into the tradition actually gives their voices, and their minds, possible resonances they wouldn't otherwise have.

STYLE

The strangest thing about a style is that it's both sustaining and self-consuming. The discovery of one's own style is an incredibly fulfilling, liberating experience for a poet. You have the sense—and it's quite true—that all of reality, the whole world, or at least the things you care about, become accessible to you.

Problems rather quickly arise, though, because in some sense the task of a style is to perfect itself, not necessarily to be inclusive. And since a vision of personal and social reality is always changing, there's inevitably a tension between the demands of style and the uses of it. Perhaps it's more easily seen in the style of an age, which sooner or later will always exhaust itself, become decadent and begin to produce artifacts in which style itself is more important than the real world. Stylistically, poetry can be seen as always moving from the transparent to the opaque, hoping for its formal dexterities to be noticed, its splendors appreciated, and the late work of any literary period can end up as merely style exhibiting itself, showing off.

And the same thing can happen to the individual poet. The greatest poets seem to be the ones who either find ways of altering their styles, enlarging them so that reality doesn't have to be radically amputated to fit them, or find a grand enough, inclusive enough style in the first place so that they can never be exhausted. Somebody like William Carlos Williams, for instance, could have lived another thirty years and still not have exhausted his style. Eliot, in contrast, stopped writing poetry, I think because he felt he'd used up the style he'd worked out over the years: he couldn't have gone on writing the way he did. His poetry would have (and sometimes did) become trivial. Once *Four Quartets* was written, I don't think he could have done anything more without some sort of extreme shift in his aesthetic, which he actually effected by turning to drama. It might be that his lyrical gift had fulfilled itself. Without finding a new approach, he'd just have been diluted his previous work. It wasn't that his style wasn't grand—it certainly was—but it didn't have within it the potential for change and enlargement, the way Williams's did or Yeats's.

SYNTAX

When I began to write the longer poems, I didn't have any particular thoughts about their syntax; what interested me was that I could work in more extended intellectual units. Once I began to work with these larger packets of meaning, though, syntax interested me more and more, and I found myself experimenting more consciously than I had been with the possibilities of more complicated syntactical structures. Syntax is both a necessity for language and thought and a part of their felicity. Syntax in poetry enacts both. For me, it's as important as poetry's more formal aspects.

THE LARK. THE THRUSH. THE STARLING.

I had loved the haiku for a long time; like most poets, I found they were a useful way of learning how image could be generated and implemented. You see differently when you're in the world of haiku: it's a precious, unique experience, and I always have a sense of good fortune to have lived in an epoch when they were available.

At the same time, the whole haiku culture can come to seem a bit much. One day I was reading a book of new translations—I forget whose—and it came to me that these clumps of words as poems were just silly, that the translator, or translators, were really ransacking poetic cultures, both Japanese and English, and coming up with seventeen syllable blobs that had nothing to do with either tradition.

And it came to me that what I'd like to do would be to "un-haiku-ize" one of the poets, and I chose Issa not only because his muscular tenderness and resignation appealed to me so much but also because I knew he wasn't a Buddhist, Zen or otherwise, which I found heartening—at least I couldn't be accused of affronting anyone's religion.

So I decided to take the core impulse of several of his haikus and reshape them into English poems that—even though they'd have basically nothing to do with what Issa had intended—would be what I could call poems and that would have none of the fake sanctity so many translations of haiku do. That's why I call them "Poems from Issa." They're not translations, certainly, and not versions: they're poems that take an image or an epiphany of Issa's to bring into American poetry. Once I got going, I had a great time. I did dozens and dozens of them, even though I wasn't sure I'd ever publish them. Then Rosemarie Waldrop asked me to do a little book for Burning Deck, and I realized that a selection of them would work well. I have no idea where all the rest of them are; I guess in my papers somewhere.

TRANSLATING

Translating poetry isn't just moving from one language to another; you're translating poetry into poetry, which isn't at all the same thing. A scholar who has a foreign language presumably will be able to translate any text into English, but translating into poetry almost always requires the special skills of a poet, and these skills often take precedence, strangely enough, over knowledge of the language being translated, something that can sometimes mightily offend critics.

There are many examples of this: the translations Galway Kinnell did of Rilke, for example, are striking, though his German is quite limited. Many of the translations of Greek tragedies in the Oxford series (for which I did *The Women of Trachis*) were by poets who didn't have Greek and who collaborated with scholars who did. And of course Robert Lowell, in *Imitations*, did a number of marvelous poems from languages he didn't have. You can see this in other languages besides English. A renowned translation of *Faust* in French is by Gérard de Nerval, who had hardly any German.

There are problems, of course, about the various levels of accuracy that can be used in translating poems, from the literal to what we've come to call, after Lowell, "imitations." And some people have gone even further, doing "versions," which sometimes can seem pretty close to pure theft, the ripping off of another poet's inspiration, without giving much attention to the intentions of the original. With Issa, I called my versions "Poems from Issa," not translations, which made me feel less larcenous.

TRANSLATING GREEK TRAGEDY

When you really get into trying to translate anything, it can appear to be a pretty hopeless project: another word for "translation" might be "failure." It's inevitable that any success you do have will be a compromise, and in art compromise is just that—which amounts to failure. Still, translation is absolutely necessary to literary culture, and besides that, it's great fun and a terrific way to learn about things you wouldn't otherwise.

With cultural monuments like Greek tragedy, translating can seem like the most outrageous hubris, but once you're into it, it's completely absorbing. Technically, the central problem has to do with finding equivalences. Greek verse is based on vowel length, ours on stress, and they're simply incompatible, so the best you're going to be able to do is to find approximations that give a sense of how much the original is determined by the complex satisfaction of conventions; you have to devise a way to convey a feeling of rigor and energy by imposing your own necessities—in my case of rhythm and syntax—on the text you're developing. Art is really always a working out of the relation between various necessities and the freedom of the mind. I suppose ultimately what I felt was that the most crucial thing at the end is not to simplify.

And you have to maintain a keen sense, when you're translating something from such a distant time and place, that you're really rewriting history. What happens in our minds in reading or seeing the play can't be what happened in the minds of the Greeks. So every aesthetic decision you make—about the choice of a word, the vividness of an image, the conveying of the emotional drama of a scene, and the reasons for it—is, if not a violation, then absolutely an alteration. I've been reading Robert Darnton, a great historian and, by the way, a great friend, and that shift from past mindset to modern is one of the things he emphasizes. Clifford Geertz, the anthropologist, someone else I've been reading a lot, talks about the same thing happening in cultural studies. Jack Zipes, the brilliant fairy tale scholar, another friend, points out that although fairy tales are assumed to say something about the universal and the timeless in the psyche, commentators are often wrong about the very people who generated the stories in the first place, who hardly fit the definition of "folk." All in all, translating can seem a rather shifty activity, a bit like grave robbing.

TRANSLATING A PHRASE

There is one little thing I'm proud about in my translation work. In Sophocles's *The Women of Trachis*, there's an odd phrase whose meaning no classicist had ever figured out, as far as I know. In the play, Heracles is commanding his son to burn him alive because he's in agony and also because he realizes that his death by fire in this way was prophesized, and that afterward he'd become a god. Herakles then addresses himself in a complicated image that has in it something about stone and something about metal.

As I say, no one, at least no one I'd heard of, had ever made coherent sense of the words. Pound translated the phrase as, "Slap some reinforced concrete on your face," which has to be one of the worst translations ever made. But it came to me that the image had to do with Greek statues, which were of course carved of stone but which also used metal accoutrements; a statue of a horse, for instance, would have a metal bit and reins. So what I came up with for Herakles to say is, "Put the steel bit in your teeth, weld it there, // clamp your lips on it, stone against stone." And according to my classicist consultants, I'd solved the problem. I suppose until someone proves I was wrong.

THE UNSAYABLE

Usually when people speak of the unsayable, they are referring to perceptions, feelings, and thoughts that are concerned with the sort of things with which religion occupies itself: intuitions of divinity, of divine presence; imaginations of emotions that would not be experienced except in the realm of prayer or theological reflections. I'm not certain that what I can state in this context here about the sayable or unsayable will have anything to do with all of that because I've never really had any experience of it. There was a time in my life when I wanted very much to experience that kind of longing, for god, for the ineffable, for the whole realm of the divine, but in truth my desire was of such a different degree that I couldn't and still can't apply it with any certainty to the way I experience anything else in my life. Even those poets I admire, Herbert and Donne primarily, who seem closest to being "religious," most often express their connection with divinity with a desire that is so dissimilar to mine that I doubt whether there was really anything in their experience that's even close to mine.

In a nonreligious sense, though, for me there's really no such thing as the unsayable—there's only the unsaid or the not-yet said. What can't be said can't be thought and can't truly be felt. What's not said isn't felt, or not wholly felt: it's only guessed at. We feel a stir, and guess there's something that might be called a feeling to go with that—"summoning" might be the best word—and that a thought might be implied by the feeling. (There's already a kind of thought attached to the feeling, what I'd call a guess, because something like a guess is instantly proposed by the mind for everything, however inarticulate, and a guess is a thought en route.)

And I think this is true as well of raw perception. We perceive something and sense there may be a feeling to go with it, and then a thought, but in most cases, almost all cases, the perception is merely registered, and then stored in memory or allowed to dissipate in forgetfulness. It's one of the functions of poetry to create connections between all these vague and disparate phenomena.

Sometimes a poem will take as its field of activity a perception. Then it will find ways to transform this perception, first into language, then into the more purely transformative aspects of poetry—figuration first of all—metaphor and simile—which, by transforming both perception and consciousness, bring the part of the self that thinks and feels into intimate connection with the thing perceived, then into one form or another of poetic music, which further transfigures the perception, and perhaps, uncertainly, moves it to another center of the brain.

What exists in the self now, having experienced the poem and its perception, was in no way sayable until the poem was said.

Poetry does the same thing with what are called feelings—which in fact are first of all, though not primarily, inner perceptions—and finally with thought. I'd say that for me thoughts are subjective speculations until they're embodied in poetry. Though this should be qualified by saying that what I'm saying here applies primarily to others to whom poetry is a central part of their life, either the reading or writing of it. For them—us—even formal philosophy's speculation, and even religion's, remain just that, speculation, until they are brought into if not the poetic then at least the literary portion of experience, that part of experience that imagines other lives and the perceptions of those lives.

THE USE OF AUTOBIOGRAPHY

For a poet, that can be a thorny problem. One of the assumptions about the use of "I" in lyric poetry is that the poet is telling the truth about him or herself. Whether it's Archilochos admitting his trepidation and flight in battle, or Baudelaire celebrating his erotic phantasms, we believe in the declarations of poets as revelations or recountings of their experiences. But the tradition of narrative poetry obviously has quite different ambitions, and very different resources. From Homer to Milton, to Browning and Tennyson and early Yeats, we recognize that there are imaginations available to the poet, we call them fictions, and just as in epic and tragedy and the novel, it's not the "truth" of the matters at hand that are important to us but the way they bring the world to our meditations. In the twentieth century, both in poetry and the novel there's a fusion of the first person and fiction and, in poetry, of the lyric and the narrative that obviates the distinctions between the genres. In Robert Frost's "The Hill Wife" or "Home Burial," for instance, the third person is obviously being used to deal with experiences or emotions Frost had himself, and we have to change our notions about what's happening in the poems in this regard.

In my own work, I'll admit that I've often used fictional elements in what are ostensibly intensely personal lyric narratives. I've never felt any compunction about this because I've always believed that the core of the experience I was considering, or elaborating, or trying to make sense of, was most crucial, and the rest, the variables, were to be considered fair game for being "fictionalized," although I dislike that term. I do feel uneasy about saying all this, because I still want the reader to experience the poems with the same trust implied in reading, say, Lowell's *Life Studies*, although I've wondered how many of the elements in those poems might have been made up.

Lowell's not alone in this, of course: what were once considered forbidden aspects of intimacy have become available to contemporary poets, and although there aren't many instances of such overt usurping of someone else's personal life as there was with Lowell, there has been a widening of the field of vision into what might be called non-sublimated expressions of very intimate matters. You can also get into quite metaphysical questions here: why we should respond at all to fictional or even mythical characters when we know very well they're the creations of authors is one of the mysteries of art—and of the human mind. It's one of the glories of our imaginations. But I suspect also that it has at least some of its basis in the enduring infantilism of our mental structures, the primitive response system that convinces us to give over decisions about our very existence to our political leaders and to identify with their symbolic legitimacy in the same way we find imaginary characters' struggles germane.

WORKSHOPS

I think workshops are a fine tradition. America society is quite fragmented, and enormous. In the England and the Continent of long ago, which are our models for such things, there were coffeehouses and cafés, where young writers could come to find people to talk to about their work, and I imagine show it around. America is culturally diverse now, and there are poets everywhere. I think many of them would stay by themselves, and suffer from it, without a place to get a larger perspective. It used to be that you could move to New York, to Greenwich Village, or to San Francisco, and find communities of artists, but that's not easy anymore, since the cities have become so expensive.

So that's one function of workshops. But besides that, I do think there's a lot to be learned about poetry. People who question the legitimacy of poetry workshops never seem to wonder about the viability of teaching painting or music, and I think what's implied by that is that poetry is something that comes spontaneously, from the heart; if you're sensitive enough you don't need any training, it will just happen. Which of course isn't true. Poetry is exactly like painting and music; there any many technical matters to become familiar with, and a workshop is a way at the very least to expose poets to issues that aren't all that obvious until they're pointed out.

YOUNGER POETS

There are a number of younger poets I admire, poets trying to find new directions for themselves, new sounds, new ways of assembling experience, often in wonderfully jagged ways. If I have noticed a tendency in some of the work by younger poets that I don't find as satisfying, it's that some seem to rely on a kind of existential irony, a mistrust of the possibility of discovering or creating meaning in the world, and a consequent resort to a wry juxtaposition of apparently irreconcilable elements of experience. Such poetry ends up embodying a world that seems to have a variant of surrealism as its epistemological first principle. Part of this surely has to do with the fact that so much of our world seems to be at risk these days, from our environment to our economic stability, and that kind of forced insouciance very well may be an appropriate response. But I do have trouble taking to heart the poems that come out of it. But who can really say? I've become very conscious lately of the fact that what I think and value is almost irrevocably determined by my own historical experience. You can't stay open to everything—any single mind can only contain so much—and it may well be that I'm just not competent to judge objectively what people thirty or forty years younger than me are doing.

PART III
The Rest

Two Encounters Early On

1. COWBOYS AND POETS

The first book I ever passionately, desperately loved, and which I read devotedly probably a dozen times, purported to be a true story. I found out later, however, it was almost entirely a fabrication, a lie. The book was *Lone Cowboy*, the autobiography of the Western writer and artist, Will James. Not *William* James—I realized this fact when I looked Will up in the encyclopedia in my grammar school library and found only the uninteresting William.

I came across *Lone Cowboy* when I was eleven or twelve. I was mad about horses then, all I wanted to do was ride and have a horse one of my own, not a very likely prospect in Newark, New Jersey. So what I did instead was to read obsessively about horses and their riders; everything in our school library, then in the branch library not far from our house, and finally in the big central library downtown. I think I read literally every book I could find that had anything to do with horses, the way ten years or so later I'd read everything I could find on the Holocaust, and after that everything by and about the various poets whose work I'd fallen in love with. But right now it was horses, and especially it was Will James; in some ways I think I almost assumed his biography as my own. As some children have imaginary playmates, I had James, and I had that book, which recounted a real cowboy's life: being born under a wagon in Montana, the mother dying in childbirth, the cowboy father so distraught by her death that he became careless of his own life and was killed a few years later by a raging steer. Then he was adopted by a French Canadian trapper, Bopy his name was, a diminutive I think of "Beaupré," who was also a cowboy during the warm months when pelts were thin.

I still remember that life so well. The winter one had two wolf cubs as pets. The gift of a little horse for a birthday. Buying saddles and boots. The slow wanderings down out of Canada. The herds of cattle, wild horses, roundups, and line camps. Then the trapper, too, disappeared, probably drowned fetching water from a flooded river, and you were on your own, to wander and work as a cowboy all over the West, from Montana even down into Mexico. Then, as vengeance for some sort of affront, you stole a herd of cattle, were caught, and ended up in prison for a time, where you begin to draw and paint seriously. And so started another life as an artist, then as an artist-writer.

The part about prison, the most seemingly unlikely yarn, turns out to be almost the only thing in the book up until then that was true. I found out years later in a study of James I happened on in another library that he had actually been a French-speaking Canadian from Quebec who'd conceived a passion for cowboy life and had gone West when he was sixteen—this would be around 1908—and become one. His tragedy began when he came to believe that in order to be an authentic Westerner you had to have been born to it, so he made up that biography, which he swore was the truth no matter what, though it meant cutting off all but the most furtive communication with his original family and though it resulted in his marriage to a woman he was obviously very attached to falling apart. The direct cause of the dissolution of his marriage was that he'd taken to serious drinking, but the author of the study hypothesizes that he had turned to drink because he couldn't bear the split between his real life and his ravening lies. He would actually drink himself to death not many years after his marriage fell apart.

I think I was too old to be brokenhearted when I found out the truth, though I certainly found it illuminating about the ways we can order our own reality according to spurious models we're not even aware have been generated for us. I suppose no great harm had come from me wanting to be a cowboy, by my working later on in the riding stables I found outside of Newark, and finally convincing my parents to buy me a hundred-dollar horse; I certainly met a lot of people and learned about a lot of things I never would have otherwise.

But thinking about James has made me wonder about the poets whose lives I've probably just as gullibly used to shape the idea of my own existence in poetry. It was certainly wrenching to find out that Rilke, one of my first poetic heroes and an enduring one, could be a terrible hypocrite, a lackey of the rich, a cad with women and, worse, with his own wife and daughter, and that he was at times a crude anti-Semite. Where do I fit all that into how much, really limitlessly, I esteem his poetry?

As for the anti-Semitism, it's all too common. A Jewish poet can forgive Shakespeare Shylock, because of that one heart-rending "Do I not bleed?" speech, but what about Chaucer versifying, *poeticizing*, a vile anti-Jewish blood libel in *The Canterbury Tales*, and what about Wordsworth choosing just that section of Chaucer to translate into modern English? And Eliot: besides his not-at-all unspoken disdain for the Jews, in prose and more shockingly in his poems, there's his cultural elitism, his royalism, and his general social contempt. And what about Yeats, another of my heroes, dabbling with fascism?

And then one has to ask about the truths, the sensitivity, wisdom, and nobility, in so much of the work that these and other great but surely flawed poets have brought forth: do I feel suspicions about that, too? No. I believe everything the poems say, every radiant image they gather, every metaphor they imagine, every nuance of experience they register, believe it all with unquestioning conviction. Yeats of *The Tower*, singing his magnificent grief at a nation and a world destroying itself; Rilke in *The Duino Elegies* finding a way to figure human spiritual aspirations in a way they never had been before, and probably never will be again: that particular fusion between an age's moral desolation and a genius's transformative brilliance happening twice is almost inconceivable. And Elizabeth Bishop, who drank too much and seemed to love so ineptly, softly recording in the intricate stanzas of "The Moose" the human microcosm, on a bus ride, of all things, that becomes a repository of human longing, resignation, and joy. And William Carlos Williams, whom I heard once on Mike Wallace's show saying that his friend Pound's raving anti-Semitic assertions might possibly be plausible: Williams's "Asphodel, That Greeny Flower," his sinuously graceful summation of a complicated marriage, and of the history, private and public, flowers and A-bombs, lived through during that marriage.

Certainly, we shouldn't be surprised that the voices that inhabit works of imagination don't necessarily jibe with the real souls who create them; we can come to feel that the sad fallibilities of even the very greatest need our forgiveness. We all make ourselves up to some extent; perhaps we can learn from the lies and sad self-deceptions of those we admire to define ourselves not by our own illusions and probably inevitable failures of generosity but by our gratitude for all the unlikely gifts the life of art generates for us.

2. SMUT

It had no title, and, as far as I ever knew, no author. As it came into my hand, there was no title page; it was a carbon, on quarter sheets of fragile onionskin paper, clipped together. The original had been typed, which meant in those days by hand, word by word, letter by letter. I suppose it would have been soiled, worn, but I only remember now the sheer miraculousness of it, of its existence, and even more of its having found me.

It's hard to believe how efficient the system of sexual obliteration actually was in those days; this would be the 1940s. At least as far as I was concerned—I was twelve, living at the edge of a small city—the whole realm of the sexual was something that happened entirely within me, in my body in shame and delight, and in my consciousness in blind secrecy, and an absolute, all but ascetic isolation. There was this *thing*, about which one inferred auras from comments adults would infrequently mumble to each other; this looming, inchoate alp of experience that evoked among one's classmates a unique kind of inexplicable, supercilious laughter, and this other thing one felt, not felt really, was taken by, wrenched, *colonized* by, awake and in sleep, in thought and whatever it is at that age that lurks beneath thought, perhaps in what comes to be what we call "fantasy," but isn't that yet, because there are no narratives yet with which to embody it.

My best friend was two years older than I was; he knew remarkably more about the world than I did and it was he to whom the work had been vouchsafed. I was sleeping over at his house; he must have said, "Look at this," and there it was: from the first half page I knew exactly what it was, knew how much, violently, without knowing I had, *needed* it, for so many now immediately self-evident reasons.

Here is the book: two women meet and are astounded to realize that they are perfect duplicates of one another, same features, same hair, exactly the same figure. (One, later in the story, will turn out to have a mole, on the underside—the *underside!* amazing—of one breast, which ultimately will add welcome complexities to their adventures.) Their names are Ruth and Louise. They go to one of their homes, undress, examine each other, caress one another, very complicatedly, even poignantly, it seems to me now, and soon conspire to change places in their lives; each of these secret sharers is married, one, as I recall, has a lover.

The story evolves. I really can't recall a single *word* of it because it doesn't come to me word by word; I don't know now if it was the kind of crude pornography that would be mass-produced in the sixties and seventies when the censorship laws were loosened, or if it was a less vulgar Victorian excretion—though is any of that really less vulgar? That's not the point: none of anything like that matters at all. It was the reading of those marvelously semitranslucent pages that remains so preciously vivid. Nostalgically, I can think of the innocent I was and of how many complexities of sexual mechanics were explicated by the text, but even that seems incidental. What still sears is the way the words came into me, with such astonishing *force*. As I remember it, I had nothing but the most blurred, uncertain image of anything actual; I suppose more precise images must have flowed now that I was reading the text, but they seemed to come *after* the words: the words were being etched, chiseled, into my . . . what? My mind, my brain, my emotions? No, something previous to all that; there was some bond that seemed to be being forged between the very core of my corporeal and intellectual existence and the act of taking experience into myself through the word. The sensuousness of the event, and there was so much, it seems, at least now—I can't care anymore what it was then—to have been divided between the erotics it flamingly evoked and my absorption of them. It was as though, as I would learn later, poets say, *I wasn't reading, but being read.*

Of course poetry has to come into it somewhere, because poetry, too, seems now to have always been there. Perhaps it was poetry, then, that existed previous to the rest—that indelible attachment to the double existence of life and art in life: act and reflection; mind and desire; passion, poem.

Literary Models
of Adolescence

I

One evening in 1957, in March, when I was twenty years old, I took the night train from Saint Sebastian, on the French border of Spain, to Madrid. A few months before, I'd left, or fled, my junior year of college. It would still be difficult for me to explain exactly why: a general sense of unease, discontent, and what I'd probably call now depression; a feeling I wasn't living the life I wanted to live; a more general suspicion that everything I did lacked meaning and resonance. I felt to myself like an empty set of manners and gestures, and I moved among other people who, no matter how much I needed them, seemed to be as inauthentic, false, and somehow illegitimated as I was. When I decided I was going to do something about all of this, namely, leave school to go back to Europe where the previous summer I'd made the standard tour with a friend, my plan was simply to go, to disappear, to present my parents and everyone else with a fait accompli. I would be an exile, an expatriate, my roots cut, my presence defined by wherever I was and whatever I was doing rather than by any demeaning connection to institution or family. But my roommate dissuaded me from so radical a cutting adrift; he convinced me to tell my parents. I did, and they, though concerned and I'm sure puzzled, gave their hesitant blessings.

I spent a wrackingly lonely few months in Paris and, finally, hooked up with a woman I'd met on the ship from New York. She was older than I was, too much so, I thought, to be a lover, but she was a good companion, and we started off South on a motor scooter. The weather in France was terrible that year, and we ended up selling the scooter in Bordeaux, took the train to Saint Sebastian, and boarded the Spanish local bound for Madrid. It was then that the most remarkable thing occurred: I felt as though, for the first time in my life, something real was happening to me.

Spain in those days was still very poor and seemed barely Westernized. The people were exotic: they dressed oddly, many spoke with a strange lisp, and they even, I fancied, held their bodies in an unfamiliar way, with a sort of haughtiness, despite their often evident poverty. The train itself was battered and ramshackle, and the aisle alongside the seating compartments was filled with people leaning out the windows, chatting or brooding into the warm, unfamiliarly scented night.

Everything was exotic, and marvelous. I ate a splendid dinner with my friend—I still remember: a potato omelet; a "tortilla" it was called—then we came back to our car where we struck up acquaintance with some Spaniards. Someone brought a bottle of wine from the dining car, and before long, a party was underway, a fiesta. We drank more wine, then, after the dining car closed, every time the slowly moving train stopped at some godforsaken station, one of the Spaniards would run out into the night to come back with a wineskin of what must have been cheap, harsh wine, but which I loved. I can't imagine how we got along so well with the Spaniards—none of them spoke English and neither my friend nor I had any Spanish—but we were drinking, singing, gabbing, arms around one another, and I was in a state of pure bliss, ecstatic. How can I explain it? In the simplest terms, I felt as though I had encountered reality at long last: I was finally *living*, in the real sense of the word. It was as though my consciousness hadn't only been heightened by all the wine and companionability: I felt like I'd just been born. I believed that I was at a turning point in my life, that a crucial initiation was being offered to me. "My god," I remember thinking to myself, "this is Hemingway." That realization wasn't in any sense a diminution of what was happening but, on the contrary, was a certification of it. This was *Hemingway*, this was authenticity, genuineness, the conquest of something, the overcoming and shedding of something else. For those hours in the Spanish night, I was a new person. Then I think I must have passed out.

2

When I was teaching a sophomore literature course some years ago, I decided to have my students read the Hemingway book I believed I had in my mind that long ago rapturous night, *The Sun Also Rises*. I know I'd read it again sometime soon after, as I'd read Hemingway's stories and the rest of his novels, but now I wanted to try to teach the book from the point of view I'm discussing it here, as a model of adolescent behavior and values. Whatever I was after, though, my students would have none of it: the book had simply no relation to any belief system they held or could conceive of holding; they found it mystifying and in certain ways even repugnant, and, much to my surprise, so did I.

The adventure that Hemingway's invented people had in Spain was for the most part empty and artificial, as far as my students and I were concerned. The characters were all rather unattractive—rich wastrels, alcoholics, sexual misfits—and the one character who was actually rather close to what I myself had been during my adventure, the brooding, romantic, oversensitive Jew, Robert Cohn, was despised by the rest. The others all conceived of themselves as somehow more authentic and more sophisticated than the Jewish nouveau arriviste. And they weren't even as young as I'd remembered them; they were moving into their late twenties and early thirties, although they certainly acted, morally anyway, like arrested adolescents. What was most distressing of all, I think, was that they all seemed as uncertain of themselves, as self-conscious of participating in an adventure that held a heightened reality, while really being hardly more than tourists, as I had been. To my surprise and chagrin, I realized I'd been more of a Hemingway character than I'd realized.

I taught the book rather half-heartedly, trying to overcome that chilling contemptuous skepticism sophomores are so able to communicate, but it wasn't until I read some of the most apparently innocuous passages aloud that I realized of what the real virtue and the real insights about adolescence consisted in Hemingway's early works. At first I'd thought it was probably the intense sense the characters had of themselves as a little nation unto themselves; the way they defined themselves as being in an ultimate we-they situation, with our side, we and our peers, determining not only their own values but the values of a generation and in fact of a world. I had long felt it must have been this which was so touched my late adolescent needs and wants, but during that class I realized the issue was more complicated, and strangely more technical. It wasn't the characters or the lives they led that had so excited my identification with them but the way in which they'd been written about. It wasn't their mild adventuring or their self-congratulatory relations with each other that had drawn me so desperately along in their wake, but the language in which they were depicted: more than anything else, what defined them was Hemingway's prose style.

For example, at the beginning of chapter 4, the narrator, Jake Barnes, is in a taxi with the great love of his life, Lady Brett. They have been partying with a group of expatriate friends and chums of friends in Paris and now have slipped off by themselves.

> The taxi went up the hill, passed the lighted square, then on into the dark, still climbing, then leveled out onto a dark street behind St. Etienne du Mont, went smoothly down the asphalt, passed the trees and the standing bus at the Place de la Contrescarpe, then turned onto the cobbles of the Rue Mouffetard. There were lighted bars and late open shops on each side of the street. We were sitting apart and we jolted close together going down the old street. Brett's hat was off. Her head was back. I saw her face in the lights from the open shops, then it was dark, then I saw her face clearly as we came out on the Avenue des Gobelins. The street was torn up and men were working on the car-tracks by the light of acetylene flares. Brett's face was white and the long line of her neck showed in the bright light of the flares. The street was dark again and I kissed her. Our lips were tight together and then she turned away and pressed against the corner of the seat, as far away as she could get. Her head was down.
> "Don't touch me," she said. "Please don't touch me."

What exactly is happening here? The passage is very typically Hemingway, in its terseness, directness, simplicity, its purity of grammar and construction. The sentences are nearly all declarative, and most of them are either simple sentences or compound sentences formed of straightforward simple phrases. Jake perceives things offhandedly, with no untoward fuss or excitement, but with a terrific sensitivity. There's a quiet drama in the flash of the lights and darks that seems to add an extra layer of makeup to Lady Brett's beauty. On another level, the place the characters move through, Paris, that always exotic, always erotically promising city, is described with absolute familiarity and objectivity. Jake doesn't say: "Wow, look at me here, in Paris, France: midnight, a beautiful woman, that church, I wonder what they call it . . . ?" On the contrary, despite the poignancy of his circumstances, his manner of speaking is entirely collected: he is an acute, dispassionate observer not only of the mysterious city around him but also of his own actions and, by implication, his feelings.

In truth, what Jake is enacting is a sort of anti-adolescence. Although, like the ordinary adolescent, he is a stranger in an alien place, a stranger with an apparently supersensitive consciousness, suffering from vague inner anguish, he manifests none of the hectic despair young people ordinarily do, and neither does he seem to feel any. He is the adolescent protagonist to the nth degree, who has nearby and apparently available to him the beautiful, seductive girl, but who isn't capable of coping with her sexually. Jake, we discover now, is impotent; he has been wounded in the war. His love for Brett and hers for him have become tragic, their longings for one another painful, their ultimate destinations chaotic and unpredictable. But through it all, unlike the young people most of us were, Jake never loses his inner composure. Hemingway has put his hero into the most extreme possible situation: Jake is a veritable apotheosis of the adolescent struggle to make sense of and deal with the difficult barriers the world presents to emotional fulfillment. But Hemingway's hero, the apparently categorical failure, becomes instead the triumph of, to use a term from another generation of adolescent stand-ins, the "cool."

Another arresting passage takes place in chapter 5, the next morning. The last sentence of the previous chapter has Jake, after Brett has left, going to bed, thinking, "It is awfully easy to be hard-boiled about everything in the daytime, but at night it is another thing." Chapter 5 begins:

> In the morning I walked down the Boulevard to the Rue Soufflot for coffee and brioche. It was a fine morning. The horse-chestnut trees in the Luxembourg gardens were in bloom. There was the pleasant early-morning feeling of a hot day. I read the papers with the coffee and then smoked a cigarette. The flower-women were coming up from the market and arranging their daily stock. Students went by going up to the law school, or down to the Sorbonne. The Boulevard was busy with trams and people going to work. I got on an S bus and rode down to the Mad-

eleine, standing on the back platform. From the Madeleine I walked along the Boulevard des Capucines to the Opera, and up to my office. I passed the man with the jumping frogs and the man with the boxer toys. I stepped aside to avoid walking into the thread with which his assistant manipulated the boxers. She was standing looking away, the thread in her folded hands. The man was urging two tourists to buy. Three more tourists had stopped and were watching. I walked on behind a man who was pushing a roller that printed the name cinzano on the sidewalk in damp letters. All along people were going to work. It felt pleasant to be going to work. I walked across the avenue and turned in to my office.

Again, declarative sentences: the world consists of facts, details, splendid in their isolation and clarity. There is no need to interpret reality, to find meaning in it; it is a given, that which is offered to us to delight in, to savor its declarations to us. Jake has suffered the terrible trauma of sexual failure, but he has absolutely overcome it. He is back in his world, with his coffee and cake: it is a world of definite articles, "the" papers—not, notice, "a" paper, which would assume a choice, a possible wavering, an uncertainty. Jake is again in the alien city but utterly composed and at home there. He passes *the* man with the jumping frogs, and *the* man with the boxers. He even knows the secret trick of the huckster: unlike the tourists who are to be gulled, who believe in the illusion before them, Jake is an insider, an initiate, almost even part of the conspiracy. He doesn't merely experience reality, he *possesses* it. Despite his heroically repressed agony, he is serene, or at least his prose, the connections between his perceptions and his language, is serene, unclouded, in fact brilliant. "It was a fine morning . . . It felt pleasant to be going to work." Reading Hemingway's prose, it becomes easier for me to understand how several generations of late adolescents could find our model for our struggle in his fictions.

3

In 1774, the young German poet Johann Wolfgang Goethe published a short novel, *The Sorrows of Young Werther*. It was a book about a young man, highly refined, terribly sensitive, frighteningly intelligent, who suffers various sadnesses—an unfortunate love affair, some career uncertainties—and who is torn mostly by a sort of metaphysical uncertainty, a philosophical despair so intense that he finally commits suicide. The book became immensely popular: it was widely read and discussed, brought instant fame to Goethe, and apparently set off a plague of suicides among young people all across Europe. The actual dimensions of this contagion of suicides is hard to know, but their legend endured, regarded usually as a curious quirk in cultural history. I think, though, it was much more than that; I think that what Werther was enacting was the invention of adolescence.

This seems an odd notion. We have become so accustomed to regarding adolescence not only as one of the natural states of human development but also, in some ways, as its most interesting and most crucial that the idea of a pattern of maturation without it seems absurd. As Philippe Aries points out, though, in his historical study on the development of the family, *Centuries of Childhood*, the family doesn't participate in what he calls an "immobility of . . . species," and neither does the individual. "It is not so much the family," he says, "as a reality that is our subject . . . [so much as] the family as an idea."

It was one of Aries's theses that, before the eighteenth century, "People had no idea of what we call adolescence, and the idea was a long time in taking shape." Aries found compelling evidence of the development of adolescence in various historical records and memoirs, but there is just as much or more in literature. Until Werther, or at least perhaps until Rousseau's *Confessions*, there is really no example in literature of an attitude that distinguished the adolescent in any essential way from the adult. Rather, there is childhood (which Aries points out is itself a more flexible concept than we usually think), then a relatively brief puberty, which is generally considered the last phase of childhood, upon which the individual moves into the adult world, with adult responsibilities, privileges, and presumably appropriate intellectual and moral attitudes.

The turmoil we would typify as particularly adolescent is neither exalted nor excused. The Bible has its teenaged kings, but the worth and greatness of a king have nothing to do with his age, only with the quality of his actions. Similarly, in the *Iliad*, Achilleus before Troy is a desperately young man. The sulk he perpetrates because he feels he has been slighted by the politically more powerful Agamemnon, which a modern novel would unquestionably be put down to his "immaturity," his adolescent touchiness, is never considered as such by Homer, who had no narrative interest whatsoever in allowing Achilleus's fateful pique to be forgiven because of his callowness. It is his character that is flawed; his age has nothing to do with it. In Euripides's *Bacchae*, the young king Pentheus brings about his own hideous death because he can't suppress the overwhelming curiosity he feels about the sexual orgies he fancies are being perpetrated by the Bacchae—who include his aunt and mother and all the other women of his kingdom. Our first response to such a clear expression of puerile, uncertain sexuality would be understanding, compassion, forgiveness; but the Greeks will have none of this: Pentheus's curiosity, his petulance and impatience, are his tragic flaws; he is destroyed by them.

The literature of the Middle Ages and Renaissance offers similar examples. Dante's Beatrice, when he first sees her and exalts her as the image of love and redemption that will inform his *Divine Comedy*, is eleven. Although Shakespeare's young lovers, Romeo and Juliet, are teenagers and act that way, they are provided none of the excuses nor solace we would assume for our own confused young lovers: their actions are considered imprudent in adult terms, in *any* terms, and they, like Pentheus, will die.

The shifts in attitude that make adolescence a definite concept arrive gradually, which shouldn't be surprising considering that such a radical change of vision altered not only our ideas of postpubescence but also, by extension, that of the child, encroaching, as Aries says, "upon childhood in one direction and maturity in the other."

The most marked of these changes date from the time of the Enlightenment and the great eighteenth- and nineteenth-century revolutions. The new epistemological concepts that evolved at the end of the seventeenth century were extreme and represented a clear rupture with more traditional ideas that had been grounded in theological rather than philosophical speculation. Locke's tabula rasa, the notion that the newborn's mind was a clean slate, a perceptual and structural void that would be imprinted with whatever impressions and values with which its society instilled it, evolved further into Rousseau's vision of the purity and innocence of the child and, then, to the concept of the possible recuperation of that innocence in a just society. If we are imperfect and corrupted, as we surely are, it is not because of either original sin nor our weak wills but, rather, because we have been perplexed and distorted by a culture that not only doesn't know how to shape judiciously its own forms but doesn't really even understand how properly to educate its citizens.

Rousseau's idea, that education is reeducation, is profound, and I believe that much of the new vision of adolescence was grounded directly in that perception. Before the eighteenth century, education, practical and moral, presumed there was a body of cultural knowledge that was to be absorbed as well as possible and then lived by. After the Enlightenment, and up to our time, practical and moral education comes to be considered a process, an investigation, a dialectic of testings between the self and society. The culture must in a sense prove itself again to each of its participants before they will share wholeheartedly and with moral conviction in the collective.

This same shift has been reinforced by political history as well. The French and American Revolutions, with their new vision of individual citizens participating in their own governance and in the creation of themselves as persons beyond whatever their inherited status might be, brought about a whole new sense of self, of the self's potentials and responsibilities. In a society in which privileges and duties are inherited, they have to be assumed at the age at which they arrive: "minority" is a much vaguer and more flexible status, much more subject to social expediency. One arrives in one's ultimate life situation in a sense "made," completed. With the age of commerce and industrial expansion, which coincided with the age of revolution and of heightened expectation, the individual's identity not only can be self-created, in most cases it *must* be. We have to be educated, and to educate ourselves, not only in order to govern ourselves but also to make our way and our place in a world that has been thrown open to undreamed of possibilities of material and spiritual ambition. And also, we should note, to undreamed of chances for failure. The disruptions and uprooting of the early age of capitalism and industrial expansion were experienced by much of the population of the West with brutal directness; the education of the self became not a luxury for the spirit but a necessity for the survival of the body. The Romantics, themselves children of the age of revolution, had to live out their disappointments and disenchantments by participating in reactionary counterrevolutions at the same time as the new common man, fighting the old fight for bread and sustenance, seemed to betray the very hopes that so shortly before had granted him freedom. As Shelley put it: "Can he who the day before was a trampled slave suddenly become liberal-minded, forbearing, and independent? This is the consequence of the habits of a state of society to be produced by resolute perseverance and indefatigable hope and long-suffering and long-believing courage." Shelley might be describing the adolescence of an entire culture. We can find the same attitude a little later in Emerson's essays, particularly "Self Reliance" and "Nature," which seem to speak directly to the insecurities and uncertainties of the young American nation and the young industrial capitalist century.

In a society charged with so many challenges, an extended period of education, maturation, and social growth was clearly needed for acquiring the strength of will needed to confront the daunting task of making a way through this new reality. Our coming to consider adolescence as a natural developmental phenomenon, rather than a cultural one, is both an expression of this and, perhaps, a complicating factor in the way we experience it. If we regard adolescence as being as natural and inevitable as physical puberty, rather than a cultural fact, perhaps we can't help but impose on it expectations that muddle even more the already difficult task of self-making. There has come to be in our culture, for example, a terrific blurring as to exactly whom should be considered an adult. Our society prescribes various passages and rituals—school, career choice, sex, and marriage, among others—but none has the definiteness of our biological life. And the question of when and how one really does achieve adulthood, in terms of both how other "real" adults deal with us and how we regard ourselves, becomes one of the crucial issues of our lives—and the most uncertain.

4

This confusion, these expectations, and the potential violation of them have themselves become the source and subject of much of the literature of the nineteenth and twentieth centuries. The configuration and quality of the family, the separation of the youthful protagonist from his or her parents, the young hero's confrontation with society, and the turbulent emotions these projects entail are the themes of a large proportion of modern Western literature. Sometimes the characters of these works are portrayed as succeeding in their struggles, sometimes they fail, and sometimes they're subjected to endless Promethean conflicts that absorb all their energies—and life itself—but the theme, what Thomas Mann called in the title of one of his works, "disorder and early sorrow," remains remarkably constant.

The approach to all this varies widely, from Goethe to Fielding, from Wordsworth to Joyce to Philip Roth, but the literature can be divided into two tendencies, what might be called "example" and "image." I mean, by example literature, works that offer, or seem to offer, guidance, direction, and helpful patterns for the project of maturation. Most popular literature is in this category: the old Horatio Alger stories, as well as all the boyhood and girlhood evocations of usually parentless adventuring through the world. Westerns are a more sublimated mode of the same thing, offering clear, however woefully misguided, enactments of heroism, as is a small proportion of more serious literature. *The Sun Also Rises*, in the sense I've discussed it, can be taken as an instance of example literature.

Works of "image" literature, which compose the greater portion of thoughtful enactments of the trials of adolescence, offer no instruction or advice, no direct routes through the quagmires of growing up. Rather, they hold up mirrors to the young by which they can behold themselves in another, behold their own consternation and helplessness, thereby, hopefully, aiding, even abetting, them on their own journey. Sometimes the images in these mirrors can be quite devastating—Byron ridiculed generations of properly educated young Englishmen in his satires—and sometimes they're more flattering, as in Wordsworth's autobiographies of himself in his changing society.

The key work of example literature during my own adolescence was J. D. Salinger's *Catcher in the Rye*. When I read the book at sixteen, it was as close as I'd ever come to revelation. Salinger's relatively simple, though tonally very complex, story about a sixteen-year- old on the verge of a breakdown shed light on so many of the dark corridors of my own life, my *secret* life, that I felt illuminated, enlightened, enchanted. In reading the book many years later, a certain imaginative sympathy is called for. The book doesn't really hold any surprises—most of the issues it deals with have by now, thank goodness, been resolved in my life—but, as with Hemingway, I realize it was Salinger's prose style that had been most meaningful for me. The book begins like this:

> If you really want to hear about it, the first thing you'll probably want to know is where I was born, and what my lousy childhood was like, and how my parents were occupied and all before they had me, and all that David Copperfield kind of crap, but I don't feel like going into it, if you want to know the truth. In the first place, that stuff bores me, and in the second place, my parents would have about two hemorrhages apiece if

I told anything pretty personal about them. They're quite touchy about anything like that, especially my father. They're *nice* and all—I'm not saying that—but they're also touchy as hell. Besides I'm not going to tell you my whole goddamn autobiography or anything. I'll just tell you about this madman stuff that happened to me around last Christmas just before I got pretty run-down and had to come out here and take it easy.

We are very far here from the prose world of Hemingway's hero. Holden Caulfield, Salinger's sad young man, is recounting his narrative from a mental institution, and though he says he is about to be released, he is still evidently in a quite agitated state. While Hemingway's narrator speaks to everyone and no one—he is alone, solitary and secure in his solitude—Salinger's Holden introduces another person, "you," someone to be with him in his story, by the second word, long before he himself, the very contingent "I," is actually introduced. There are *no* simple and declarative statements in Holden's speech. His sentences are contorted, turning in on themselves, going on and on past where anyone in a normal state of mind would end a thought to start another. Compared to Hemingway's world, which is purified of almost all adjectival activity, everything in Holden's speech is modified." Probably . . . and all . . . all that . . . kind of . . . quite." Holden is thinking very fast, too fast, with a complexity that's almost beyond him; he can barely keep up with himself, even without his little slip about his parents, "They're *nice* and all—I'm not saying that," it's clear that his relationship to his family is overwhelmingly complicated.

Holden is conscious that he offers nothing like a good example of anything, and he will even take a swipe at another fictional character who does, who is in fact a key character of the literature of example, David Copperfield, Dickens's ever resourceful, ever ethical, never neurotic or overly libidinal hero whose goodness and good deeds in the end conquer all adversity. Holden, later in the book, will try to deflate another potential literary hero, one of Hemingway's this time, from *A Farewell to Arms*: "It had this guy in it named Lieutenant Henry that was supposed to be a nice guy and all. I don't see how D.B. [Holden's writer-brother] could hate the Army and war and all so much and still like a phony like that."

It's not always so easy, however, to distinguish between the literatures of example and image. Mark Twain's *Adventures of Huckleberry Finn* not long ago was the center of a controversy about just such a difficulty. Some in the African American community have objected to the apparent racism of Huck, to his mistreatment and belittling of the runaway slave, Jim. Huck seems genuinely to love Jim, and even saves his life, but his response to Jim's actual humanity is contaminated by his acculturation, by the very language he uses to speak of his relations with Jim, and it is this that has been most abrasive. I feel that Twain meant Huck's essential conflict to be precisely his attempt at moral self-awareness, his beginning to understand what racism and intolerance have really meant to his society and to him. But Huck's ironic hectoring of Jim and the outright racism of most of the adult characters in the book are depicted so vividly that it's easy to see how the question of whether Twain meant Huck to be an image, a pedagogical device, as I feel he is, or an example—a depiction of malign racial attitudes—as those who protest the book believe, is hard to resolve.

Huck, at any rate, is a prototypical adolescent, with a part of him still in childhood and a part straining to bring him to the moral consciousness of maturity. Twain clearly grasped the issues of the new adolescence: the self, set adrift from family, trying to cobble an acceptable identity for itself in a community of adults that has no precise definition for him. Some adults treat Huck as one of themselves, others regard him as still a child. Along with this, Twain satirizes the absurdities of much of the example literature of the time. When Huck is trying to free Jim from captivity, his even less mature friend, Tom Sawyer, finds the adventure insufficiently exciting and proposes adventuresome complications that have their origins in literature. Tom chides Huck: "Well, if that ain't just like you, Huck Finn. You *can* get up the infant-schooliest ways of going at a thing. Why, hain't you ever read any books at all?—Baron Trench, nor Casanova, nor Benvenuto Chelleeny, nor Henry VI, nor none of them heroes? Who ever heard of getting a prisoner loose in such an old-maidy ways as that?" And poor Jim's situation becomes even more fraught as a result of Tom's fantasies and meddling.

As I've pointed out, Twain was only one of many nineteenth-century writers who concerned themselves with adolescence, and once literature began to produce reflections of the turmoil and illusions of adolescence, young people began to respond to them in shaping their own lives; the phenomenon becomes a kind of hall of mirrors. Some of our greatest literature deals with the problems adolescents have with these complicated interchanges between life and art. Raskolnikov, in Dostoevski's *Crime and Punishment*, who is Huck Finn's near contemporary, is driven not only by the intolerable social situation in Tsarist Russia, nor by his own repressed and turbulent sexuality: he is also led, or misled, by the radical literature that was being produced throughout Europe at that time, particularly by his reading of Nietzsche's *Thus Spake Zarathustra*. Nietzsche, in his best-known work, promulgated an überman who would inaugurate a new morality, based on a more accurate reading of human psychology rather than on the delusions of metaphysics and religion. Nietzsche's exhilarating ideas mean to redeem the lost hopes of the age of revolution: in his vision, it will not be society that produces his new man because society is incurably corrupted. But the enlightened individual, the Zarathustrian hero, will leap past those who are unconfident and self-demeaning as a result of their unexamined moral compromises. In some ways Nietzsche's Zarathustra, the character himself, can be regarded as a sort of ultimate adolescent: in his petulance and bravado, as well as his flamboyant brilliance, he is the apotheosis of example literature. Raskolnikov, to his sorrow, takes him as even more than this, attempting by his own act of absurd violence to unmoor himself from the pettiness of his culture.

The heirs of Raskolnikov, and of Huck, are not to be found only in our literatures. The new vision of life, of moral development and of social potential, and the dark underside of all these hopeful promises—disruption, disjunction, uncertainty, loss of security, and the terror of a moral nihilism—have been endured by the young for several centuries now. The Bohemian, the Dandy, the Dadaist, the Surrealist, the Beatnik, the Hippie, the Punk, the Rapper: all have been offered as images of fulfillment and completion. Toward the end of my own adolescence, Jack Kerouac delineated characters who were much like Hemingway's tight-lipped, ill-rooted heroes but set absolutely adrift in their own country, fleeing themselves in joyrides across the continent, voyages that are no longer travels towards anything, no longer a search for meaning or certainty, but ends in themselves, an incessant series of arrivals and departures, frantic attempts to shake loose and be set free into the process if not the reality of self-revealment and self-creation.

Now, hardly more than a few generations after Kerouac, the situation of the young is yet more complex and more acutely dire. The conflict today between the models our adolescence have bequeathed to them and the reality they have to endure has intensified the tensions of their quest. The young today must cope with readily available hard drugs, those deceptive, wily, and maiming means of evasion and escape. And they must deal with a culture that has commercialized the very act of rebellion that was once the treasured possession of the young. Today's adolescents can behold themselves on television and the Internet and can behold, too, enactments of their most outrageous fantasies. Gestures of revolt are readily available, but at the same time their desperate energy is radically disvalued by their very accessibility.

And the social-political world toward which the young strive resonates with anxiety and despair. Aside from the cynicism with which the terrorist threat has been used as an excuse for everything under the sun, to many young people, the adult world seems almost frenziedly stupid in its refusal to deal in constructive ways with the social and environmental havoc it has perpetrated. The youth of our time set out in life in a situation of extreme economic uncertainty; the uncertainties of globalization, a slash-and-burn economics that is being used to inaugurate the most regressive and mean-spirited reactionary programs: the young can feel, perhaps properly, that our whole culture is being frighteningly manipulated and it is they who experience this most painfully, and most passionately.

It occurs to me to wonder whether what we're glimpsing now might be the end of adolescence as we've known it: as a quest, an exploration into the potentials of a rich adult life. Might we instead be going through a transition at the end of which there will be nothing available to the young but the darkest aspects of adolescence: uncertainty of identity, radical and often futile attempts at self-assertion, an indefiniteness of prospect, an elusiveness of the very concept as well as the attainment of maturity? Perhaps our culture, without quite consciously recognizing it, has come to shape its institutions in so constraining a way that soon we will have no release or respite from a conflict that perhaps once never existed. We will be allowed only to be old, without ever having become adults.

Paris as Symbol, Idea, and Reality

I

The first time I came to Paris, I was nineteen, on a trip around Europe with a friend. I don't remember how we happened to end up there, but we parked our tiny Renault 4 in the rue Jacob and stayed in what was then a cheap hotel on the corner of rue Bonaparte. It's difficult to explain to myself, even now, but from the moment we arrived in the city, and especially when I walked out of the hotel and up the rue Bonaparte to the Saint German square, I fell in love with the place and suddenly felt that for the first time in my life I was where I belonged.

I'd wonder now if it had something to do with the fact that I'd written my first poem a few weeks before and had absurd inklings that perhaps writing was something I would want to do with my life, but even that doesn't really make all that much sense: I had only the sketchiest idea of the way Paris had affected other would-be or actual writers. It was much more instinctive than that—the city just grabbed me, and attached me to it; I walked through it in a trance of infatuation. I didn't know then that I was hardly the first to whom this had happened, but by the middle of the next school year, I knew I had to go back, left school, and did.

I stayed in the same hotel, and despite the exaltation of being in the city, I was often lonely, and when I couldn't sleep I'd get up and walk aimlessly through the nearby streets. I didn't know then, and wouldn't until decades later, when I'd finally notice a plaque on a building on the next street, the rue du Seine, that the Polish poet Adam Mickiewicz had lived there for a number of years. Mickiewicz was the greatest Polish poet of the nineteenth century: he fled Poland, which was then under Russian occupation, for Paris and lived there from 1831 to 1855 (though he died in Turkey, where he'd gone to organize a Polish regiment to fight in the Crimean War).

I learned the dates of Mickiewicz's stay in Paris by calling another Polish poet, a friend whose name is Adam, too: Adam Zagajewski, who also fled Poland. In the dark 1980s, he went to Berlin, then Paris.[1] There aren't any satisfactory translations of Mickiewicz's poems in English, but there are many of Zagajewski's, some of which I (a poet from America, from New Jersey, who also lives much of the year in Paris) helped translate. Zagajewski wrote a poem in honor of still another Pole, Joseph Czapski, a much admired writer and painter, who survived prison camps under the Nazis, then in the Soviet Union, and who when he was finally freed from all that came to Paris and lived in or near it until his death a few years ago. Zagajewski's poem takes place on the edge of the city, in Saint-Cloud. It begins:

CRUEL

In the Parc de Saint-Cloud, birds sang.
Alone in that vast, narcissistic forest
that looks out on Paris,
I pondered your words:
The world is cruel; rapacious,
carnivorous, cruel.
I circled the Parc de Saint-Cloud, east to west,
west to east,
I strolled through the leafless
chestnuts, bowed to the dark, bowing cedars,
heard pinecones cracked
by sparrows and wrens.
No beast of prey in the park,

---

1. Since this essay was written, and since the great changes in Middle and Eastern Europe, Zagajewski has returned to Poland.

other than time, just then changing
from winter to spring, stripped,
an actor flinging his costume away,
in the cold wings backstage . . .
(Translation by Renata Gorczynski, Benjamin Ivry, and C. K. Williams)

The intellectual and aesthetic model and mentor for Zagajewski has been another Polish poet, Czesław Miłosz. Miłosz, born in Lithuania, lived through the Second World War in Poland, and after the war, a committed left-liberal, he became part of the new socialist-communist government in Poland, serving as cultural attaché first in Washington, DC, then in Paris, where he defected from a government he had come to find unbearably oppressive. He wrote a book about Stalinism, *The Captive Mind*, which remains one of the most spiritually generous anti-Communist critiques we have, and stayed on for some years in Paris, where he'd already visited in the 1930s when he came to seek out his cousin, O. V. Miłosz, yet another Lithuanian-Polish poet residing in Paris, who, a brilliant mystic, lived most of his life there, and wrote his poems in French. After Paris, Miłosz, Czesław, that is, went to Berkeley, where he taught until his retirement. While there, he wrote a poem about that first long ago visit to Paris:

BYPASSING RUE DESCARTES

Bypassing rue Descartes
I descended toward the Seine, shy, a traveler,
A young barbarian just come to the capital of the world.
We were many, from Jassy and Koloshvar, Wilno and Bucharest, Saigon and Marrakesh,
Ashamed to remember the customs of our homes,
About which nobody here should ever be told:
The clapping for servants, barefooted girls hurry in,
Dividing food with incantations,
Choral prayers recited by master and household together.
I had left the cloudy provinces behind,
I entered the universal, dazzled and desiring.
Soon enough, many from Jassy and Koloshvar, or Saigon or Marrakesh
Would be killed because they wanted to abolish the customs of their homes.

Soon enough, their peers were seizing power
In order to kill in the name of the universal, beautiful ideas.
Meanwhile the city behaved in accordance with its nature,
Rustling with throaty laughter in the dark,
Baking long breads and pouring wine into clay pitchers,
Buying fish, lemons, and garlic at street markets,
Indifferent as it was to honor and shame and greatness and glory,
Because that had been done already and had transformed itself
Into monuments representing nobody knows whom,
Into arias hardly audible and into turns of speech.
Again I lean on the rough granite of the embankment,
As if I had returned from travels through the underworlds
And suddenly saw in the light the reeling wheel of the seasons
Where empires have fallen and those once living are dead.
There is no capital of the world, neither here nor anywhere else,
And the abolished customs are restored to their small fame
And now I know that the time of human generations is not like the time
    of the earth. . . . .

                (Translation by Renata Gorczynski and Robert Hass)

In this poem Miłosz uses his experiences in Paris to meditate on the false promises of "universal, beautiful ideas." The illusion that Paris is the capital of the world, that there can be a capital of the world, that is, a place, any place, that would actually embody those political ideals that the poet refers to as "the universal," is something Miłosz learned is seductive but, in the end, pernicious, tragic. Still, the democratic ideals inaugurated by the French revolution were an irresistible attraction for young idealists through the turbulent political history of the nineteenth and twentieth centuries, and they were drawn to Paris from all over the world.

For example, what is considered by many the greatest novel in Guatemalan literature, a harrowing tale of political corruption and oppression titled *El Presidente*, was written in the 1930s by Miguel Asturias. Though it takes place in Guatemala, it was composed in Paris, recited aloud every evening in a Spanish-language bookstore to a group of Asturias's fellow exiles from Latin America. (Asturias, like Miłosz, went on to win a Nobel Prize in Literature.) *El Presidente* was one of the models for another book, *The Autumn of the Patriarch*, the author of which, yet another Nobel Prize winner, Gabriel García Márquez, also came to

Paris to live and study and starve, as many of the young writers and artists who arrived there over the generations have starved. (I had the pleasure of meeting García Márquez a few years ago; we spoke of Paris, and to my surprise he told me he hated the city, that he loathed his memories of his time there when he was unknown and desperately poor.)

It would be interesting to know how many of those who came to the city, as Miłosz says, "dazzled and desiring," full of grand hopes, have ended up feeling less than positive about it. Another Latin American exile in the thirties was the Peruvian César Vallejo, one of the great poets in Spanish of the twentieth century. Vallejo was a committed Communist, probably because there were no alternatives to the vicious social and political systems in Peru in those days. He came to Paris as a journalist, also went hungry, visited the Soviet Union, returned still poor but full of hope, a hope we know now was frighteningly illusory. At one point he wrote a wonderfully sad poem about himself and Paris, "Testimony," which has been translated by an Irish poet, Paul Muldoon, who's also written several poems that take place in Paris, though he's never lived there for very long.

TESTIMONY

I will die in Paris, on a day the rain's been coming down hard,
a day I can even now recall.
I will die in Paris—I try not to take this too much to heart—
on a Thursday, probably, in the Fall.

It'll be like today, a Thursday: a Thursday on which, as I make
and remake this poem, the very bones
in my forearms ache.
Never before, along the road, have I felt more alone.

César Vallejo is dead: everyone used to knock him about,
they'll say, though he'd done no harm;
they hit him hard with a rod
and also a length of rope; this will be borne out

by Thursdays, by the bones in his forearms,
by loneliness, by heavy rain, by the aforementioned roads.

(Translation by Paul Muldoon)

César Vallejo did indeed die in Paris, on a Thursday, in the hospital called Hotel Dieu, in the rain, or so the legend has it. Whatever the truth of that, we can be sure that many poets and writers less well known than Vallejo died in Paris, as well, some in despair, some perhaps still graced with the dreams that brought them.

The greatest poet of the century in German, Rainer Maria Rilke, came to the city in his mid-twenties, already celebrated. He first arrived with his much older and notoriously unconventional lover, Lou Andreas-Salomé, Russian by birth, who had been living part of the time there. Rilke had gone off to live in an artists' colony, where he married, and then came back to Paris, leaving his wife and new child behind. Through his wife, an artist, he'd met and then become the secretary of the renowned French sculptor Rodin, for whom he worked a few years and about whom he wrote a splendid monograph. The building on the rue de Varenne that was Rodin's last home and studio and now houses the Rodin museum was found for Rodin by Rilke. Rilke wrote many of his most notable poems in Paris, and he also wrote his semi-autobiographical novel, *The Notebooks of Malte Laurids Brigge*, which recounts the difficult solitude he experienced in his new city and speaks as well as any book that's ever been written about the trials and exaltations of the young artist.

"I am in Paris," Rilke's character Malte writes,

> those who learn this are glad, most of them envy me. They are right. It is a great city; great and full of strange temptations. As concerns myself, I must admit that I have in certain respects succumbed to them. I believe there is no other way of saying it. I have succumbed to those temptations, and this has brought about certain changes, if not in my character, at least in my outlook on the world, and, in any case, in my life. An entirely different conception of all things has developed in me under these influences; certain differences have appeared that separate me from other men, more than anything heretofore. A world transformed. A new life filled with new meanings. For the moment I find it a little hard because everything is too new. I am a beginner in my own circumstances.

Then Rilke writes, as though it explains anything unclear in what he's just said: "Do you remember Baudelaire's incredible poem, 'Une Charogne'? Perhaps I understand it now."

It can seem strange and unlikely to explain so many tangled emotions by a single poem. Yet it and several others from Baudelaire's *Les Fleurs du Mal*, particularly "Le Cygne," "Les Sept Vieillards," and "Les Petites Vieilles," are among the most influential artistic productions of the nineteenth century and were essential to the inception of a new vision of art and life, what has come to be called much too often and reflexively modernism. Rilke, in Malte, makes what I believe is the most succinct and accurate statement of the responsibilities and opportunities of the art of modernism. "It was [Baudelaire's] task, he writes, "to see in this terrible thing, seeming to be only repulsive, that existence which is valid among all that exists."

This is the beginning of "Une Charogne," translated by William H. Crosby.

A CARCASS

Do you recall the thing we saw once, my own,
    One summer morning fair and fresh:
The pathway turned and there, upon a bed of stone,
    A great hulk of decaying flesh,

Its legs upthrust to mock female lubricity,
    Seething and sweating its pollution,
Its open belly, cynically and carelessly
    Venting a gaseous corruption?

The sunlight burned intensely through the rottenness
    As though to render it well done,
Returning thus a hundredfold of Nature's largesse
    By multiplying what was one;

And God in heaven gazed up this splendid corpse,
    Luxuriating like a flower.
The horrid stench had almost felled you in the gorse,
    So overwhelming was its power.

Flies in droves descended on that putrid belly
    From whence exuded black brigades
Of larvae trickling slowly like a liquid jelly
    From end to end along its shreds;

All of it heaved and fell as smoothly as the sea
   And writhed and rustled in its motion;
One might surmise the corpse, breathing uncertainly,
     Survived in the proliferation.

2

Although presumably the majority of writers who came to Paris came for the sake of their art, there are other reasons why so many came and continue to come. Mickiewicz's flight to the city had nothing to do with his aesthetic aspirations: he was a political refugee, and though it's interesting to wonder whether he ever read *Les Fleurs du Mal*, which was published while he was in Paris, for him the city was a refuge, a sanctuary, a base of operations. It was also that for the great German poet and social critic Heinrich Heine, a refugee from other sorts of political and cultural oppression. The fact is that despite the conservative reactions to the French Revolution that continued on and off through the century, France more than anywhere else had incorporated the ideals of the democratic revolution in its very tissues and remained a place of relative freedom. There's another plaque on a building, near where I used to live in the Tenth Arrondissement, that quotes something Heine, who lived in the building, wrote just after he first arrived: "If someone asks how Heine is doing in Paris, tell him, 'like a fish in the sea.' Or better yet, tell him that when a fish in the sea asks another fish how he's doing, let the second answer, 'Like Heine in Paris.'"

The image of the city as both a political refuge and a shining symbol of ideals of toleration has persisted. The first major poet who wrote in English of the new age of revolution was Wordsworth, who, still a very young man, happened to arrive in France for a walking trip the day before the Bastille fell and came back a year or so later. Not long afterward he expressed succinctly the best ideals of the revolution in his autobiographical poem, "The Prelude":

Distinction lay open to all that came,
And wealth and titles were in less esteem
Than talents and successful industry.

Wordsworth also coined the phrase that encapsulated that time of amazing hope better than anything else: "Bliss was it in that dawn to be alive." (It was perhaps especially blissful for Wordsworth—he fathered an illegitimate daughter while he was in France.)

Among others who migrated to the city later on was Ho Chi Minh, the leader of North Vietnam during and after the Vietnam War, who was also a poet and had studied in Paris, where he worked for a time as a busboy in a restaurant. The great Syrian poet Adonis has lived for many years in Courbevoie, just outside the city, and more immigrants arrive all the time: Kurdish refugees from Turkey and Iraq; Tamil driven here by the endless civil wars in Sri Lanka; political and economic immigrants from various African, Arab, and sub-Saharan countries and from the Near and Far East, Eastern and Central Europe—just about everywhere.

American writers for the most part have had the luxury of not having to flee to Paris but, instead, choosing to live there, everyone from James Fenimore Cooper to Henry James to James Jones. Henry James wrote to a friend on arriving: "I am turning into an old, and very contented, Parisian: I feel as if I had struck roots in the Parisian soil and were likely to let them grow tangled and tenacious there." And much later the raucously candid and endlessly energetic Henry Miller fled his depressing Bohemian life in New York for Paris, writing on his arrival: "I love it here, I want to stay forever . . . I will write here. I will live quietly and quite alone. And each day I will see a little more of Paris, study it, learn it as I would a book . . . The streets sing, the stones talk. The houses drip history, glory, romance." Miller stayed on for a number of years, until he was driven back to America by the impending Second World War, and he did manage to get out into the world a little, as anyone knows who's read the gloriously tumultuous *Quiet Days in Clichy*.

Probably the most notorious of the Americans who've lived in and written about Paris is Ernest Hemingway, who first came as a young journalist but returned many times. Later, he would say of those first sojourns, when he had just begun to write fiction, was still poor and newly married to the first of his several wives, as the happiest time of his life. He circulated in the community of writers who lived there then. Among them were Gertrude Stein, who influenced Hemingway in the development of his prose style, Ezra Pound, and later Hemingway's sad literary sibling F. Scott Fitzgerald. Fitzgerald, like quite a few others, came to Paris to find a party. Find one he did: it went on for years and all but destroyed him. Hemingway—he was an awful hypocrite—despised Fitzgerald for his flightiness, but certainly the festive aspect of Paris, its wildness and bohemian libertinism, was a good part of the seductiveness the city held for him, too. Hemingway tragically never did manage to leave his own party behind him, to abandon his arrested adolescence: his wealth and fame gave him the opportunity to maintain his jejune self-indulgence until it destroyed him.

Pound, coming almost directly from the University of Pennsylvania, wrote a poem in Paris, about Paris, that would come be regarded as the signature poem of the imagist movement.

IN A STATION OF THE METRO

The apparition of these faces in the crowd;
Petals on a wet, black bough.

Pound commuted between Paris and London for decades. He became friends with Sylvia Beach, the owner of the bookstore Shakespeare and Company (the name of which, if not its serious spirit, still endures), convinced her to publish James Joyce's *Ulysses*, then invited Joyce to come to Paris, which of course Joyce did, to stay for the rest of his life.

T. S. Eliot had arrived before he knew Pound and remained long enough to write some of his poems in French. They're mostly very undistinguished, but a passage of one,

Phlébas, le Phénicien, pendant quinze jours noyé,
Oubliait les cris des mouettes et la houle de Cornouaille,
Et les profits et les pertes, et la cargaison d'étain:
Un courant de sous-mer l'emporta très loin,
Le repassant aux étapes de sa vie antérieure . . .

Eliot translated it and it became part of the section of *The Waste Land* called "Death by Water."

Phlebas the Phoenician, a fortnight dead,
Forgot the cry of gulls, and the deep sea swell
And the profit and the loss.

A current under sea
Picked his bones in whispers. As he rose and fell
He passed the stages of his age and youth
Entering the whirlpool.

The list of American writers who've come to the city, some to stay, some to be nourished by it and take their experiences home with them, is impressive. Sherwood Anderson, Thornton Wilder, Paul Bowles, passed through; Chester Himes and James Baldwin came to escape the intolerable racial tensions in America; Elizabeth Bishop set some of her early poems there; John Ashbery and Paul Auster came to do what amounted to apprenticeships before they returned to New York; Diane Johnson still lives part of the year on rue Bonaparte, and the great Canadian Mavis Gallant came and never went back.

From the rest of Europe, too, the talented and tormented migrated to the city. The brilliant Russian poet Marina Tsvetaeva came in the twenties, and lived in the Russian exile community, mostly in miserable poverty, through the thirties, until she finally went back to the Soviet Union during the very worst time of Stalinism, and finding life there even grimmer than she'd conceived it could be, committed suicide. She'd written at length about Paris, and one of her poems recalls Pound's.

READERS OF NEWSPAPERS

It crawls, the underground snake,
crawls, with its load of people.
And each one has his
newspaper, his skin
disease; a twitch of chewing;
newspaper caries.
Masticators of gum,
readers of newspapers.
And who are the readers? old men? athletes?
soldiers? No face, no features,
no age. Skeletons—there's no
face, only the newspaper page.

> All Paris is dressed
> this way from forehead to navel.
> Give it up, girl, or
> you'll give birth to
> a reader of newspapers.
>
> (Translation by Elaine Feinstein)

Another Russian poet, Yvgeny Esenin came as well, dragooned from Moscow by his paramour, the American expatriate dancer Isadora Duncan. When I first came to Paris in the fifties, Duncan's brother, Raymond, still managed the eccentric art institute he and Isadora had established on the rue de Seine, and you'd see him walking the streets of that neighborhood in the Greek robes and sandals that were the getup of some of his and his sister's more curious fantasies.

Later, the Polish poet, Zbigniew Herbert, also living in Paris, would write about Duncan leaving the Soviet Union, which she had idealized, glamorized, propagandized for, and then jilted, taking poor Esenin with her when she left:

> Unfortunately she had to bid farewell to the Land of Hope
> as consolation she took a costly poet with her
> the half-conscious Esenin cursed loved howled

Poor Esenin, who was still nearly a child, driven to distraction by Duncan's carryings-on, went back to the Soviet Union, and shot himself in a hotel room. So many suicides.

The roster is vast. The Romanian Celan, the Hungarian Radnóti, the Czech Kundera, the Argentine Cortázar, and the South African Breytenbach. Even some of the most innovative Japanese poets of the century spent time there, and several years ago the Nobel Prize was won by the Chinese novelist and painter Gao Xingjian, who has long lived in Paris.

3

There seems to be obvious question here, which is, Why? What is it that has made Paris over these last hundred and fifty years or so the place to which so many have been drawn? Certainly there are other great cities in the world; some have had their moment as thriving artistic centers, but only Paris seems to have consistently maintained its allure. It's often been said that there's something about the way Paris wears its passage through time, one might almost say flaunts it, that is intrinsically inspiring. e. e. cummings, who, though he lived the rest of his life in New York, recalled forty years later the Paris of his youth:

> I celebrated an immediate reconciling of spirit and flesh, forever and now, heaven and earth. Paris was for me precisely and completely this homogeneous duality: this accepting transcendence; this living and dying more than death or life. Whereas—by the very act of becoming its improbably gigantic self—New York had reduced mankind to a tribe of pygmies, Paris (in each shape and gesture and avenue and cranny of her being) was continuously expressing the humanness of humanity. Everywhere I sensed a miraculous presence, not of mere children and women and men, but of living human beings.

It's been said that the history Paris is embedded and embodied its very stone, rather than in the cultural and personal memory of which the buildings of a city are a symbol. But, however compelling, this is only a metaphor. Rome, in fact, is older than Paris and manifests its age just as or even more dramatically. And though Rome has had its moments as the place for which artists longed (many Frenchmen among them), most recently the reasons for this seem to have less to do with Italian culture and more with the delightful Italians. New York, too, has at times been a locus of aesthetic creation and commerce—as it is now—and London, too; and Florence and Amsterdam have had their moments as well. Yet though each city certainly has its urban splendor, none has so fused its history with its artistic heritage, and none has conveyed through the voices of those who've dwelled in it the mysterious sense of being a cosmos in itself, a unique and infinitely promising reality, a reflection, or an enactment, of essential mysteries.

Walter Benjamin, the German critic and thinker who meditated so profoundly on the new age of the modern, took Paris and Baudelaire as the key to a comprehension of its many disparate and perplexing contradictions. The city always intrigued him; he wrote in his "Paris Diary" in 1929: "No sooner do you arrive in the city than you feel rewarded. The resolve not to write about it is futile." Benjamin, too, suffered from the city's tendency to inflict solitude: "The rendezvous to which loneliness, that old pimp, invites me." But he goes on, almost ecstatically:

> Of course—what an easy matter it is to overlook this city! It is as easy as overlooking health and happiness. You can't imagine how uninsistent it is . . . Just think how the streets here seem to be inhabited interiors, how much you fail to see day after day, even in the most familiar parts, and how crucially important it is, more so than anywhere else, to keep crossing from one side of the street to the other . . . What is the source of this unassuming exterior that seems oriented toward the needs and talents of the most insignificant members of society?

Benjamin is particularly acute in understanding the larger implications the new vision of the city implied. Describing the Parisian panorama, he speaks of "an enormous crowd in which no one is either quite transparent or quite opaque to all others." This remains an illuminating description of walking the streets of any modern city. Again, about Baudelaire, but really about any enthusiastic urbanite: "Baudelaire loved solitude, but he wanted it in a crowd."

(Benjamin in another context quotes the French poet Paul Valéry on the same theme. Valéry, Benjamin points out, "has a fine eye for the cluster of symptoms called 'civilization.'" Valéry writes of city life: "The inhabitant of the great urban centers reverts to a state of savagery—that is, of isolation. The feeling of being dependent on others, which used to be kept alive by need, is gradually blunted in the smooth functioning of the social mechanism. Any improvement of this mechanism eliminates certain modes of behavior and emotions." Benjamin comments on this: "Comfort isolates," a scarily prescient observation about what it is to live in a suburb, that most recent avatar of human social organization, in which isolation, under its code terms "privacy" and "self-sufficiency," is promulgated as the primary virtue of social and political being.)

Until the nineteenth century, no one wrote of the city, Paris or any other, for its own sake: the gathering of stone and souls that comprised the urban reality was incidental to the events going on among them; the city's nature wasn't a mystery, it was simply taken for granted. If a character in a Molière play goes out into the street, the name of the street won't be mentioned, and neither will anything else about it. The urban space is the passage from one place to the other, and the city is merely the repository of these passages; what happens of importance happens indoors.

What occurs in the nineteenth century, around the time of Baudelaire and after, that so changes the very definition of the city, for the artist, and everyone else? We well know there are many cultural and political factors: the social order had undergone a profound rearrangement when government by democracy, in whatever form it took in particular countries, became the referent for political aspiration. Religion, as a part of the same shift, became a much less active force in people's lives: religious belief as the primary element in ethical considerations was becoming being radically questioned, and a new belief in the aesthetic as a moral force in its own right was evolving.

On a more pragmatic level, the economic texture of society was changing: the way goods were manufactured and bought and sold, as well as the environments in which people confronted or evaded one another in this new system of mass commerce and popular consumption. The department store was invented, to which the burgeoning middle class came to see and be seen as well as to shop. People in the new commercial reality became more visible to each other, and the split between rich and poor, the exalted and neglected, became much more evident.

In Paris, this new visibility still was hidden behind the old structures of the city. Freud developed his geology of the mind with its "unconscious" later in the nineteenth century, but Paris already seemed the city that best embodied the distinctions implied in Freud's nomenclature. More than any other modern city, it was a place of concealment, in which every building has a courtyard, or two or three—inward, often dark places where lurk things unseen and possibly—in those days probably—forbidden. And the city still, despite Haussman's sanitization of it, has narrow lanes and alleys that abruptly slice through rows of presentable facades, where things go on about which one doesn't like to think too much, as, according to Freud, one doesn't like to consider too closely the similar secret places in the self. In the way it conceals certain activities, and reveals others, Paris is perhaps very like modern consciousness itself. As Benjamin says, you have to pay crucial attention, you have to keep crossing the street. The facade, that which is before your eyes, is merely picturesque, and therefore incidental. You have to go more deeply in to find what's really before you and what might be behind you.

So Paris came to seem to many of those who came to it not merely a place where the unconscious can be enacted but an unconscious in itself, seductive and menacing, a realm where desire is frankly manifest, and the violence behind desire always drones as a shadowy resonance. And though it's true that the gentrification of Paris has muted much of the force of all this—the courtyards are as likely as not to have art galleries or clothing boutiques in them as anything else—there are still neighborhoods where certain shadowy passageways are definitely uninviting to exploration.

4

To what degree artists or writers affect changes in a culture is of course a complex question. Was Baudelaire manifesting in "Une Charogne" social tendencies that were already underway, or was he, however indirectly, inventing them? We can't know for certain, but we can know that by the time Rilke's Malte was reading the poem, and reconceiving himself through it, the poem and the world of consciousness it implies had become central to the aesthetic world.

The most crucial element of the poem, and of its method, is quite evident. As Rilke remarked, it was certainly the most repulsive poem that had ever been written, but its project he notes, its purpose, is the transformation of the repulsive, and by extrapolation, of ordinary reality as well, into the beautiful. And the poem is indeed beautiful: formally elegant, its grotesque, repellent images are lush; it's both a love poem and a meditation on mortality and temporality—and beauty.

But its transformative force is what's most striking: the hideously rotting carcass, its decomposition, the description of what swarms over and around it are the perceptions of a poetic mind that, precisely because it can transfigure such horror into a moral meditation, is vastly different from anything before it. It is this radical transformation that characterizes the aesthetic choices and the moral norms of the age of the modern in which we still live.

For in the modern, the transforming imagination itself becomes moral. Always before, imagination had served intellect. From a strictly ethical perspective, the beauties of art were ultimately most useful in illustrating and illuminating conclusions already effected by theological or philosophical reflection. Now, though, the imagination in its transformative mode takes the realm of the moral as its dominion, too; it assumes the traditional functions of religion and philosophy as its own. The modern, we might say, as Baudelaire conceived it and as Rilke elaborated it, is just the imaginative transformation to which I've alluded.

In the literature of the modern, the principle means of transformation is metaphor, and metaphor in itself implies a consciousness that differs in essence from logical reflection. In metaphor, the positioning of a perception or sensation in relation with another apparently unconnected to it implies, actually demands, the existence of a mysterious, unpredictable, nonrational process in the mind, something that exists previous to consciousness and is inexplicable to it. The rational aspects of consciousness, intellect and logic can't predict the movements of the imagination as it moves through its metaphors. In modern poetry, more than those of the past, this is particularly striking because here metaphor works primarily by bringing together not similar things but things that are radically unlike.

This is the beginning of a poem Rilke wrote in the Jardin des Plantes in Paris. Might anyone, by means of any train of logic, have predicted its metaphor?

THE FLAMINGOS

With all the subtle paints of Fragonard
no more of their red and white could be expressed
than someone would convey about his mistress
by telling you, "She was lovely, lying there
still soft with sleep."

(Translation by Stephen Mitchell)

The place in the mind from which the metaphor came to Rilke is a place simply not available to ordinary thought. In this new epoch in which imagination is in some senses set free, the mind is intrinsically less constrained than it had ever been.

Only a few years after Rilke, Apollinaire, and then the Surrealists, would make the passionate commitment to metaphor—and the unconscious that metaphor implies—the foundation of their epistemology and the aesthetic morality they elaborated from it. Apollinaire is its chief theoretician, most notably in his masterpiece, "Zone," which begins:

In the end you are weary of this ancient world
This morning the bridges are bleating Eiffel Tower or herd
Weary of living in Roman antiquity and Greek
Here even the motor cars look antique
Religion has stayed young religion
Has stayed simple like the hangars at Port Aviation
                              (Translation by William Meredith)

Bridges like sheep, the Eiffel tower as a shepherdess, religion as simple as an airplane hangar? In Apollinaire, the city, Paris particularly, and its inhabitants become the vehicle of the imagination; anything and everything can become not what it believed it was, but the vehicle of a metaphor, its irrational element, whose workings are like those of dream.

Many lifetimes later, the Romanian, Paul Celan, living in Paris, writing in German, is hyperconscious, too, of what the city might mean:

MEMORY OF FRANCE

Together with me recall: the sky of Paris, that giant autumn crocus . . .
We went shopping for hearts at the flower girl's booth:
they were blue and they opened up in the water.
It began to rain in our room,
and our neighbor came in, Monsieur Le Dream, a lean little man.
We played cards. I lost the irises of my eyes;
you lent me your hair, I lost it, he struck us down.
He left by the door, the rain followed him out.
We were dead and were able to breathe.
                              (Translation by Michael Hamburger)

Walter Benjamin's project for the last part of his life was a study of the "passages" of Paris, the series of commercial arcades within buildings that were constructed as a means of vitalizing new neighborhoods in the north of the city. The mysterious inwardness of the passages intrigued Benjamin; their existence reinforced certain aspects of the urban reality that already existed. The entire city seemed to have acquired an unconscious of its own, one in which were revealed symbols and implications it had kept hidden even from itself until the poets and writers arrived to reveal them. Even today, strolling or stalking through the city seems to involve some kind of problem of mind, a project of imagination, even if we aren't aware of it. Merely strolling in Paris can seem to have a meaning, a resonance, as though one were a note of a great, inaudible chord. (Miłosz wrote: "Then I gave you the eyes of various people, so that you could look at the same city.") And if we are involved in a project, that of keeping our eyes open and our imaginations acute, aren't we making a kind of progress as we advance through the streets, or through our imagination of the streets? Aren't we making headway through certain elusive systems of self, a self that, now that it has a vast city as a symbol embodying it, has also to be larger, possibly vast, too?

So Paris becomes the city of the soul, a place of profound spiritual struggle; it becomes an agent of transformation, perhaps the most powerful. Isn't this why Rilke's Malte comes to Paris in the first place? To be able to enact his intuition that the essential task of the heart now is the transformation of itself and everything else, of all existence? And the first thing Rilke learns in his desolate young poet's loneliness is that the city will both wound and abet him in this project because the city demands transformation; to a sensibility like Rilke's, it is intolerable as it is, untenable, swarming with desire and death, with time and decay, with human sadness and ecstasy.

Here is Rilke in the fullness of his genius, in Malte, articulating the terrible dramas the city can reveal.

> But the woman, the woman: she had completely fallen into herself, forward into her hands. It was on the corner of the rue Notre-Dame-des-Champs. I began to walk quietly as soon as I saw her. When poor people are thinking, they shouldn't be disturbed. Perhaps their idea will still occur to them.
>
> The street was too empty; its emptiness had gotten bored and pulled my steps out from under my feet and clattered around in them, all over the street, as if they were wooden clogs. The woman sat up, frightened, she pulled out of herself, too quickly, too violently, so that her face was left in her two hands. I could see it lying there: its hollow form. It cost me an indescribable effort to stay with those two hands, not to look at what had been torn out of them. I shuddered to see a face from the inside, but I was much more afraid of that bare flayed head waiting there, faceless.
>
> (Translation by Stephen Mitchell)

"An indescribable effort." Yes, that is what our transformations demand. But really, isn't this finally why everyone, all, come to Paris, the real city or the one of our hopes? Because nowhere else is the transformation of self, and the mysterious unknown possibilities of self, so apparent? Yet the city, in its transformative mode, will always stay out ahead of us, always in some sense elude us, the way consciousness itself can elude us, so that often the way through the city, just because it promises so much, can be loneliness, pain, unbearable compassion, and a constant and acute sense of what life might be, and isn't.

"The shape of a city changes," Baudelaire writes in "Le Cygne," "faster, alas, than a human heart." (*La forme d'une ville change plus vite, hélas! que le coeur d'un mortel.*)

Letter to a German Friend

This essay was written over a period from 1998 to 2001 after a stay of some months at the American Academy in Berlin. It was subsequently published in a different form in Germany and the Netherlands. After the attack on the World Trade Center, it seemed to me to have become somewhat dated—primarily of historical interest—and I presumed I would save it to publish one day in a collection of essays.

There are two elements that have made me decide to publish it in English now.[1] *First, the resurgence of anti-Semitism in Europe and the Middle and Far East, and perhaps in America as well, if many of the commentators on the recent (2004) film* The Passion of the Christ *are correct in their evaluation of it.*

And of course since 9/11 and since our ill-conceived war on Iraq, Americans have had to begin to come to grips with the sad fact that our country has become "symbolic" in the same sense in which I use the term in this essay to describe the Germans. Americans are troubled and confused just as the Germans are, since so few of us feel we've ever participated in even the most distant way in any of the offenses of which our nation is presumed guilty by those who see us now as a symbol, more than a people. We are being forced to examine our history and our common conscience in a way we never expected

---

1. "Now" refers to fall 2004, when this essay was originally published in *Salmagundi*.

we would have to. *If our symbolic identity does not have, or does not have yet, as much sway over our perception of ourselves as it does to German and Jew, it is no longer something to which we can afford not to attend, and we have certainly realized already that it is not an uncomplicated matter to try to shed such definitions.*

1

Another television documentary about the Holocaust, this one made by Germans. Some recently unearthed films, the usual horrors; one which I found especially rending of a mother being herded like a sheep away from her crying child, just a toddler, eighteen months or so, like my youngest grandson—awful. Then several German war veterans speaking of atrocities, some who claimed to have seen nothing, and done nothing, some who had seen, yes—one nearly tearful as he recalled an old Jew holding his two daughters against him as they were shot—but done nothing themselves, but no one who had both seen and done anything. Many recited the usual litany: were the Germans guilty, are they still guilty? Yes, no, yes. None of the poor old men realized that what troubles them has little or nothing to do with guilt.

I thought of you, naturally, of your work, of our conversations. I thought, too, of how complex the connection still is between German and Jew. Even us: we're close friends now, we have no apparent conflicts or tensions, nothing either of us wouldn't say to the other, yet it can still feel as though there's some mystery between us, perhaps not so much as individuals, but certainly as representatives of our two peoples: the German and the Jew. We can seem to be terribly different from one another, embodying radically divergent realities. Sometimes it can even seem we're *demonstrations* of something; I'm not sure what. Perhaps human beings always signify more than we think we do, or intend to. This can be a good thing, when we're regarded as admirable, but even then it can be distressing because it has more to do with what the world thinks of us than how we conceive ourselves.

I think that's why I'm writing this, because no matter how we put to one side what happened between the Germans and the Jews, there's still something almost inevitably awry in the way we are in the world together, and I'd like to find a way to better situate us in that complex, possibly saddening affiliation.

It would be good to be together again to talk about all of this, especially if it could be in Berlin. I miss Berlin. That's a statement a few years ago I'd have been taken aback to find myself making; I probably never would have come to the city at all if I hadn't been invited for a residency, and I'm still surprised at how sympathetic I found it to be and how quickly my affection for it grew. Needless to say, from time to time I questioned my feeling of warmth towards a Germany city, and occasionally I've thought that the source of my positive feelings was due at least partly to the feeling I often had when I was in Berlin that *I wouldn't be harmed*. I was certain, and at some level was quite taken aback to be certain, that although I was in the very heart of what had once been the heart of evil, I was in no jeopardy; I even felt somehow protected, like a child whose vulnerability is taken into account by those around him.

And I wasn't harmed, even at the farthest edges of my spirit, even in those parts of me that can be as sensitive as unknit wounds. Not only most of the people I met, but the ambiance of the city, its streets and parks, its forests—so many unlikely hectares of trees—seemed to want to be sure that none of my ancient suppurations would be so much as breathed upon.

Wouldn't be harmed. Amazing. For in other times and places in Germany I had been harmed. When I visited Dachau when I was in my twenties, before I'd even really begun to meditate on what took place there, I knew I was being hurt, injured, that my spirit was being irrevocably afflicted with an anguish I would take to my grave. It was so desolating to be in a place that was the very incarnation of iniquity, in which one's ethical meaning as a human seemed sullied and rent. As I gaped at those strands of wire, those decrepit barracks, that plaque in the earth marked "Ash-Grave," I had the impression that I was supposed to *do* something, and when I didn't, because I had no inkling of what I might do or what might be done, I realized for the first time how powerless we can be in our moral universe.

Yet in Berlin, the place where so much of that evil was conceived, even in Wannsee, where I lived, and where the notorious Wannsee Conference took place, where men actually sat around a table, with cups of coffee, I imagine, to plan the annihilation of races—even in Wannsee I was exultantly unwounded; nor at the Savignyplatz, nor the Literaturhaus, nor the Altemuseum with its gorgeous Greek platter depicting Achilles solicitously bandaging Patroclus's arm. Even in the old synagogue in Mitte, which, because it was located too perilously close to other, blameless buildings to be blown up or burnt down during the war, instead had been degraded by being turned into a stable—even there; nowhere did I feel betrayed by the least moral or historical toxicity.

But my time in Berlin wasn't completely untroubled; there were things that did disturb me—some directly, some more obliquely, abstractly. While I was there, a well-known German author gave what quickly became a controversial speech about German Holocaust guilt, during which he expressed more than anything else how sick and tired he was of it all. He said he believed the Germans' "historical sensitivity" was being exploited by people whose motives were "nefarious at worst, monetary at best." There was a response by the head of the German Jewish community, the argument escalated, and soon became, as such things mostly do, sensational and rhetorical and off the point. I heard nothing I hadn't heard before, although the author's tone, his frank irritation and animus, was new to me.

What interested me much more while I was in Berlin, and made me more uncomfortable, sadder, I suppose I should say, was the perplexity I sensed still afflicted my German friends about the Holocaust, about what their obligation was to its memory, what the limits of that obligation should be, and whether there should be any enduring sense of responsibility at all. I came to feel that there was something the Germans, even the most perspicacious, even you, didn't quite understand about themselves, which I thought I might.

For a long time now the Germans have argued with the world and among themselves about Germany's guilt, or lack of it, but it seems to me that what the Germans haven't comprehended is how much in a peculiar, and essential, way you're like the Jews now. That is, how much you've become, like the Jews, a symbolic people.

We both know all too well that when one even mentions German and Jew together in our time, the Holocaust immediately intrudes. It can seem absurd that events that occurred more than fifty years ago should continue to be so pressing and to generate so much intense feeling on all sides. There have been enough catastrophes in our past; if the word "genocide" has come to be used too freely, certainly some atrocities well merit the term. Sometimes I think the reason the Holocaust retains such vitality, and appears so absolutely singular, might be aesthetic as much as moral. Perhaps we cling to it so much more tenaciously than to any of those other horrors because none of them has as much purely dramatic coherence. I mean "dramatic" in the strictly theatrical sense of the term, because all that happened during the years of the Third Reich can seem to have a certain unity, a self-containedness, like Greek tragedy. Just as the classical tragedies have a temporal coherence that makes them strikingly apprehensible to the imagination—all taking place in the course of a day, from dawn to night—so the twelve-year period of the Nazi epoch has a similarly cohesive, comprehensible structure. It had a well-demarcated beginning, when Hitler was appointed chancellor of the republic, and an equally definite ending, when Germany was overrun, Berlin destroyed, Hitler's corpse burnt on the ruins of the city, the death camps revealed to the world, and their remaining prisoners released. The period even has some of the near-ritual quality of tragedy, in the way its plot inexorably unfolds, with shifts of tone and texture as the crimes accumulate and begin to generate their own retribution; the whole narrative seems to take place close to the very essence of the psyche, the way myths do: Oedipus or Antigone, Moses or Christ. None of the other disasters of our recent and even long ago history is so structurally coherent, and surely this is one of the reasons why they don't have quite the same emotional and moral fascination for us; none has what might be called the tragic *glamour* of the Holocaust.

And of course there are intrinsic reasons why the Holocaust still burns so for us. The sheer numbers involved, the brutal, methodical industrialization of murder, the overt moral malignancy of the Nazis, their apparent dedication to situating themselves, and all Germany, in contempt of ordinary norms of civilization—not to speak of those images recorded on film, then after the war in words, that seem etched into consciousness itself: the faces of people on their way to the gas chamber; the gaunt, ravaged bodies of the survivors, with their hollow, stricken gazes; men bludgeoned to death in public; women and children shot by high-powered weapons intended for the battlefield; starvation, degradation. They're distressingly reliable, these little playlets of horror and dread—the alertness they evoke, the vehemence of attention: they demand an utter absorption from us. Like the erotic, they're irresistible, and they feel connected to that fundamental place in us where good and evil and beauty and ugliness are grounded. Our historical grief for that time is very much like grief for a person: just as after months, years, decades, the memory of a loved one can erupt with freshened sorrow, all the hours of mourning coming together to inform this new sadness, so these racks and tangles of corpses, these ashes eternally burning their way towards the molten center of existence emerge in us, and in a hideous epiphany we are forced to think again: *This happened, this really did happen!*

2

> I am not "guilty," I experience neither "guilt" nor "shame," I am quite convinced all of those dreadful matters which happened so long ago have nothing to do with me, and yet I feel afflicted, and, I feel, too, that the world, or certain elements of it, wish me to feel afflicted.

This is the essence of what I heard when the famous writer stirred up his tempest while I was in Germany; he implied, of course, that he wasn't alone in this, that many if not most Germans feel the same way, and I believed him. *The Germans are "normal" now,* he was saying, *why can't I, we, be allowed to live normally?*

What he had not understood, I think, was that the Germans have been for several generations, and will continue to be for at least some time, not a normal nation, like the French or Italians, but, as I have said, a symbolic people, like the Jews, one of those social groups whose definition in the minds of others is not who they are, nor what they do, but what they stand for. As much as human beings can be, they are emblems, signs.

To be emblematic, symbolic in this way isn't necessarily always a bad thing. Sometimes the connotations that inform the symbolic identity of a group can be positive, particularly if they are evaluations the group has generated for itself. Thus the Jews considered themselves the "chosen people" long before that notion came to have the opprobrium attached to it that signified those who had refused and continued to refuse the new spiritual cosmos Christ inaugurated. But for the most part, and certainly in this context, symbolic characteristics attributed to groups are negative—so the fact that the Jews defined themselves as a unique, "chosen" people, surely added to the intensity of gentiles' antipathy towards them. Similarly, the apparent wholeheartedness with which the Germans welcomed Hitler's promises of racial purity, and their eager acceptance of his depiction of them as conquerors, destined to dominate Europe and the world, intensifies the negative force of the symbolic identity you must bear now.

It's been remarked that some people who have been blind their whole lives and recover their sight feel resentful to realize that during the time they were blind they'd been visible to other people, without their having been asked and without having suspected what being "seen" consisted of. There has to be an equivalent perturbation in confronting that one isn't what one thought one was but, rather, a symbol of something else. I feel genuine solicitude for Germans, at least those like you who've seriously tried to understand their place in history, when I think of the confusion you'd have had to feel in realizing at some point in your process of maturation that you were enwrapped in an invisible, seemingly gratuitous robe of emblematic identity, something that meant nothing to you and too much to too many others.

This is a discovery the children of despised minorities make early on, nearly as soon as they intuit their place in their social world, and there can be something affecting in how unprepared Germans seem to be when you comprehend that you're burdened with this double self. The realization must be exacerbated by how late it can dawn on you, in most cases probably only when you begin to reflect seriously on world and self. Such matters occur in a place very close to the core of self-evaluation and sense of worth, and for many, this recognition has to be appalling. The symbolic personality, which exists outside but along with the life one actually lives, must feel at first so inessential, so supremely trivial, like the beginning of a toothache. Unlike Jews or Blacks, whose symbolic definition is an ongoing dilemma that demands a dedicated and often maddening attention, a German can easily conceive of living his entire life without having to consider the implications of symbolic identity at all, and probably most Germans do precisely that.

For most of us our symbolic identity always arrives unexpectedly, with a kind of pounce. It came to me when I was eight or nine and a friend and I had been wrestling, as we all often did. My friend had tripped me up, I'd fallen, he was holding me down, we were both laughing, and then suddenly he slapped my face—*Jew-Bastard!*—hard, on one side, then—*Christ Killer!*—still harder on the other, and he kept at it until I would admit as he demanded that I was a "dirty Jew," that I'd "killed Christ." A tiny story, entirely a cliché by now, but still, it bothers me to this day. Not my defeat—I'd lost fights before—but my sense of utter astonishment, which was accompanied by feelings not of outrage but of despair. What had changed so much in my friend so that an ordinary afternoon in a park became an occasion for such wild animosity?

I still can't understand. Was it his little experience of power, of having me momentarily helpless, that transmogrified him from an amiable chum to a thug, and me to his foe? Perhaps he'd never experienced the surge of confidence and certainty that goes through us when we've triumphed, even on such a minor scale. Maybe he felt himself released into that state of mind, which I can only imagine, where one no longer has to heed those wearisome prohibitions of good and evil, should and should not. To be not burdened for once by compunction and restraint, by those irritating injunctions from conscience that keep us oscillating in our vision of ourselves between admirable and detestable: all the ordinary exasperating turmoil with which we are afflicted. Perhaps what was so alluring to him was just that, the chance to elude the strictures of conscience and, at the same time, to be other than and greater than he knew he really was. He must have felt for that moment that he had been transformed—he was both himself, and an infinitely more significant other. An ordinary person becoming . . . What? A warrior? A soldier? An SS man? As for me, I'd known for a long time I was a Jew. My parents had told me, and of course, I'd begun to attend synagogue occasionally, and Sunday school. Now I understood what it really could mean. (How uncanny to realize that this happened just at the time when Auschwitz was most ravenously devouring lives.)

But what does it feel like to a German to have it come upon you that you are a sign, a representation, rather than a coherent, unified person? Certainly, it can seem unreasonable that after all the decades that have passed the Germans should still have to bear any symbolic onus. All those things happened long ago, they're finished, the Germans since then for the most part have manifested an impeccable rectitude: why then should the ignominy stay so alive, so current? Why shouldn't that writer be able to say, as he did, "Enough," and have it be the last word on the subject? The answer is relatively straightforward: it's because symbolic thinking is not like other acts of consciousness; in ordinary thought, facts proven wrong move into the category of error and in one way or another are put aside, and ordinary events in the past have a different sort of reality from those of the present and can be forgotten, or repressed. Symbolic thinking doesn't work that way. Symbols have no need for reasons. They're no more susceptible to logical explication than the elemental phenomena of perception. This is precisely the force of symbolism in religion and art. Symbols affect the emotions and the mind more primitively and more profoundly than do ideas. They're *facts*, not arguments. They subsume and obviate analysis and neutralize the possible effect of any rational objection. Dante realized and embodied the uncanny power of symbolic thought in his great *Comedy*; he intuited that our entire spiritual universe could be transfigured to a representative realm and, ultimately, exalted.

At the same time, one of the more sinister potentials of the human mind is how readily actual living people can be transformed to symbols, and how effective this can be in affecting presumably objective thought. A physics textbook published in the Nazi Germany era attacked Albert Einstein as the perpetrator of "Jewish physics," charging that his "theories were meant to reshape and dominate the whole science of physics, but when faced with reality, they lost all shred of validity." Moreover, symbols, even the most pernicious, can stay in effect long beyond what seems reasonable: one of the aspects of symbolic thinking is its timelessness, its inability or unwillingness to allow what is in the past to lose its currency and force.

I have to say it's hard for me to know how Germans actually experience being defined symbolically. For one thing, to feel a conflict within oneself between the nature of one's symbolic identity in the world and one's self-conception isn't at all the same as encountering the active prejudice other more traditionally symbolic peoples confront. There can be few people left anywhere who would turn on their heel and leave a room when a German enters, but there are still many who, confronted with a Jew or a black, for instance, readily revert to stereotypical thinking. When I was in Germany in another city, at a reception after a poetry reading, an editor who had been drinking quite a bit referred to a writer about whom she and another editor had been speaking, as "that Jew." The remark was wholly gratuitous; it had no connection whatsoever to what was being discussed. I said nothing—being a symbolic person demands such alacrity, such velocity of thinking, and you're rarely alert enough to respond as you'd like to—but I must have flinched, or given some sign of distress, because a young television producer with whom I'd been chatting sensed it and asked me, "Are you Jewish?" When I replied I was, his attentiveness immediately increased; I could tell I was *interesting* to him now in a way I hadn't been before.

Although there was nothing negative in his response to me, rather the contrary, I was to him now first and foremost a Jew, and what's more, he had no sense of how my ethnic-symbolic identity had taken precedence over everything else he knew about me, just as the drunken editor had less benevolently recast her characterization of the writer she mentioned so that his Jewishness preceded everything else about him.

Precedence. It's always startling: one stops being one thing and becomes another. For the other person a kind of mask comes over you, and now there are a fresh set of assumptions about you, having to do with qualities that come before your actual character and experience. For a moment, one seems to be nothing at all, an absence, a conditional, while the other arranges his perception to resituate you in his new scheme of things. And in this drama, whatever else comes to pass, there is one attribute you know for certain you will no longer possess, which is uncomplicatedness, and that therefore you can no longer be a part of an unselfconscious relationship with the other person. It's not that you're defined as less accessible to the other; it's just that you are much less real, and he or she don't even necessarily realize it.

In America, when the civil rights movement was getting under way, many African Americans recounted incidents in which as children they would all at once be made to realize that they were "different." By the nature of their physical being they were now defined by the world of whites, the majority world, which determined for the most part the values of their whole society, as *other*, and this otherness had dreadful connotations. Suddenly they had had to discover that there were conditions to existence, conditions that had no basis in logic or ordinary modes of understanding. We don't always appreciate how troubled children are by disruptions of logic; the young learn early on that the pathways through mind have intimate connections to the world beyond: we've hardly set out in life when we realize how precious the equations of cause and effect are in interpreting and affecting the world. The child experiencing prejudice, realizing that he is being disvalued in another's eyes for no apparent reason, suffers more than hurt; he is confronted with the disintegration of what he has been taught is the essential premise of existence—cause and effect. The heart stutters to learn that all of that is invalid now, that you are being regarded through tangles of assumption about which you can do nothing, that you are no longer as you once were in the causal world. It shouldn't be surprising that the children of oppressed minorities have more difficulty getting themselves into accord with the norms and procedures of the majority educational system. They have learned that reality is not what they had been taught it was, so why should they devote attention and energy to an alien set of beliefs about the relation of mind and world, however useful society tries to convince them it might be?

The annoyance some Germans express about the way they're perceived by the rest of the world, and about how little responsibility they feel they have for that perception, can be both touching and exasperating. The Germans have endured their symbolic onus for several generations—the Jews have had the same fate for a score of centuries, and continue to be a resource to whom demagogues everywhere from the Duma in Moscow to Iran can turn when they need to dredge up a scapegoat. But still, the desire for "normality" does seem like a straightforward aspiration to be like everyone else, neither more nor less—though this issue, too, is monumentally complicated. Isaiah Berlin once said that to be normal means to feel that one isn't being observed, and it certainly can be irksome to feel always on display as an odd or unusual phenomenon. But being normal might also be defined as being not bound to a symbolic identity, not being a demonstration or proof or disproof of something beyond the self. Normality implies that one has the right to assemble the qualities about oneself one decides are essential for evolving identity, even if they're not necessarily comforting. The mortification of becoming a symbol is that one's entire being is compressed within new parameters, that one is no longer perceived as what one has striven to be. Feelings understandably can become intense; when the matrix of the conflict from which symbols have been generated is so tragically compelling as the Holocaust, the knots of emotion can appear inextricable.

Truly, the Third Reich had a frightening genius for bringing forth symbols of radical figurative force, phenomena that still resonate with a charge of violence and fear. The swastika; the yellow star, and the pink and red; the panzer, the Stuka, the Luger, the jackboot, the lager; even the words: lebensraum, blitzkrieg, Kristallnacht. Even in translation the words retain their power: master race, the Night of the Long Knives, book burning. And all this is beside the imagery of that time, the glimpses of inhumanity that have such convulsive force for us: the cattle cars, the barracks, the gas chambers and ovens and chimneys;

even the greasy smoke that was said to permeate the very earth of country around; even the odors, the singular stench of human bodies burning. What other moral system is characterized even by its odors?

All of these symbols have entered the lexicon of historical and ethical reflection. We can believe these dreadful evils were a wild aberration, the result of a particular historical happenstance or anomaly, but they are still facts that humans have to explore in the world and in ourselves in order to be certain that our moral vision is as comprehensive as it must be. How long they will maintain their intensity, their power to put conscience in a state of alert, will probably depend on what new desecrations human beings find to inflict on themselves. But in our time we're derelict if we don't take them into account in our ethical meditations. World War II and the Holocaust have become references, measures, scales; they are the very essence for us of unreasonable violence, of malignant and limitless political rapacity. Further, even the relatively peaceful period leading up to the Reich, the apparent atmosphere of tolerance during that time as contrasted with what came after it, embodies other paradoxes our societies still confront. That Germany was so apparently civilized a nation, with so consummate a culture, and that so much evil could be regurgitated from beneath that decorous veneer, makes it integral to any consideration of collective moral hypocrisy.

When certain Germans plead in essence to be left alone, to be normal, they're not only being naïve in their assumption that we can select the symbols we wish to have attached to us, but they misread history, innocently attributing to it more solicitude and generosity than there is much evidence it has. The unfortunate truth is that one isn't allowed by the world to renounce one's symbolic identity: its qualities and resilience are determined by others. The reasons history keeps alive or allows a symbolic identification to fade away is complicated, not to say capricious.

The image of the relentlessly vindictive SS man still ineluctably informs the German symbolic identity, but even ordinary Germans of that time evoke daunting issues of individual choice and will. It has never really been explained how Hitler managed to induce an entire nation to perpetrate the kind of savagery, the gross depravity and corruption that it did. Did Hitler have some knowledge more effective than that possessed by any emperor or king or barbarian chieftain that allowed him to cajole his people—his subjects, I suppose they should be called—to sanction crimes inconceivable to the most madly cruel and arbitrary tyrant? It's occurred to me that Hitler himself, even in his life, may have been in some ways an entirely symbolic creature, to have neither had nor wanted any other sort of existence. We know his body was never a source of pleasure for him. Early on he gave up any commitment to the corporeal: no real sex, no delight in eating; at the end a doctor in constant attendance to keep his physical shell in order, but no more. This sense of himself as a symbol might help explain his obsession with the Jews, whom he had designated as his adversaries, we might say his symbolic opposites, and why he was willing to sacrifice so much—the entire German nation, really—in his combat with them. It might also help to understand why admirers coming into his presence found themselves affected with something like vertigo, the sense of losing their spiritual bearings. Some explained this as a result of Hitler's magnetism, or their awe before his power, but perhaps it wasn't merely power Hitler manifested towards these lesser beings, but scorn, for their existence as mere personalities, afflicted with ambiguity and need, rather than having been elevated beyond all such banal concerns as he had been.

Yet none of this answers the question of the Germans' homicidal then suicidal fealty to Hitler. Yes, Depression, yes, debilitating war reparations, inflation, yes, all the propaganda, but still, again, how *that*? It is an abiding quandary and surely one of the reasons why there is an ever ongoing analysis of the German psyche of that time. Some of those inquiries have been distressingly crude, positing an eternal and all-determining anti-Semitism on the part of the Germans. This conclusion is morally repugnant in itself and slights the larger question of how any group of people could have been so radically submissive, allowing themselves to be associated in any way with such clear ethical transgressions.

Some—many—Germans did refuse to participate in the vileness, and this makes the questions even more complicated. In fact, the "Good German," too, has come to have a symbolic connotation almost as intricate as that of the German war criminal: the people who tried and sometimes succeeded in protecting their Jewish acquaintances or helping them to escape, the several priests who sacrificed their lives by sermonizing against the regime, the officers in the failed plot to assassinate Hitler, and, most touching, the "Edelweiss Pirates," the tiny movement of dissident adolescents, most of whom were betrayed and hanged.

Yet still, the exclusionary nature of the term itself, "Good German," implies that there weren't enough, that more Germans should have resisted, protested, done something, anything. We ask a great deal of those ordinary Germans, though, those who after all were so much like us, our neighbors, our families, ourselves. We ask of them that they should have been stronger, more heroic, to have taken greater risks. The word "risk" won't do, though, because given the efficiency and extent of the gestapo's surveillance, to do anything at all meant to be prepared to sacrifice one's life. Dare we ask ourselves whether we would have the valor to attempt resistance in such a situation? In the sheltered and privileged environment I live now, I'm aware that within meters of where I live, there are poor people, some desperately so, who suffer political and social neglect and contempt, and yet I forgive myself the fact that I do essentially nothing for them, and rationalize my inaction by telling myself that these problems are too great for any one person's efforts, that they are issues for specialists who in democracies are appointed to attend to them. But in my heart I know that I am in truth no more ethically scrupulous, courageous, or "good," than the Germans were back then.

3

No wonder Germans can feel put upon by the assumptions made about them and the demands that ensue from those assumptions. Certainly it's distressing to have a single component of your existence, something that you don't necessarily feel has much to do with you at all, become the resolving fact of the way your life is evaluated. This is the ineluctable predicament of symbolic identity, and there is no way to experience it without anxiety. Jews, as I've said, have known this for a long time, having been characterized for centuries by our cultural and "racial" difference: a people to be at best tolerated, at worst rejected, expelled, and finally wiped out.

It's no small irony that the Germans should find themselves symbolically bound to a people who have themselves been symbols for so long, and that many Germans don't at all appreciate how intricately their destiny is interwoven now with the destiny of the Jews. As long as the Jews are designated as a symbolically distinct entity, then so may Germany remain in the memory of humanity as those who kill Jews, a unique instance of destructiveness and malice. The Jew as victim has as its antithesis the German as perpetrator, and this is naturally more irritating to Germans than to Jews, not only because of its moral accusation but also because the Germans are just less used to such things. A Jew can feel both sympathy and a sense of vindication at beholding the Germans struggle with this, but it can also seem pathetic, even repellent, to hear Germans bemoan their inability to rehabilitate their symbolic fate and to extricate themselves from any association with that particular act of the Jewish epic of suffering.

Isn't it the most short-sighted vanity to believe that one can assemble one's own destiny and be able to get shed of the portions of it one doesn't find agreeable because one had no participation in their choice? Destiny by definition is precisely what arrives on us despite our intentions and acts. Perhaps the most complex issue the Germans have to deal with is whether they are symbols not only to the rest of humanity but to themselves as well. One can play the game of shame and repentance and still not accept the intricate personal implications such a complex identity entails; the one attitude that is clearly unacceptable is to believe that "this has nothing to do with me."

This is not, I think, about "guilt." The very word "guilt" has been eviscerated; instead of clarifying, it can obfuscate. Rather than specifying a moral condition, it can arise from and serve political expediency. But perhaps the concepts of guilt, or shame, can regain their efficacy if they are considered as processes rather than as states, as stages of the healing of historical lesions, on the part both of those whose group committed wrongs and of the world in which they must exist. I doubt whether there is any kind of atonement or any vow or act of repentance that the Germans can make to extirpate the reality of that period, but there's no question that symbols, even entire peoples as symbols, do lose their brute force over time. Who can surmise now what the menace of the Huguenots was to the orthodox of sixteenth- and seventeenth-century France that brought about so many deaths? Or reimagine the passion of the Crusaders as they slaughtered the Arabs of Acre, or the homicidal fervor of the missionaries to numberless European colonies in the face of the recalcitrance of their "heathens." There are shifts of affective structures, perceptions alter, a nation or race or cult no longer has the meaning it did, but it's crucial to understand that this shift is never because the designated people themselves desire it: there has to be some significant historical shift, a change of worldview, before the imagery and resonance of a symbol provokes no feeling, or at least no intense feeling, and reinforces no prejudice. The Jews of nineteenth-century Germany went to enormous lengths to alter the perception of their symbolic selves, even resorting to the debasing recourse of false conversion, and yet we know too well how shallowly in the psyches of their countrymen these alterations were actually perceived. The Germans will have to recognize that it's neither by active repentance nor by passive hope for forgetfulness that they'll be released from the onus of their symbolic definition.

Even as I write this, a part of me suspects that the memory of the Holocaust will someday lose its capacity to evoke outrage, that it will come to have an interest more aesthetic or anthropological than moral, and that the Germans will be freed of their burden as symbols long before the Jews. The Jewish symbolic identity is engraved so deeply into the historical psyche of the world that there seems no way in which the Jews will ever be disregarded, ever be entirely normal or unobserved in the way Isaiah Berlin meant.

If finally there is anything that remains to be asked of the Germans by the Jews, I suppose it would be that, even if their own symbolic identity comes to be expunged by history, the Germans continue to acknowledge to themselves that their past remains part of a syllogism that includes the historical torment of the Jews and that this acknowledgment must be accomplished with good grace.

"Good grace": such an odd little phrase. I don't know if anything like it exists in German, or if it can be easily translated. With forbearance, courtesy, and a recognition of the community constituted by the asker of this forbearance, and the asked. There have been indications that many Germans are aware of this, the memorials and the museums, but there have also been clear cases of the contrary as well. The famous writer who issued his complaint about being put upon by having to remember Auschwitz and who cast the blame for it on those who were using the Holocaust for their own repugnant purposes proposed, as a certain amount of German discussion seems to, that the problem be resolved and the bothersome debate ended by having the Jews in Germany once and for all "assimilate." I don't believe that even in his exacerbated annoyance the writer understood what he was implying by his statement. When you bid someone to assimilate into "your" society, isn't what you're really saying something like this: that if you, you others, will give up, renounce, or at the least profoundly revise who you are—not just the symbolic identity that constitutes you now but your *essence*—we will be agreeable to accepting you as one of "us." In other words, we will deign to not regard you any longer as primarily symbolic, and *our* symbolic identity will be neutralized, or at least minimized, as well.

If this is an indication of the Germans' notion of what will be their "normality," then perhaps if anything is to be asked of them then, it is precisely that they *not* be normal, but *different*, *unlikely*, that they find ways to demonstrate that the awareness of being in association, if not complicity, with a wrong like the Holocaust can become a positive moral force.

But perhaps that is the task for all of us, not only the Germans: that we dwell on that demented time of death not because it allows us to imagine ourselves morally superior to anyone else—that would be something like a pornography of dread—but because we still live in a world in which there is always somewhere in effect a violent symbolic loathing of one sort or another. The human animal has sustained its apparently limitless capacity for transforming neighbor into detested other, subject if not to overt violence then to subtler economic and social oppression. This is a truth that tears at us: it is the ground of our moral dejection and of our covenant of grief. Whether the Holocaust was or was not the worst atrocity ever committed in history isn't finally terribly important. What is crucial is that our reflections on it rouse us to demand more accountability from our institutions, and ourselves, for otherwise we are, again, perhaps for the last time, lost.

Nature and Panic

The first evidence we have of any human doings with nature other than utilitarian artifacts for hunting and fishing are the Paleolithic paintings in caves in France and Spain. These great works of art were created over a period of twenty thousand years, and then stopped; we don't really know why they first began to be created or why they didn't continue.

I think most of us have been tempted to play the game of trying to intuit the vast number of individuals who were born and died during those uncountable millennia and to imagine what a single person's life, a "first person" in both senses of the term, would really have been. For me, the daydream invariably leads me to picture my poor ancestor living in almost constant fear of threats to life and well-being: the predators, the droughts, the erratic cold that sometimes descended and stayed for thousands of years, and sometimes, for reasons we still don't understand, didn't. "Nasty, brutish and short," to quote the Hobbesian cliché.

So, were those people really that much more anxious for themselves than we are? To return to the Paleolithic paintings: there's little evidence of anguish or dread in their subject matter and execution. The creatures in them are depicted with accuracy and detail and with that breathlessly assured brushwork that could have been acquired through nothing but aesthetic dedication and love. There are almost no depictions of nature as threatening. In one painting there's a lion, but she's treated with a whimsical humor; in another two, someone seems to have been killed by a bison, the beginning of what some researchers suspect may have been a series of myths. The only truly malignant matters that are recorded in the caves are a few mysterious and so far uninterpreted recumbent human figures, riven with what seem to be spears: they were possibly murdered, perhaps even tortured. But generally, if the society in which these artists lived was fraught with fear, it certainly isn't manifested in their work. Even their span of years, it turns out, wasn't as short as was once thought: the most recent evidence suggests that people during these eras regularly lived to the age of fifty or sixty.

At the same time, if we pull back a little and consider larger currents of human existence, there does seem to have been ample reason for anxiety. The climate, as I mentioned, often dramatically changed in those epochs. There were long droughts and, at some point, the almost total dying off of reindeer, which had been humans' primary food—with what precise consequences we probably will never know, beyond that humans somehow adapted, and survived.

And we also can't possible know whether any single person, or group, or group of generations would have been aware, and especially daunted, by these grim developments. Perhaps one year, winter came earlier; perhaps another year, the reindeer migrations arrived later, then not at all. Would there have been a history to contain these matters? We don't know that either, but if there was, what would have been the emphasis of those who recorded it? Would they have been depressives, manic-depressives, optimists, pessimists?

I'll continue on a more personal note. Like many people I know, I often have a somewhat—no, a wholly—frightening vision of the future of humanity and of our earth. There are periods when I live in a state of acute anxiety, indeed, near panic, about what awaits our children and grandchildren. Last year, I realized one day that every poem I was writing, or attempting to write, had global warming and its consequences either as its overt or implied theme. Sometimes I'm depressed beyond writing or saying anything at all; I fall into a funk that sometimes threatens never to end.

Given all the evidence that's being accumulated about global warming and its ramifications, this seems a perfectly reasonable response to the only future in sight. However, I've also had to realize over the course of my life that I'm intrinsically somewhat of a depressive person, about much else besides the end of the world, and that my instinctive response to fear, or threat, or despair is to plunge deeper into the darkness that so readily takes me. It required a long time for me to notice that many people respond differently; some friends, for instance, who, when deeply concerned about large matters, can turn readily away from them to a relatively cheerful vision of existence, while I go on brooding, frightened, trembling. And certainly not unsensible public figures can manage to convey a bright vision that confounds personalities like mine. One of my favorite recent examples is Fred Kavli, a wealthy scientist philanthropist who recently established a program of million dollar prizes for scientists and who announced at the first presentation ceremony: "The future is going to be more spectacular than we ever can imagine." I hope with all my heart that he knows something I don't.

I've come to wonder lately what the implication of all this is for my life and work as an artist, a poet. Certainly the traditions of literature, particularly in the last century and a half, have had their fair share of dark personalities—more than mere pessimists, sometimes outrageous nihilists. One of my most enduring poetic influences has been Baudelaire, hardly a paragon of healthy thought. Don't I have a right to express my own sadnesses? I have often enough, lord knows, in the past, and I'm sure I will again, but at the same time, mightn't there be some responsibility in my artistic endeavors I hadn't suspected, hadn't conceived of, until now?

Surely the most extreme vision of the future in recent literature is Cormac McCarthy's novel *The Road*. McCarthy is a novelist of craft, with a powerful gift for verisimilitude, and in his book he puts all his talents at the service of the literally darkest non–science fiction fate that has ever been conceived for human beings. The earth—land and sea—is black with soot and ash, utterly silent except for the wind, some mysterious intermittent explosions, and the several words, most of them threats, human beings still manage to pass between them, before, in many cases, they devour each other. Those of you who have the read the book know that the word "grim" hardly begins to do justice to the sheer horror McCarthy inflicts on the planet, and on us, his readers.

I use the word "inflict" intentionally. I'm not the only person I know who's expressed regret at having ingested the book: I feel sometimes indignant that I have to have it in my consciousness. If there ever was a book that embodied the extremity of the emotion we call panic, this has to be it. I find it's like having a piercing scream in my mind, one that, when the book comes to mind, which it does more often than I'd like, goes off like a siren.

Another recent, much different, book that deals with the possible dark times ahead of us is Gretel Ehrlich's *The Future of Ice*— also a book of premonition and dire prophecy. I'll admit that when I began reading it, I thought I wouldn't be able to go on. Ehrlich's prognostications about the grim future in store for the world seemed mostly to consist of information I already possessed—reading it felt like watching an autopsy of a living body. As I went further into the book, though, I was taken with its intimacy, its presentation of an actual person living a real life while at the same time reflecting on so much melting away, and I found the book finally inspiring, precisely perhaps because it doesn't manifest the kind of annihilating cosmic panic that McCarthy's book does. It tells of the passions and sadnesses of experiencing, having to experience, the fear of knowing what may come to us, but all of that is tempered by the dailiness of the life and loves of the author. *The Future of Ice* contains its own epigraph, its own enduring motto: "Beauty saves me." Until I went back to look for the phrase to quote, I had remembered it as "Beauty saves us," and I've allowed myself to keep it that way.

I find it a bit odd to be using the word "beauty" this way. I've never thought terribly hard about the concept, certainly not as a theoretician, which I'm emphatically not. We all, though, have ideas about what is beautiful and what isn't, and generally we think we know why. And it is, or at least was, tempting, as a poet, to try to be an aesthetician rather than an artist: there's an aura of immediate authority associated with the one that isn't associated with the other. I know that at any moment I'll be able to think and talk for five or ten minutes about beauty: I never know whether in the next five or ten minutes or five or ten years I'll be able to create any.

Beauty won't save the world from the depredations with which it's already been savaged, but it can save us from the enervating despair that is the outcome of panic, that paralysis that might keep us from doing what we can to confront what's before us. We'll never know how our ancestors, so put upon by the enormous unknown world in which they found themselves, persevered and survived, but we do know that they bequeathed to us, and probably infused into our genes, the conviction that the dream and execution of the beautiful made the world ours in a way nothing else could.

However it happens—by whatever complex, forbiddingly imprecise, dauntingly imperfect means—all over the world, if not every day then in every age, art is created and beauty manifested: beautiful paintings and poems and pieces of music and buildings are generated. One can almost imagine small flaring lights on the surface of the earth, like those seen in photos from space, though they are much sparser and more scattered than the illuminating devises that bespeckle our globe. And then over time these embodiments of the beautiful are harvested, amassed, collected in books, in museums, in concert halls, to be distributed into the lives of individual human beings, to become crucial elements of their existence. Often, our experience of beauty will be the first hint of what each of us at some point will dare call our soul. For don't those first stirrings of that eternally uncertain, barely grasped notion of something more than mere mind, mere thought, mere emotion usually first come to us in the line of a poem, a passage of music, or the unreal yet more than real image in a painting?

And isn't it also the case that beauty is the one true thing we can count on in a world of insufferable uncertainty, of obdurate, relentless moral conflicts? I've wondered sometimes if humans invented gods not to tend to our moral or immoral selves but to have something appropriately sensitive and grand and wise enough to appreciate these miraculous nodes of beauty that are so different in material and quality from anything else in the world. Might gods have first been devised not to assuage our fears and hear our complaints and entreaties but for there to be identities sufficiently sublime to understand what those first painters and sculptors, and surely, though the words and tunes have been lost, those poets and singers had wrought?

Perhaps this is why those first great art works were executed deep in caves, so as to be certain the divinities who were their audience wouldn't be distracted by the wonder of the natural world, and so lose the concentration necessary to glory in, and be glorified by, these singular human creations that equaled and even surpassed what had been given by nature for meditation. And perhaps that's why poets and painters, who may half-remember such matters, go off into what can look to others like solitary caverns, shadowed with loneliness, but which surely aren't. Beauty saves us. Beauty will save us. The world, though, is still ours to cherish, and ours to protect.

On Being Old

A novelist friend of mine published an essay a few years ago called "On Being Beautiful." I was inspired by her to try a similar title, one that might hearten me to be as frank as she was. Although a few readers grumbled about the possible vanity implied in my friend's words, she is indeed beautiful, as I am indeed old.

I remember the first time I was referred to in print as a "young poet"—it happened just about the time I thought I'd moved into early middle age. For some reason poets continue to be called young for a both gratifyingly and irritatingly long time, then you're not anything in particular, and finally you're referred to as . . . well, like me, old—or worse, elderly, a word that seems to have lurking in it various horrendous decrepitudes. So I'll begin by noting that the hardest part of being old is admitting to yourself you actually are. That sounds more aphoristic than I mean it to be: the truth is it's a duel, a savage battle. Ten or a hundred times a day sirens wail to remind you that for a minute or two you may have forgotten you're seventy-something and that you'd better face the fact more realistically. Except there are no instructions as to how to do this: you just know you're kidding yourself if you slip into the benign indifference to passing time we're allowed to enjoy most of our lives.

The rest of aging, at least so far, isn't as bad as it might be. My body hangs together pretty well—the only time it's a bother is when I happen to catch sight of myself in a mirror, especially late at night after too much sight-clearing wine. The upsetting thing then is how in its softenings and sags the body looks simply *stupid*. It doesn't understand the way it once did how important a personage it's lugging around—otherwise it wouldn't dare appear in this gnarled disguise.

It occurs to me to wonder how some of my poet heroes would have looked undressed when they were old. One of the ones I most admire, Robert Frost, I actually met when I was twenty and he was eighty-three. I had a little fling with his granddaughter and had the chance to spend some time with him. I was so awed that I had no idea what to say to him; I just watched. Physically, by then his face was like a sculpture of itself: something in the public rather than the private realm. His granddaughter I might add was my first critic. I'd just begun to write and had never shown a poem to anyone but a few nonpoet friends. She'd read a lot of poetry, and when I read a poem to her, the second I'd ever written, she said, "That's awful," and I knew she was right.

Which is another thing about looking back from so far: wondering how it all happened to happen. I remember the first time I wrote a reasonably successful poem, but not what I'd had to learn in order to write it. I had an inspiring teacher in college, Morse Peckham, who was then just writing a book on the close reading of poetry, and I learned at least how to read a poem from him, if not how to write one. I also got to know the great architect Louis Kahn quite well: he was a fanatical worker, and I took from him how dedicated you had to be to your art. I came a little later to meet some poets around my age, who taught me a lot. But it still remains a genuine mystery to me how I ever spun a competent poem out of so much snarl.

But I was speaking of the time before all that, when I was subjected to Frost's granddaughter's painful appraisal. I survived that, and worse over the years, but one of the benefits of having lived this long in poetry is that one comes, gratefully, to feel quite distant from the theatrics of criticism. Even if I might still squirm a bit from jabs at my work, I've attained a certain equanimity—except, I should add, when it's clear that a critic hasn't read my poems carefully, or at all. That can happen surprisingly often, and still makes my teeth grind. Mostly, though, it's hard not to perceive the sheer absurdity of the stance of many critics, the way they assume they're more intimate with the genre about which they're commenting than mere practitioners. Certainly critics "know" things, sometimes quite well, but the conviction some have that what they know is more germane to the production of poetry than the poet can be irksome, to say the least. This is almost never the case when poets write criticism. The greatest poet-critics, like Auden, Heaney, Mandelstam, and Brodsky, always inform their considerations with an awareness of how difficult is the accomplishing of poetry, and how hard it is even to think fruitfully about it.

Young poets, in contrast, can be pretty obnoxious about it all. The poet friends I mentioned above—one of whom had already at eighteen published a book, the fact of which woefully intimidated me—had a sincere passion to protect the world from what they considered bad poems. *Danger*! they'd cry. *Don't even look! You might turn to poetry stone*! I never could share their fervor and contempt, not because of anything I can call generosity but because I didn't have the confidence to be that certain about anything. I still mostly don't—I've become over the years more and more conscious of the vagaries of taste.

How shifty a thing taste can be, how shitty, even one's own. I tremble to remember the poets, like Elizabeth Bishop, I dismissed out of hand, whose greatness dawned on me only later. Then there are poets I once admired and who opened ways through thickets for me, but whose work now I find clumsy and shiftless. I think we all tend to believe we can see through the vagaries of our moment to some absolute standard of judgment—this must be a characteristic of human consciousness itself—but the conviction is absurd. So, I never blab anymore about poets whose work doesn't or no longer moves me. But there are, however and thank goodness, poets the power and force of whose work once nearly knocked me down with delight and envy, and still does, so that when I read them again I feel again like an apprentice. About whom here's a poem:

WHACKED

Every morning of my life I sit at my desk getting whacked by some great
  poet or other.
Some Yeats, some Auden, some Herbert or Larkin, and lately a whole
  tribe of others—
oi!—younger than me. Whack! Wiped out, every day . . . I mean since
  becoming a poet.
I mean wanting to—one never is, really, a poet. Or I'm not. Not when
  I'm trying to write,

though then comes a line, maybe another, but still pops up again Yeats,
   say, and again whacked.

. . . Wait . . . Old brain in my head I'd forgotten that "whacked" in
   crime movies means murdered,
rubbed out, by the mob—little the mob-guys would think that poets
   could do it, and who'd believe
that instead of running away you'd find yourself fleeing towards them,
   some sweet- seeming Bishop
who's saying SO-SO-SO, but whack! you're stampeding again through
   her poems like a mustang,
whacked so hard that you bash the already broken crown of your head
   on the roof of your stall.

. . . What a relief to read for awhile some bad poems. Still, I try not
   to—bad, whackless poems
can hurt you, can say you're all right when you're not, can condone
   your poet-coward
who compulsively asks if you're all right—Am I all right?—not wasting
   your time—
Am I wasting time?—though you know you are, wasting time, if you're
   not being whacked.
Bad poems let you off that: the confessional mode now: I've read reams,
   I've written as many.

Meanwhile, this morning, this very moment, I'm thinking of George
   Herbert composing;
I see him, by himself, in some candlelit chamber unbearably lonely to
   us but glorious to him,
and he's hunched over, scribbling, scribbling, and the room's filling
   with poems whacking at me,
and Herbert's not even paying attention as the huge tide of them rises
   and engulfs me
in warm tangles of musical down as from the breasts of the choiring
   dawn-tangling larks.

"Lovely enchanting language, sugar-cane . . ." Whack! "The sweet
   strains, the lullings . . ."

> Oh whack! Lowell or Keats, Rilke or Wordsworth or Wyatt: whack—
> fifty years of it,
> old race-horse, plug hauling its junk—isn't it time to be put out to
> pasture? But ah, I'd still
> if I could lie down like a mare giving birth, arm in my own uterine
> channel to tug out another,
> one more, only one more, poor damp little poem, then I'll be happy—I
> promise, I swear.

It's not only one's taste that changes over the course of one's life. In the early years of my literary education at university and just after, there was a vogue for myth, folklore, primitive religion, preliterate song—*The Golden Bough*, *The White Goddess*, *Technicians of the Sacred*, all that. The poets and intellectuals I knew then weren't much interested in history, or only insofar as it manifested in poetry and art. Wars, revolutions, social movements, evolving or regressive: all were peripheral to the seriousness of what we thought of as our larger interests. Looking back now, I see those thankfully few years as a distraction from the real world in which I was living. Because about then in America, the civil rights movement dawned, then the Vietnam War was launched, and though such historical upheavals could be enriched by thinking of them in a context of collective unconscious and all that, you could no longer pretend to think seriously about or write about the world without a knowledge of society and history, real history.

Of course, one's own life takes place in history and generates a history of its own. For a poet, this can be difficult. It's very hard to grasp realistically the trajectory of your own writing life in relation to the world around you, mostly because you've been so preoccupied with the daily, monthly, decadely obsession of writing poems. And then there are times these days when the niggling question surfaces of whether one might actually have written enough poems.

In a sympathetic and intelligent (the second word devolves directly from the first) review of my last book, the poet-critic ended his otherwise favorable observations by remarking that he found the book a third too long. Of course I disagreed, and besides, how many books are there about which something similar couldn't have been said? But still, I wondered whether there might be a model the writer had in mind that my book had violated. And, even more discomfiting: if there's a model for how long a book of poetry should be, might there be a template for a career in poetry? Is there, as the insurance companies put it about medical expenses, a lifetime limit on the number of poems one is allowed to write?

Then there's that old expression, "something to say." Might one come to a time when indeed one might have nothing more to say? At the same time, did one ever really start a poem with something to say? William Carlos Williams once published a book called *I Wanted to Write a Poem*, and before Williams became one of my masters, I despised its title, so much so that I wouldn't read the book. In the muddle of my misguided ideals, I believed you weren't supposed just to want to write a poem: poems were meant to germinate from and enact some urgent philosophical or spiritual intuition—their actual composition was somehow incidental to that larger purpose.

I don't know how long it took me—I suppose fortunately not all that long—to grasp that writing a poem—*writing* a poem—was what everything was about. To be a poet isn't to distill ideas, however grand, into verse language; rather, in the simplest terms, to write poetry is to sing. And the task of the poet is to learn to sing, then to do it, then learn it again, and do it a little differently . . . Of course you do realize as you go along that the song is most compelling when it embodies issues beyond poetry that are crucial to you, and perhaps to others.

The question of whether I might be inflicting poems on the world, though, is less trying than convincing myself that it's worth the effort to write another poem. Writing poems is hard work. Not writing them is even harder. No wonder one comes to think: Why bother? Why am I doing this? Then: what have I done with my life? Written poems? Written poems when there was so much to be done in the world that needed greater doing? But wait, isn't this the abiding question of lyric poetry, the poetry of an "I"? Who am I, thinking about temporality, mortality, beauty, or death? Who am I, falling in love? Who am I, wandering through the world with nothing much to do, like Whitman, whose work shows you can make yourself and the world and other people monumental by strolling around without much to do?

But in the worst moments, this doesn't relieve the galling sense of repetitiveness and futility. Sometimes it's easier to convince myself to keep at it by thinking of painters or musicians who just seem to do what they do with no fuss. Monet, in his hoary old age tottering out to his garden or pond to do one more painting. Or Titian, in his ancientness still working. That's what you do, that's all. You paint another painting. Or if you're a musician you write another sonata, or symphony, or whatever. The Japanese painter and printmaker we know as Hokusai gave himself thirty different names during his lifetime. In his seventies he referred to himself as "The old man mad about art"—that's heartening; I like that. It was also around then that he projected a life for himself in which at a hundred he would finally learn how really to paint, and then, he said, at a hundred and thirty "every dot and stroke I paint will be alive." He died at eighty-nine.

In my daily life, though, none of this woolgathering is very useful in revealing what my next poem will be. Yeats wrote, in "The Circus Animals' Desertion," "I sought a theme, and sought for it in vain." And that's it exactly. It used to be that "themes" came tumbling from all directions, you just had to get out of the way. But now . . .

And what makes it even pricklier is how quickly I can fall into a funk when nothing is happening at my desk. This isn't anything new: my editor at Farrar, Straus and Giroux, Jon Galassi, who's also a good friend, tells me I've been complaining in much the same way for the nearly forty years we've known each other. Lately, though, I think I've figured out where my desperation comes from.

I used to believe what I thought was a metaphor about writing poetry: that it's addictive, like a drug. But I understand now that composing verse is actually, not metaphorically, addictive: there really is a kind of rush, to use the addicts' term, when you're generating or revising a poem. Busy the mind is, scurrying this way and that, spinning and soaring, and, as is apparently the case with stimulants, there's an altered experience of time and of the self as it moves through time—I'm sure other poets know what I mean by this. And they must know, too, that when one isn't working on a poem, doesn't have any poetry work to do, there are real withdrawal symptoms. In my case, I fall into something like depression, and as in other depressions, I begin to doubt, to ask questions I shouldn't, about my work, my life—all I grumbled about just now. Goethe put it succinctly: "The poet's requisite trance is the most fragile element in his armory."

The other realization I've had recently was that some of this, paradoxically, has to do with the years I've practiced my craft. I'm more efficient now when I work; it doesn't take me as long to make decisions about a poem, to revise or reconceive it. This is all well and good, and I certainly won't complain, except that my proficiency leaves me with more time on my hands to suffer the absence of the excitement of poetry labor. I sit and stare, I close my eyes, I read other people's poems or don't, it doesn't matter. Of course reading great poems, especially for the first time, has its own addictive thrill—it's almost as good as going at one's own work—but there aren't all that many great poems that after all these decades haven't already found me. So it can be a relief when a friend sends me a poem to make suggestions about—at least I'm doing something.

One thing that does keep me going in the end is change, the sound of my poems changing: their tone, voice, velocity, general shape. Knowing how or why these changes come about I've always found impossible to describe: they just happen, and I tag along. After my most recent book, *Wait*, I found myself writing poems unlike any I'd written before. There seemed to have arrived in them an element of not only the irrational but also the absurd, a willed goofiness that for some reason pleases me. "Whacked" is an example of this. Maybe I'm tired of being logical, rational, lucid, "mature." I knew all along I was never any of these things: sanity was always a kind of armor I donned before I went into the fray of composition—and of life, too, I suppose. When I hit seventy or so, it came to me that I hadn't changed a bit since I was eighteen—Yeats once said something similar—or even since I was twelve. I often feel as chartless as I was then, meandering through the world without much definite sense of direction. As a kid that was mostly okay, until the tornado of adolescence whirled me into the mind I had to live with for the next fifty years, when I finally landed where occasionally I can relax and be myself again.

"Being oneself." Isn't that the most absurd phrase? As though there's a choice? In the life of art, though, every day can feel like a choice. Who am I today? Am I a poet today, one who might write a poem? Or am I that clod who dared cultivate the desire to string words together in a poetic way? So, again: Will I finally be myself today? Or is today's "myself" the same poet who wrote with certain musics until now, and will I have to write in those musics, which may by now be utterly tedious, again?

It may well be that the self I am today just doesn't want to make the same damned noise. Maybe that noise has become boring. How do I change it? Do I invent a different poet? Do I study the music of different poets from those I've known? Don't I know them all? Besides, if the poems do change, as I say mine recently have, is it really because of some choice? Have I ever chosen the music of a particular poem? Isn't it always rather that the music of the poems seems to choose me? Which me? A choiceless choice.

All right: after all the poetry business, how can an old man speak of life without coming sooner or later to death? Dear death, our faithful lifelong companion. But before I consider death itself, it would be cowardly not to confront the worse-than-death. I mean the other, more dreadful fates that lurk in one's quickly diminishing future: the horror shows of dementia, amnesia, aphasia, even the mostly unremarkable memory loss, the last of which already afflicts me, leaving me occasionally stricken with embarrassment before people I know well whose name all at once isn't there.

The worst of these soul killers, Alzheimer's and its kin, are believed by many of us who work with our minds to be worse than merely dying. It would be pleasant to be amusing here, to find a tone sufficiently flip to distance myself from the terrible implications of this, the way Philip Larkin did it in "The Old Fools." It's a terrifying poem, where old age is characterized finally as "The whole hideous inverted childhood" but in which Larkin still manages to employ his inimitable tone of detachment, irony, self-mocking—stances I find to be utterly beyond me. My own poem about these matters, I suppose, has quite a bit less detachment:

RAT WHEEL, DEMENTIA, MONT SAINT MICHEL
for Albert O. Hirschman

My last god's a theodicy glutton, a good-evil gourmet—
peacock and plague, gene-junk; he gobbles it down.
Poetry, violence; love, war—his stew of honey and thorn.

For instance, thinks theodicy-god: Mont Saint Michel.
Sheep, sand, steeple honed sharp as a spear. And inside,
a contraption he calls with a chuckle the rat-wheel.

Thick timber three meters around, two persons across,
into which prisoners were inserted to trudge, toil,
hoist food for the bishop and monks; fat bishop himself.

The wheel weighs and weighs. You're chained in; you toil.
Then they extract you. Where have your years vanished?
What difference? says theodicy-god. Wheel, toil: what difference?

Theodicy-god has evolved now to both substance and not.
With handy metaphysical blades to slice brain meat from mind.
For in minds should be voidy wings choiring, not selves.

This old scholar, for instance, should have to struggle to speak,
should not remember his words, paragraphs, books:
that garner of full-ripened grain must be hosed clean.

Sometimes as the rat-wheel is screaming, theodicy-god
considers whether to say he's sorry: That you can't speak,
can't remember your words, paragraphs, books.

Sorry, so sorry. Blah, his voice thinks instead, blah.
He can't do it. Best hope instead they'll ask him again
as they always do for forgiveness. But what if they don't?

What might have once been a heart feels pity, for itself though,
not the old man with no speech—for him and his only scorn.
Here in my rat wheel, my Mont Saint Michel, my steeple of scorn.

But then, again, after everything, death. How death shape changes over the decades. My own most intimate relationship to death occurred in my twenties. Death then was with me all the time, as a threat, and also, as I've said, a companion, a possible savior, but in whatever guise it took, it was there. I remember thinking at one point that the most appropriate title for my first book of poems, the book I never finished writing, should have been *The Book of Dying*.

It's different now. Death only takes me occasionally these days, and doesn't hang about the way it did then. It comes instead in sudden, dire surges, in which everything is infused with death, flooded away. During those times, usually at dawn when I wake too early, death possesses reality, not as fear, but fact, inevitable, unavoidable, complete. And along with this, or just subsequent to it, I'm jettisoned into time in an unfamiliar way. In that early light, I often find myself ranging restlessly over my past as I never used to. I'm back in my twenties or thirties or even before, taken by spookily animated memories. All the thoughtless and stupid things I said, years ago, decades ago, I find have been dutifully stored in some cesspool of conscience that only now has taken to overflowing, so that my selfishness, my awful insensitivity, all which at the time I thought were a portion of how one was in the world, return with distressing clarity.

The journeys I make through time aren't only in own my life, though. I also find myself traveling through larger cycles as well. I refer a lot in my mind to the far past, to history, and even to pre-*Homo sapiens* existence. I keep trying to give credence to the fact that my own personal ancestors were these hairier other humans, the possible lives of which I find so engrossing.

Then, again, more often, I find myself spun out into the future. I obsess about the future much more than I ever did before, much more than I'd like to. What terrible possibilities await us, or, more poignantly and painfully, our heirs. I remember the first time I heard the term "global warming." I felt a chill: it was clear that we, all of us, were involved in a destiny much larger than any we'd ever imagined. The survival of the planet as we know it was going to be our responsibility. These days I think a lot about this, I dwell on its terrible plausibility. Sometimes I can't think about anything else—I find myself too often writing mostly wretched poems about it.

Galway Kinnell has a poem, "There Are Things I Tell to No One." A lovely title, to which in my memory I'd found I'd somehow added a phrase, "But the Poem." Except I find now that there is indeed much, very much, I not only don't tell the poem but don't tell anyone else either. I have a wife I love unreasonably, a son and a daughter, three grandsons and a son-in-law, and many beloved friends. I worry about them, and I don't want to tell those closest to me how dire my vision of the future is for fear of terrifying them. I'm not bringing any news to them, surely, but they respect what I think, and feel, and I'm afraid my anxieties will only intensify their own. There are times I'm almost relieved that I won't have to live to see the worst of it, and others when I almost wish not to perceive what's out there right now. Trying to save our world has become, in America at least, a partisan political issue, contaminated by the cynical cultivation by the Right of willful superstition. I find this to be the most atrocious example of corruption that we've had to behold in our already harrowing historical moment.

The rest of our communal madness goes on, as usual. Watching the news, realizing again how such and such number of people had been killed in one country then another, I wonder how many times in our media-saturated culture we hear that word "killed" spoken, and how difficult it still is to grasp the reality that each occasion represents a person with a consciousness of the mysteries of existence exactly like our own, which will no longer be a consciousness but a void. Horrible thought.

And in its way a childish one. Children think like that, one thing at a time. It takes us a long time to learn to abstract from the instance. But not that long. When he was three, my grandson Sully asked his mother, "When you step on an ant, does it say 'ouch?'" "Ants don't talk," my daughter answered. "Yes," Sully said, "but does it say 'ouch' in its mind?"

We come to know this thing called mind quite early on, and we also at some point much later come to realize how much our minds aren't susceptible to being what we'd like them to be. As I've aged—"matured" I suppose would be the word—I've become more and more aware of the parts of myself that don't arrive at anything like what's implied by that grand term. The older I am, the more I've become aware of how trapped I am in a mind that in its perceptions, its impulses, its emotions is very much still a child's. I've spent so much time, so much labor trying to tame this thing called mind, trying to cajole it to be more reasonable, more sensible, less absolute, less simply silly. But the task seems hopeless because my child's mind, the mind that lurks beneath all the others I like to think determine who I am, experiences the world in brute, crude, utterly unsophisticated systems of feeling and thought: it wants, it wishes, it desires—things, feelings, states of being—and when it isn't granted them to possess, or at least hope for, it becomes depressed, or flies into a tantrum. And, worse, it's not satisfied with halfway: it admits no partials, no gradations, no compromises or concessions. To it, accommodations are capitulations, failures, precursors to defeat.

Furthermore, that the world beyond me is not as my child's mind wishes it to be, imagines it can be, is passionately convinced it absolutely should be, throws it into a frenzy of frustration, exasperation, indignation, umbrage, so that I, trapped for so much of the time in this, my mind, am offended, embittered; I disapprove, I sulk, I become petulant. When I look out into that world, when I peer out between my petulance and my sulk at that world that at once lacks and is in danger—how can it not be that I am fraught? How can my mind not be frightened—not only of the world but also of itself, this child's mind that inflicts the imperfect world on itself?

But then, sooner or later, again and again, I ask myself how can the world's ultimate facticity, the simplicity of it, its purity, not be dimmed, diminished, thrown out of focus, distorted by a surrender to myself, by my helplessness before myself? I see the world as it is, its space, its people, its things; I see it glowing in the astonishment of pure being, yet the emotion I draw from that glow, from that blaze, is worry, concern, anguish; is anxiety, terror, then sadness, then, again, despair, that despair which seems not merely to perceive the world beyond itself but, in its imagination, to consume it.

And so I mostly shut up about my despair. Sometimes perhaps telling a poem about it, but mostly struggling to keep it to myself.

As I will here. And return to death, which, in this context, can sometimes be, as I've said, solacing. Not to have to behold the rains stop, the deserts advance, the glaciers melt, not to experience the violence and suffering that may well ensue from such disruptions.

And yet reality, our reality, is here: it beckons, it hasn't lost a bit of its glorious clarity, its colors, its sounds, its scents, those simple miracles that are more miraculous in the complexities that science has revealed are woven beneath them. I desire this world with the unquestioning, unconditional force of a love that forever wends a way through the interstices of disappointment, dissatisfaction, foreboding.

And poetry. It doesn't seem absurd after all to have given one's life to poetry. To have been allowed to participate in the grandeur of its traditions, to have experienced so profoundly so many inspiring poems, so many poet-geniuses, so many glimmers of something greater than anything I could have imagined life would offer, life would be. Even unto death, poetry can go on, will go on.

WRITERS WRITING DYING

Many I could name but won't who'd have been furious to die while
    they were sleeping but did—
outrageous, they'd have lamented, and never forgiven the death they'd
    construed for themselves
being stolen from them so rudely, so crudely, without feeling themselves
    like rubber gloves

stickily stripped from the innermostness they'd contrived to horde for
    so long—all of it gone,
squandered, wasted, on what? Death, crashingly boring as long as
    you're able to think and write it.

Think, write, write, think: just keep galloping faster and you won't even
    notice you're dead.
The hard thing's when you're not thinking or writing and as far as you
    know you are dead
or might as well be, with no word for yourself, just that suction-shush
    like a heart pump or straw
in a milkshake and death which once wanted only to be sung back to
    sleep with its tired old fangs
has me in its mouth!—and where the hell are you that chunk of dying
    we used to call Muse?

Well, dead or not, at least there was that dream, of some scribbler, some
    think- and write-person,
maybe it was yourself, soaring in the sidereal void, and not only that,
    you were holding a banjo
and gleefully strumming, and singing, jaw swung a bit under and off to
    the side the way crazily
happily people will do it—singing songs or not even songs, just lolly-
    molly syllable sounds
and you'd escaped even from language, from having to gab, from hav-
    ing to write down the idiot gab.

But in the meantime isn't this what it is to be dead, with that Emily-fly
    buzzing over your snout
that you're singing almost as she did; so what matter if you died in your
    sleep, or rushed toward dying
like the Sylvia-Hart part of the tribe who ceased too quickly to be and
    left out some stanzas?
You're still aloft with your banjoless banjo, and if you're dead or asleep
    who really cares?
Such fun to wake up though! Such fun too if you don't! Keep dying!
    Keep writing it down!

Acknowledgments

"Unlikely Likes: George Herbert and Philip Larkin": an earlier version was published in the *Yale Review* 88, no. 4 (October 2000): 121–38.

"Amichai Near the End": an earlier version was published as "We Cannot Be Fooled, We Can Be Fooled" in the *New Republic* (July 3, 2000).

"Autobiography with Translation": originally published as "On Lowell's Imitations," *Salmagundi*, nos. 141–42 (Winter–Spring 2004): 110–12.

"Lowell Later": an earlier version appeared as "Listening to Lowell" in the *Threepenny Review*, no. 97 (Spring 2004): 14–15.

"Odd Endings": originally given as a talk at the University of Chicago's Poem Present series (April 20, 2006).

"Some Reflections on Tragedy": revised version of a talk, "Beyond Euripides," delivered at a translation conference, Princeton University (April 23, 2004) and later published in the *Yale Review* (October 2012), forthcoming.

"Letter to a Workshop": an earlier version appeared in *American Poetry Review* 36, no. 4 (July–August 2007): 31–34.

"Two Encounters Early On": part 1, "Cowboys and Poets," was first published in the *Boston Globe*, June 14, 1998; part 2, "Smut," was published in *Lost Classics*, edited by Michael Ondaatje (New York: Anchor Books, 2001).

"Literary Models of Adolescence": revised version of a talk delivered to a meeting of the Philadelphia Society of Adolescent Psychiatry, 1990.

"Paris as Symbol, Idea, and Reality": revised version of the talk "Poetry and Place," at Reid Hall, Columbia Global Centers, Paris (1999).

"Letter to a German Friend": originally published in *Salmagundi*, nos. 144–45 (Fall 2004–Winter 2005): 156–73.

"Nature and Panic": revised version of a talk delivered at the conference "Human : Nature" at the University of East Anglia (2008).

"On Being Old": Poetry Society Annual Lecture (May 26, 2011), commissioned by the Poetry Society of London, published in the *Poetry Review* (Winter 2011) and forthcoming in the *American Poetry Review* (July–August 2012). The poems in the essay appear in the forthcoming collection *Writers Writing Dying* (New York: Farrar, Straus and Giroux, 2012).